Alexander Hamilton's

PUBLIC ADMINISTRATION

Alexander Hamilton's

PUBLIC ADMINISTRATION

RICHARD T. GREEN

The University of Alabama Press
Tuscaloosa

The University of Alabama Press
Tuscaloosa, Alabama 35487-0380
uapress.ua.edu

Typeface: Baskerville and News Gothic

Cover image: Alexander Hamilton illustration; iStock © GeorgiosArt
Cover design: Michele Myatt Quinn

Library of Congress Cataloging-in-Publication Data

Names: Green, Richard T. (Professor of public administration), author.
Title: Alexander Hamilton's public administration / Richard T. Green.
Description: Tuscaloosa : The University of Alabama Press, [2019] |
Includes bibliographical references and index.
Identifiers: LCCN 2018032200| ISBN 9780817320164 (cloth) |
ISBN 9780817392567 (ebk.)
Subjects: LCSH: Hamilton, Alexander, 1757–1804—Political and social
views. | Political science—United States—History. | Republicanism—
United States—History. | Public administration—United States—
Philosophy. | United States—Politics and government—1775–1783. |
United States—Politics and government—1783–1809.
Classification: LCC E302.6.H2 G787 2019 | DDC 973.4092—dc23
LC record available at https://lccn.loc.gov/2018032200

To John Rohr, my mentor and friend

Benigna cor, sensus oculorum est

Contents

Acknowledgments

My odyssey through the works of Alexander Hamilton began long ago with my doctoral research. That was a very different project from this one and more ambitious than it should have been. Nevertheless, it started my academic career on a sound footing for thinking more deeply about American public administration. I revisited Hamilton's work, and the burgeoning literature on him, periodically until at last I felt ready to begin this new project in earnest. The intervening years benefited me a great deal, with forays into both theoretical and practical aspects of contemporary public administration. Theory and practice must inform each other in professional fields, and the mix helped me appreciate more fully the insights Hamilton had to offer. I am thus indebted to a large number of practitioners as well as academics with whom I have interacted over a long career. They are too numerous to name, but my thanks to them all is heartfelt. There are, however, a few colleagues whose insights rise to such significance that I must at least acknowledge them here.

Chief among these is John Rohr, to whom this book is dedicated. He put me to work on the founding period and urged me to study Hamilton especially. I cannot thank him enough for his sage advice and uncanny insight. His passing in 2011 was a major loss to the field. He is sorely missed. Early on, he introduced me to a group of colleagues whose work has informed so much of mine. Doug Morgan has been a trusted friend and coauthor on works addressing the constitutional moorings of public administration. Influential too are several of his colleagues at Portland State University, especially Phil Cooper, who delves ever so deeply into the complex relations of law and public administration. David Rosenbloom's extensive constitutional scholarship has also informed much of my perspective, as has Brian Cook's fine historical work on the constitutive aspects of public administration. All of them in a way led me back to Hamilton.

I must thank the anonymous reviewers of this book for their incisive critique and numerous suggestions. They have dramatically improved the outcome. Dan Waterman at the University of Alabama Press should be credited for their selection and for so ably steering me through the revision process.

Finally, to Mal, for her endless patience with my distractedness and long hours sequestered from so many things we normally do together, I am ever in her debt.

Alexander Hamilton's

PUBLIC ADMINISTRATION

Introduction

Though we cannot acquiesce in the political heresy of the poet
who says:
    "For forms of government let fools contest—
    That which is best administered is best,"—
yet we may safely pronounce that the true test of a good
government is its aptitude and tendency to produce a good
administration.
                    —Alexander Hamilton, *Federalist* essay 68

All interesting administrative questions are political questions.
Age-old political and constitutional problems now present
themselves as problems of (or in) public administration.
                    —Herbert Storing

At the time of this writing, an extraordinary hip-hop-styled play about
Alexander Hamilton hit Broadway and riveted the nation's attention.
The play, *Hamilton*, by Lin-Manuel Miranda, has made Hamilton's life
and genius accessible and even attractive to modern Americans from
all walks of life. Miranda adapted it from Ron Chernow's highly ac-
claimed biography of Hamilton[1] and framed him appropriately as a
poor, orphaned, immigrant bastard come to America—the land of opportunity. "This is a story about America then, told by America now,"
Miranda explains, "and we want to eliminate any distance between a
contemporary audience and this story."[2] As Rebecca Mead of the *New
Yorker* describes it, Miranda is "telling the story of the founding of his
country in such a way as to make everyone present feel they have a
stake in their country. In heightened verse form, Shakespeare told
England's national story to the audience at the Globe, and helped
make England England—helped give it its self-consciousness. That
is exactly what Lin is doing with *Hamilton*. By telling the story of the
founding of the country through the eyes of a bastard, immigrant orphan, told entirely by people of color, he is saying, 'This is our country.
We get to lay claim to it.'"[3] The play is a remarkable achievement, not
only for its timeliness and faithful rendition of Hamilton's life and
times through novel hip-hop style and syntax but also for drawing out
the dramatic and attractive aspects of one of our most controversial

founding fathers. Historically, he has often been demonized as an arrogant elitist, a friend of bankers and commercial interests as well as of the rich and wellborn, and for treating the masses with disdain.[4] In his time, his enemies accused him variously of scheming for monarchy and subverting the new republic, of harboring aristocratic pretensions, of wishing to end states' rights, and of trying to establish an imperial empire. Amazingly, he was alleged to have attempted these things through his role as the nation's first secretary of the treasury (1789–95)—in other words, as a bureaucrat. Miranda's play illustrates Hamilton's monumental achievements in this subordinate role as part of the drama of designing and establishing a new nation, and along the way captures the resulting controversy, intrigue, and tragedy that haunted him to the end of his life at age forty-nine.

Hamilton's tenure as first secretary of the treasury is significant in large part because, as one of the leading apologists for the new Constitution, he attended more than any other founder to the Constitution's capacity for sound and effective administration. He was our first and foremost administrative theorist as well as preeminent practitioner. With President Washington as his essential aegis, he mounted an extraordinary campaign to put the new union on a stable and secure footing. He carved out a dominant role in the new republic because he understood the necessary connection between one's vision for the nation and the particulars of its public administration. This is not to say that his vision was the only right vision for America. It certainly was not, but his vision prevailed in the early going because he understood institution building and administration better than any of his colleagues. His arch political rival, Thomas Jefferson, conceded as much in his lament that it would be impossible to remove Hamilton's funding system.

Hamilton's administrative acumen drew him to the most unwanted, reviled position in the new government. The Treasury offered the greatest advantage due to its financial connection to every department and policy arena. The financial institutions he established would constitute the financial spine of both government and the developing economy, and he heavily influenced the designs of virtually every other new agency, as well as the content of most early policies, with effects that lasted well beyond his time and even to the current day.

Why This Book?

Hamilton's work illustrates Dwight Waldo's profound point that a theory of public administration is a theory of politics.[5] American public administration has inherited from Hamilton a distinct republican framework through which we derive many of our governing standards and practices. His administrative theory flowed from his republican vision, prescribing not only the how of administration but also the why and the what should be done. Administration and policy merged seamlessly in his mind, each conditioning the other. His Anti-Federalist detractors clearly saw this and fought his vision tooth and nail. That conflict endures, because Americans have not settled on just one vision of the American republic, and it seems unlikely we ever will. The difference today is that the battle is now waged mainly on Hamilton's ground, whereas during the founding period it was the reverse. That is why Hamilton must be a pivotal figure in our current reckoning. If we want to more fully understand ourselves and our ways of governing today, we must start by understanding him, and we cannot do that without exploring his administrative theory and practice in depth.

That is the project of this book. It deals with Hamilton both as a founder of the American republic, steeped in the currents of political philosophy and science of his day, and as its chief administrative theorist and craftsman, deeply involved in establishing the early institutions and policies that would bring his interpretation of the ratified Constitution to life. Accordingly, this book addresses (1) the complex mix of classical and modern ideas that informed his vision of a modern commercial and administrative republic, (2) the administrative ideas, institutions, and practices that flowed from that vision, and (3) the substantive policies he deemed essential to its realization. The analysis flows from immersion in his extant papers (running thirty-one volumes) and in the many thematic and biographical works on his life. It aims to provide a comprehensive explanation of his theoretical contributions and a richly detailed account of his ideas and practices in historical context.

History matters in the sense that it helps us understand how and why ideas and agendas emerged and reached prominence. It draws on our fascination with the interplay of ideas and the machinations of power, the relevance of social mores and conventions, and the impact of technique and invention. Understanding more about these matters helps us to reach judgments about their significance beyond their time, drawing us into a dialogue of sorts with our past as we argue over what should be and how we should conduct our affairs today. This book does not pretend to address every implication of Hamilton's administrative theory. Readers will find many to consider in their own way and hopefully will contribute insight about them far beyond what I might discern. This work intends to provide a great deal more grist for reflection by students and scholars as they wrestle with the roles and conundrums of American public administration today. My own thoughts on these matters emerge in part through the analysis in each chapter, and I use them in the concluding chapter to assess what I see as both the salience and the limitations of Hamilton's theory.

Plying a Constitutional Perspective

David Rosenbloom has often stated that his extensive contributions to the field rest on the basic conviction that the Constitution still matters in the work of American public administration. I share that conviction and associate with a group of scholars now described as the Constitutional School of public administration. They bring a wide variety of perspectives to bear on the relation of the Constitution to public administration, so there is no particular orthodoxy touted other than that the document engenders a juridical approach to values and processes rooted in a conflicted constitutional tradition.[6] I use the term "juridical" in its most basic sense as administration of and by law, as well as in the complementary sense that it engenders and disciplines administration through legal principles and processes. Hamilton personified the juridical approach to administration. He was the leading legal mind as well as administrative theorist of his day, and drawing from broad constitutional language, he fused legal and administrative ideas into a vision of a powerful national republic. His work was preeminently constitutional and administrative and therefore is especially relevant to current political mantras and arguments about restoring the Constitution.

It is common to hear critics assert that the Constitution nowhere mentions the public administration, as if this were some kind of damning indictment. But the Constitution fails to mention a lot of things, including political parties. Few people today think of parties as contrary to the Constitution, even though the vast majority of the founders despised them as a form of vice—and then promptly exploited them for their own agendas. A great irony arises here, because Hamilton, with Madison and Jay, penned the eighty-five essays of the *Federalist*, and there employed the term "public administration" more frequently than any other. The analysis provided in the following chapters demonstrates that Hamilton treated the Constitution as the superstructure of American public administration. Furthermore, his conception of it emphasized the capacity, through its blending, or "partial agency," in the powers of the three branches, to produce an amaz-

ing degree of cooperation among them, along with a relatively harmonious integration of their powers in subordinate agencies for narrowed purposes. Media portrayals today would have us believe that
American government and politics are thoroughly gridlocked by conflict. That is hardly the case despite all the heated rhetoric and partisan strife. Such portrayals treat the tip of the iceberg as the whole of
it, and a lot of people get misled in the process.

This is important because public administrative institutions per-
vade our lives, so much so that many of them form an environment
much like the air we breathe and are almost as vital. We seldom think
of them, but they form much of the infrastructure of political society.
Most of us can name but a few of the thousands of governing units
that dot the landscape, much less explain what they do or how they
function. They operate below the surface of our attention. It is only
when they seriously fail that we realize what we have taken for granted.
One need only consider the panicked reaction of residents in Flint,
Michigan, upon discovering that changes to their water system had
poisoned them with lead to realize how important public service is
to our lives. We become quite animated when good policing breaks
down, when public schools fail to properly educate, or when the financial system blows up in our faces. People want these things to operate
smoothly and effectively, without having to think too much about them.
That desire to take them for granted presupposes extensive public cooperation and deep trust, and that has everything to do with Hamilton's approach to public administration. The following pages explain
the theoretical and practical nuances of that approach and illustrate
the central, constitutional role that public administration played in
his designs.

The Literature on Hamilton

Attention to the founding fathers flourishes today in part because
Americans continue to invoke their ideas and principles as normatively binding. Such invocations in public discourse often amount to
wild assertions about what is *constitutional* or *unconstitutional* about
governmental powers and official actions, and at times they display a
cultic aspect marked by vehement and dogmatic claims. Such claims
reveal more in the way of ignorance and misunderstanding than they
do of sober appreciation for the conflicting and often unsettled views
that the founders actually embraced. Amid all the wild assertions, however, there exists a residue of serious popular interest in the found-

ers, piqued by a train of exhaustively researched biographies written in a dramatic and engaging style. Ron Chernow's 2004 biography of Hamilton exemplifies the genre. It is the most recent and thorough of Hamilton biographies and presents a lively portrait of the man in relation to his family, his colleagues and rivals, and the times. The work is cited throughout this book, along with many earlier and still useful biographies. Beyond these, an extensive literature of varying quality exists on Hamilton in historical accounts, as well as in myriad thematic and topical analyses.

The literature focusing on his administrative ideas and practices, however, is much smaller though not insignificant. By far, the most well-known work in the field of public administration is Lynton Caldwell's *The Administrative Theories of Hamilton and Jefferson*. Originally published as Caldwell's doctoral dissertation in 1944, and then as a second edition in 1988, the book provides a concise review of the central ideas and principles in Hamilton's theory and then compares them with Jefferson's. The book remains quite useful as a shorthand account of their theories. However, as Caldwell conceded in his 1988 edition, "there is more to be said about their continuing relevance to American government."[7] Quite so.

This book takes advantage of a variety of subsequent scholarly analyses and perspectives that examine historical and philosophical antecedents and reveal much more about Hamilton's administrative thought and practice. Especially noteworthy are books such as Michael Federici's *The Political Philosophy of Alexander Hamilton*, Harvey Flaumenhaft's *The Effective Republic: Administration and Constitution in the Thought of Alexander Hamilton*, Karl-Friedrich Walling's *Republican Empire: Alexander Hamilton on War and Free Government*, Peter McNamara's *Political Economy and Statesmanship: Smith, Hamilton, and the Foundation of the Commercial Republic*, John Lamberton Harper's *American Machiavelli: Alexander Hamilton and the Origins of U.S. Foreign Policy*, Michael Chan's *Aristotle and Hamilton on Commerce and Statesmanship*, Thomas McCraw's *The Founders and Finance: How Hamilton, Gallatin, and Other Immigrants Forged a New Economy*, and Stephen Knott's *Alexander Hamilton and the Persistence of Myth*.[8] Among these works, Harvey Flaumenhaft's *The Effective Republic* stands out for its focus on Hamilton's idea of an administrative republic.

Flaumenhaft's careful assessment of Hamilton's constitutional theory of administration, gleaned from Hamilton's extensive writings, influences aspects of most chapters in this book, along with previous works by Gerald Stourzh and David Epstein.[9] However, Flaumenhaft concentrates on Hamilton's political science in terms of his "analysis of the republican problem and its possible solution" and thus excludes attention to his theory of political economy and public finance, as well as to military and foreign policy.[10] These are treated here as integral to Hamilton's theory of effective republican administration.

Flaumenhaft's work is valuable as well for showing how Hamilton treated administration as an aspect of our constitutional life. He rightly observes that "previous studies of Hamilton's political thought neglect the administrative thought located at its center, while studies of his administrative thought inadequately locate it within the political thought surrounding it."[11] This is an important point and calls to mind the insight of Flaumenhaft's mentor, Herbert Storing, that "age-old political and constitutional problems now present themselves as problems of (or in) public administration."[12] The founders wove the conundrums and disputes they wrestled with, and often failed to resolve, into the fabric of the Constitution and thereby confined or sublimated them as issues to be coped with through administration. Administration in its broadest sense, then, is the arena of our politics.

This point will carry through all the chapters of this book and explains in part why Hamilton's theories of political economy and finance, and of military and foreign affairs, factor heavily into his administrative theory. They are vital for understanding many of the administrative institutions he established and why they set important precedents for institutions and practices later on. My analysis of Hamiltonian political economy relies heavily on Forrest McDonald's work.[13] His explanations of the sources of Hamilton's economic and financial thought remain unrivaled. I rely on additional works, especially those by Walling and Harper, to explain Hamilton's military and foreign policy.

Additionally, this book draws insights from Federici and Walling to address the practical wisdom or prudence evidenced in Hamilton's writings and public decisions. Particular attention is paid to Federici's analysis of Hamilton's moral realism as influenced by classical and Christian sources rather than by Machiavelli. I argue that Hamilton's moral realism undergirds his theory of administrative responsibility and his approach to public policy. Administration and policy were simply two sides of the same coin for him and thus were not abstracted from one another as separate endeavors, as they are today. He had much to say about determining the administrative feasibility and prudence of good policy given the nature of the human condition and the particular situations he addressed. He also formulated ideas about obligations in public life that give shape to a distinctive, though not wholly separate, sphere of public morality. Aspects of this morality are mentioned in several chapters and are treated at length in chapter 4, on administrative responsibility.

Organization of the Book

Immersion in these and many other works have led me to a significant expansion and reframing of Hamilton's administrative theory well beyond that provided by either Caldwell or Flaumenhaft. I treat Hamilton's administrative theory, first, as a work of political theory in its own right and, second, as one that is not only *bound* by the principle of rule by law but also *enabled* by it as a platform for the future development of the country. The book therefore opens with chapters on Hamilton's theory and philosophy of republican governance, on his *energetic executive* in constitutional context, and on his constitutional and administratively oriented jurisprudence. Subsequent chapters address his sense of administrative responsibility and public morality and how these support a significant degree of autonomy for the public administration, for the roles he articulated for public finance and political economy, and for military and foreign affairs. The final chapter explores his legacy and provides an assessment of the salience as well as limitations of his administrative theory.

Assessing how Hamilton, or any other founder, might view the subsequent development of the American republic is hazardous at best. So is trying to discern the lines of influence of their ideas through history. As a dominant and controversial founder, Hamilton's ideas have been invoked by countless public figures in pursuit of all kinds of agendas that may or may not coincide with his intentions. Politics and administration are suffused with mixed and ulterior motives. We can likely agree that many of his ideas have been influential in some fashion—that they have made an impact—but we will never be able to untangle the specifics. What we can do, however, is continuously elucidate his and other founders' ideas and visions for the country going forward. Many historians, biographers, and essayists conclude that we live closer to Hamilton's vision of a feverish commercial republic than to any other. If that is true, and I think it is, then we had better understand the implications and thereby discern its perils as well as its promise. It is a mark of Hamilton's wisdom that he readily noted the dangers of his vision while pursuing its promise. I call attention to both throughout the text.

Hamilton's Administrative Genius and Prescience

Biographers and historians generally consider Hamilton the administrative genius of the period. His great reports, letters, pamphlets, legal opinions, and, of course, the *Federalist* essays together constitute the philosophical and constitutional/legal foundations for "energetic" public administration. Leonard D. White observes that it was Hamilton "who first defined the term in its modern usage and who first articulated a philosophy of public administration."[14] Lynton Caldwell describes Hamilton as "pre-eminently the architect of the administrative state."[15] Clinton Rossiter and Harvey Flaumenhaft argue that Hamilton, more than any other founder, shaped and gave life to the Constitution primarily through his idea and practice of energetic administration. Both address Hamilton's constitutional interpretations as an enduring legacy, one that Rossiter says continues to influence our society, our government, and our plans for change.[16] Ron Chernow concludes that in "contriving the smoothly running machinery of the modern nation-state—including a budget system, a funded debt, a tax system, a central bank, a customs service, and coast guard—justifying them in some of America's most influential state papers, he set a high-water mark for administrative competence that has never been equaled."[17]

Hamilton provided a rich and visionary constitutional theory of public administration in the sense that he intended it to suit a much larger and more complex political society than existed at the time. Forrest McDonald observes that Hamilton saw the need not only for the political revolution that brought the new Constitution into being but also for a social revolution that would fit the population for life in a commercial republic.[18] His public administration thus carried forward a constitutive agenda that he believed flowed from the underlying premises as well as clauses of the founding document. These informed his great reports as well as the institutions and policies they engendered.

Studying Hamilton's extant reports conveys a strong sense of his prescience. His *Report on the Subject of Manufactures* (hereafter *Report on Manufactures*) envisioned an entrepreneurial society marked by tremendous diversity in occupations and pursuits that would enliven opportunities and improve living conditions for all inhabitants. Manufacturing would provide the necessary stimulus, leading to a mixed and prosperous economy. But he also warned of the dangers that typically accompany such prosperity. It could bring about "insolence, an inordinate ambition, a vicious luxury, licentiousness of morals, and all those vices which corrupt government, enslave the people, and precipitate the ruin of a nation"[19]—concerns shared by his critics and expressed by growing numbers of people today.

Unlike most of his colleagues, Hamilton anticipated the development of a powerful public administration. This public administration should maintain fiscal integrity and stability through financial administration in much the same way that John Maynard Keynes would advocate one hundred and fifty years later. He anticipated the creation of regulatory agencies overseeing the production of quality agricultural and manufactured products. He anticipated the work of agencies such as the Federal Trade Commission and the Consumer Financial Protection Bureau in calling for measures designed to "prevent frauds upon consumers at home and exporters to foreign countries."[20] He saw the need for a sound and respectable foreign policy based upon the protection and interplay of national interests, both political and economic. The principles he laid down shaped early American foreign policy and anticipated twentieth-century foreign policy as espoused by Walter Lippmann, George Kennan, Hans Morgenthau, and others of the so-called realist and nationalist schools of diplomacy.[21] Above all, Hamilton anticipated the need for administrative efficacy and what he called "system" in public administration.[22] He brought organization to all levels of administration, at times concerning himself with even technical details, as evidenced in his many Treasury circulars, which reformed both treasury and customs operations down to the street level.

Finally, in his advocacy of system and study toward the improvement of public administration, he anticipated the formal study of public administration. He planned in his later years to write a treatise on it as the core of modern political science.[23] Sadly, his early death deprived the nation of that project.

These examples, and many others, have led biographers and analysts of Hamilton's work to conclude that he anticipated America.[24] Ron Chernow puts it this way: "If Jefferson provided the essential poetry of American political discourse, Hamilton established the prose of American statecraft. No other founder articulated such a clear and prescient vision of America's future political, military, and economic strength or crafted such ingenious mechanisms to bind the nation together."[25]

Hamilton's Life and Character in Brief

Hamilton spent his boyhood in the British West Indies and coped with the stigma of an illegitimate birth.[26] He received only informal education there and initially worked as a clerk for his mother. At St. Croix, he gained work as a counting house clerk for Beekman and Cruger, an import-export business. The job gave him invaluable experience in the world of business finance and trading. As Chernow describes it, the island was situated on one of the busiest trading routes in that part of the world, and the job "afforded him valuable insights into global commerce and the maneuvers of imperial powers," and their mercantilist policies. The job required him to "mind money, chart courses for ships, keep track of freight, and compute prices in an exotic blend of currencies." The owners steadily increased his responsibilities as they discovered his abilities.[27] There he also witnessed firsthand the cruel and degrading treatment of slaves, and it sharpened his opposition to the practice as a whole. He became one of the early and most vocal abolitionists during his subsequent life in the United States.

Hamilton educated himself during these years, avidly reading everything he could get his hands on, including substantial works in poetry, philosophy, religion, and history. The Reverend Hugh Knox quickly recognized his brilliance and ambition; he opened his library to the voracious reader and afforded him an avenue for publishing some impressive poetry and a stirring account of a hurricane that devastated St. Croix and nearby islands. The account brought him significant acclaim on the islands and opened an opportunity to travel to the American colonies.[28]

He attended preparatory school in Elizabethtown, New Jersey, to take "cram courses in Latin, Greek, and advanced math to qualify for college" and was found to be "a fantastically quick study."[29] He took copious notes in English, Greek, and Latin (he was already fluent in French) and committed much of his study to memory through recitation while he paced about. Chernow noted that his lifelong penchant for "talking *sotto voce* while pacing lent him an air of either inspiration or madness."[30]

At Elizabethtown, he encountered Whiggish views about the state of the colonies in relation to the English Crown and parliament and, through letters of introduction by Hugh Knox, began meeting and impressing people of higher social standing and influential opinions. They encouraged him to apply to Princeton, a "hotbed of Presbyterian/Whig sentiment," but he was turned down because the school would not grant his request for a program of accelerated study. King's College (later to become Columbia University), a royalist-leaning institution in New York, accommodated his wishes, admitting him in 1774. There he studied under an ardent Tory, Dr. Myles Cooper, the president of the college. Hamilton was thus exposed to both sides of contention early on and witnessed all the ferment and conflict erupting in New York City. He could understand and sympathize with both sides, but he steadily leaned in the Whig direction as tensions moved toward conflict.

At King's College, he raced through Greek and Latin classics, rhetoric, philosophy, history, geography, math, and science. He read Enlightenment theorists such as Thomas Hobbes, John Locke, Baron de Montesquieu, and David Hume, as well as great legal minds such as William Blackstone, Edward Coke, Hugo Grotius, Samuel von Pufendorf, and Emmerich de Vattel. Along the way, he and his friends formed a literary club that met weekly to refine their writing, speaking, and debating skills. His friend and roommate, Robert Troupe, noted his "extraordinary displays of richness of genius and energy of mind."[31] His oratorical skill and growing sympathy for colonial resistance to British oppression became legend with his *Speech in the Fields* by the liberty pole near King's College on July 6, 1775. Thereafter, he identified with the republican cause, and at age twenty, he commenced his career as one of America's most brilliant pamphleteers with *A Full Vindication* and *The Farmer Refuted,* the latter providing an exhaustively researched critique of unjust British laws and actions against the colonies and a cogent justification of colonial actions (such as the Boston and New York tea parties) in response.[32]

Hamilton cut formal study short to enter the Revolutionary War. He rapidly schooled himself in military history, tactics, and drill. His astute observation of conditions in the colonies led him to conclude that the best military strategy for colonists would be to "harass and exhaust the [British] soldiery by frequent skirmishes and incursions than to take the open field with them, by which means they would have the full benefit of their superior regularity and skills." Chernow characterizes this as an "intuitive judgment of the highest order" and one that "captured in a nutshell" General Washington's strategy even before hostilities commenced.[33]

In 1775, Hamilton joined a militia company dubbed the Hearts of Oak, shaped it into one of New York's finest artillery units, and distinguished himself and the unit with some remarkable battlefield accomplishments.[34] He attracted the attention of several military leaders, including General Washington, and in 1777 was promoted to the rank of lieutenant colonel and appointed Washington's aide-de-camp. He became Washington's most trusted aide, taking on extensive administrative responsibilities. Many of Washington's memoranda, field instructions, and exhortations to Congress came from his hand, with Washington's approving signature.[35] The position prepared him for leadership and the administration of foreign relations, finance, and public service. The experience also convinced him of the grave inadequacies of government under the Articles of Confederation. Accordingly, he joined an influential group of colleagues in search of a more effective design for popular government.

During the long winters of the war, Hamilton educated himself further in history, political philosophy, political economy, and finance. He corresponded with Robert Morris and other financial experts and served as Washington's liaison with Congress on financial and organizational matters. By 1781, he was urging development of executive organization and financial reforms and was publishing political tracts in support of empowering the Congress to run a national government free of state interference. His *Continentalist* essays of 1781 and 1782 laid the foundation for his subsequent efforts at establishing energetic government and foreshadowed his work in the *Federalist*.[36]

Shortly before the end of the war, Hamilton left Washington's side for a much-desired field command. He participated heroically at the Battle of Yorktown and shortly thereafter, in 1782, retired from active military duty to study law and serve as Continental receiver of taxes for New York. He urged the New York legislature to pass a resolution calling for a general convention of the states to amend the Articles of Confederation. He also became a delegate to the Continental Congress. From 1782 to 1786, he urged reform of the articles, practiced law, wrote legal and political essays, and acquired more knowledge of public finance.

In 1784, Hamilton published his controversial *Phocion* letters criticizing the New York legislature's passage of the Trespass Act, which violated peace treaty articles prohibiting confiscation of loyalist property.[37] The action appalled Hamilton, and he warned of the broader implications of denying Tory loyalists their property rights. His defense of them at court incurred wrath from an inflamed public who saw him as a traitor to the American cause. In his most famous case, *Rutgers v. Waddington*, he defended the rights of two British merchants by invoking the supremacy of national law, the law of nations, treaty law, and even natural law over New York State law and framed an early argument for judicial review to overturn such laws. As Chernow described it, "Hamilton articulated fundamental concepts that he later expanded upon in the *Federalist*, concepts central to the future of American jurisprudence."[38]

In 1786, as a member of the New York assembly, he was named one of six commissioners to meet at Annapolis to frame trade regulations in the general interest of all the states. Hamilton, with James Madison, played a central role in transforming what they viewed as a futile exercise into a call for a constitutional convention. They looked beyond commercial arrangements to the critical flaws in the structure of governance under the Articles of Confederation. A new federal government was needed, they argued, with powers adequate to the "exigencies of the union." Hamilton's written *Address*, toned down at Madison's urging, garnered unanimous support.[39]

Hamilton attended the Constitutional Convention in 1787, but his contribution was modest given his talents. His only substantial speech before the Committee of the Whole occurred on June 18 in the midst of deadlock over the Virginia and New Jersey plans. It was the longest speech delivered at the Convention (six hours) and one that would haunt Hamilton throughout his later life. In it, he offered an extremely nationalistic plan of government that would clearly establish the national government's supremacy. The speech was likely intended to jolt the delegates out of their deadlock, but his proposals generated distorted rumors and accusations that he sought the complete abolition of the states in favor of a unified, monarchical government. Though not true, the accusations stuck.[40] Hamilton's devotion to supporting and defending the republican document that eventually came out of the convention was perhaps rivaled only by Madison, but that did not stop his enemies from continuous accusations of monarchism. Chernow concludes that "in the end, nobody would do more than Alexander Hamilton to infuse life into this parchment [the Constitution] and make it the working mandate of the American government."[41]

Shortly after the convention, in anticipation of the New York Ratifying Convention, Hamilton began publishing the *Federalist* with John Jay and James Madison. He took the lead in defending the proposed constitution clause by clause. The eighty-five essays remain the most authoritative commentary on the Constitution, with fifty-one attributed to Hamilton, twenty-nine to Madison, and five to Jay. George Washington averred that "the work will merit the notice of posterity,"[42] and so it has, with a force exceeding any of their hopes. Remarkably, the content and style of the writing made it seem as though the essays came from one mind, even though the authors independently fired off their essays without time for review. Also remarkable is the consistency of Hamilton's thought relative to his other work. Chernow's assessment seems accurate: "Those who criticize Hamilton for having engaged in a propaganda exercise in *The Federalist* must reckon with the tremendous continuity that connects the *Federalist* essays to both his earlier and later writings."[43] Despite the rhetorical force of the essays and of Hamilton's many orations, it took ratification by Virginia to finally break the deadlocked New York convention with a vote of 30 to 27 in favor.

In 1789 Hamilton gained appointment as secretary of the treasury in the new government. He ignored exhortations from friends to seek more distinguished and less perilous positions. The ability to reach into all governmental affairs through that office overcame any reservations he may have had.[44] Although no hard evidence exists to show that Hamilton directly influenced the content of the Treasury Act of 1789, it seems very likely that he did. The resulting design clearly met his expectations. His allies in Congress, especially Madison, were sure to carry them into the debate on the bill.[45]

Hamilton's tenure as secretary of the treasury (1789–95) is fully addressed in succeeding chapters. His herculean efforts in that office set the new government into motion, but it also stimulated intense resistance and contributed substantially to the development of political parties that coalesced around the leading figures of the era. Most hurtful and shocking to Hamilton was the defection of James Madison to the Jeffersonian-Republican cause. Though they had united in common cause to develop and ratify a new constitution and to establish the first three great departments of the new government (Treasury, War, and Foreign Affairs), they actually held different visions for the future of the young nation and for the role of the national government. As partisan divisions crystalized, Madison gravitated toward the Republicans, while Federalists rallied around Hamilton. Each felt deserted by the other.

By 1795, Hamilton had achieved much of what he wanted, but he also had become dispirited and worn down by political controversy and internecine administrative battles. He worried increasingly about his own financial situation (his meager public salary made it difficult to support his growing family), and so he resigned to resume a more lucrative legal practice and work behind the scenes politically.[46] In fact, he remained a major force in Washington's cabinet. Washington continued to consult him, the Federalists begged his leadership, and his political writings increased.

From 1798 to 1800, Hamilton served as inspector general of the army, preparing the United States for an impending war with France, while arguing against joining hostilities with any of the European empires. From 1801 until his death in 1804, he practiced law and continued to meddle in New York politics, always in battle with Governor George Clinton as well as his ultimate nemesis, Aaron Burr. In a twist of irony, he supported Jefferson in the tight election of 1800 against Burr. He could not take partisanship so far as to support someone he viewed as an unprincipled demagogue. His machinations against Burr resulted in the duel at Weehawken, New Jersey, that ended his life. His last years were marked by a combination of personal tragedy (due to the loss of his beloved eldest son, Philip, to a duel in 1801) and despair about the folly of state and national politics at the time.

If there is one best way to characterize Hamilton's life, it is that he advocated American union above all else and sought a great and honorable reputation for it at home and abroad. He believed this to be the surest way to protect liberty and justice for Americans over the long run.

On Hamilton's Character

Hamilton exuded passion and intensity. He was so agile of mind and speech that he often displayed impatience and was known to be quick-tempered. His friends would often counsel restraint and moderating language when he wanted to assail the heart of a matter. One gets the impression that he was a person so brimming with ideas, so quick to grasp the heart of issues, and so intellectually curious and intense that he could not contain himself. And yet most of the time he did so with remarkable discipline and, surprisingly, with charity. He displayed remarkable tenderness and passion with his family, friends, and colleagues and usually treated his opponents with politeness and sincere respect. He took them seriously and preferred to engage their ideas and actions on their merits rather than through political intrigue. This wonkish tendency got him into trouble when opponents twisted his words for political effect. His enemies did wear him down at times, to the point where he lashed out. In his late career, he meddled too much in the affairs of the Adams administration and vehemently attacked his enemies in the press. Political adversity and family tragedies weighed so heavily on him that some scholars speculate that he went to his duel with Aaron Burr ready to die.

Hamilton was also very kind to those in need, whether they be friends, clients, or even strangers who crossed his path. He had enjoyed much kindness growing up under tough circumstances, and he returned it readily throughout his life, especially in the pro bono work he performed at his law office. His generous spirit likely influenced his vision of an opulent republic marked by liberality toward the dispossessed. It certainly informed his own sense of public-spiritedness while in office. He sacrificed his own personal fortune for the sake of his public duties.

Those who believed Hamilton to be an arrogant elitist got it wrong. The characterization stemmed in part from his willingness to stand against the popular mood when it resulted in unjust actions against individuals and their basic rights, as well as from his wonkish candor. At times, he seemed naive about the effect of his words, and his political rivals fully exploited these moments. Their labels stuck, and Hamilton's reputation has suffered ever since. The truth about him is much more complex. If any label may fairly be applied, it is that he was a dedicated meritocrat, and in this he was joined by many of his founding colleagues. They embraced the idea of a natural aristocracy—of people with ability, wisdom, virtue, and noble ambition.[47] In more recent times they have been called "the best and the brightest." They come from no particular class, and bloodlines are irrelevant. Biographers note Hamilton's early attempt to break the class-based system of military promotion in order to bring more talented enlistees into the officer ranks. He also joined with his friend Henry Laurens in advocating the enlistment of slaves and granting them freedom upon completion of their military service. He was an early and ardent opponent of slavery and averred that Africans were likely as intelligent and capable as any other race of people—a highly controversial view in his day.[48] He also advocated universal male suffrage and eligibility for office. This hardly fits the caricature of an arrogant Hamilton. In many respects, he was well ahead of his more privileged colleagues as a man of the people.

However, this did not stop him from also fiercely criticizing throngs of people moved by anger and other destructive impulses. He feared that mob impulses would dominate the politics of a republic, especially if stirred by disingenuous leaders. He believed the American people to be well suited for republican government, but he sought arrangements of governance that could dampen an excessive democratic spirit, and most other founders joined him in the effort. The horrors of the French Revolution dramatically illustrated their concern soon after ratification.

Hamilton has also been characterized as the great defender of the wealthy. That his policies favored the wealthy in many ways cannot be disputed, but this was more for the instrumental purpose of securely establishing the early republic. Even Charles Beard, in his economic interpretation of the founders' motives for establishing a new constitution, acknowledges that Hamilton "was swayed throughout the period of the formation of the Constitution by large policies of government—not by any of the personal interests so often ascribed to him. . . . He saw that by identifying their [the wealthy class's] interests with those of the new government, the latter would be secure; they would not desert the ship in which they were all afloat."[49] He looked upon the rich as a useful asset for a newly established nation with few developed resources. He would use them for public benefit, but never did he join them in schemes calculated purely for their own interest. As Broadus Mitchell characterized it, Hamilton's "only client was the whole country."[50] To conclude, it may be fair to say that Hamilton's character was fit for what America would become, a land teaming with immigrants in search of opportunities to make a good life and to distinguish themselves in the affairs of the republic through initiative, hard work, and public-spiritedness. That is the image Lin-Manuel Miranda captures in his remarkable play.

1
Hamilton's Constitutional Republic

> There is something noble and magnificent in the perspective
> of a great Federal Republic, closely linked in the pursuit of a
> common interest, tranquil and prosperous at home, respectable
> abroad; but there is something proportionately diminutive and
> contemptible in the prospect of a number of petty states, with the
> appearance only of union, jarring, jealous and perverse, without
> any determined direction, fluctuating and unhappy at home,
> weak and insignificant by their dissentions, in the eyes of other
> nations.
>
> —Alexander Hamilton, *The Continentalist,* 1782

> Alone among the statesmen and political thinkers of his
> generation (and indeed of several generations after his death),
> he understood the importance of administration to the success of
> popular government.
>
> —Clinton Rossiter, 1964

The concept of republican government is by no means simple or clear. This was as true during the founding period as it is today. James Madison, in *Federalist* essay 39, described many uses of the term. Hamilton did the same during the New York Ratifying Convention and later in defending himself against charges of being a monarchist.[1] That the founders employed a variety of terms to describe the government they were constituting just added to the confusion. They frequently employed terms such as "popular government," "republic," or "republican government," and somewhat less frequently the terms "democratical government," "elective government," "free government," and "representative government." Hamilton may have been the first to use the term "representative democracy" to describe American government more precisely,[2] but he used "republican" and "popular" government most often.

Hamilton and his colleagues derived their republican ideas from a confluence of historical, theoretical, scientific, and philosophical insights, which had coalesced in Europe to form a new, modern liberal conception of political society. Though its antecedents reach far back into history, modern liberalism bore a new political science and an era characterized as the Enlightenment. Its ideas found expression in the writings of luminaries such as Niccolò Machiavelli, Thomas Hobbes, John Locke, David Hume, Francis Hutchinson, Baron de Montesquieu, Adam Smith, James Steuart, and Jean-Jacques Rousseau. Their work represented a radical departure from traditional classical and Christian conceptions of political order. At root, it posits a state of nature that exists prior to the establishment of civil society and in which individuals are driven psychologically by a fundamental passion for self-preservation. Civil societies are formed by individuals through a *social contract* to protect the *natural right* to survival by protecting life, liberty, and property. Passions drive people more than reason does, though reason can be employed to channel the passions toward productive ends. A modern liberal regime focuses and limits the aims of government on the material conditions and virtues required to ensure a peaceful and orderly society. It eschews ancient or classical regime aims to cultivate higher virtues, which serve some notion of a summum bonum, or ultimate good, for individuals and their place in the community, or polis. Individuals are instead free to determine their way in life through social institutions of their choosing or on their own.

The American framers enjoyed the rare opportunity of forming a political society based on these modern liberal ideas more than any other regime in history. Moreover, they could form such a society on republican principles exclusively, without need for the mixed forms of government (e.g., combining monarchy, aristocracy, and democracy) that had evolved in some European countries, especially Great Britain. Though many founders admired the British model, most were convinced that Americans would only accept a government based purely on republican and *democratical* ideals. At the state and national levels, they applied the Aristotelian distinction between a republic and a direct democracy. Aristotle treated direct democracy as a form of popular government prone to mob rule. Republics, on the other hand, contained mechanisms of restraint against mob rule, primarily through representation and structural innovations in governing form. Americans practiced both direct and representative democracy at local levels throughout colonial history but were disinclined to establish direct democracy for state and national government. Their focus centered on the design of representative government and on whether and how a republic could be sustained on a large or extended national scale. Historically, republics had been small city-states, so no precedents existed upon which to base an extended republic, and this led to fierce arguments between advocates for preserving a confederation of smaller state republics (Anti-Federalists) and those wishing to establish an extended and united national republic (Federalists).

Hamilton, with Madison, Washington, and other *nationalists*, vigorously advocated for the extended, united republic despite individual differences over the policies it should eventually pursue. For Hamilton, an extended republic put effective leadership and administration at its core alongside the separation of powers and checks and balances that to this day receive far more attention. Furthermore, Hamilton's conception of an American republic retained some elements of classical and Christian thought. He was not as extremely modern liberal as some scholars have suggested. For example, he rejected the notion of a social contract in favor of classical and Christian views of the individual as historically rooted in collective life, "born into a world in tension between order and disorder" and bound by the dictates of a moral natural law.[3] These older ideas informed his designs and his theory of administration in significant ways. An explication of his republican theory can be derived from his brief but thoughtful definition of a republic offered in a letter to the *New York Evening Post* in 1802:

> The truth seems to be, that all Governments have been deemed Republics, in which a large portion of the sovereignty has been vested in the whole, or in a considerable body of the people; and that none have been deemed Monarchies as contrasted with the Republican standard, in which there has not been an *hereditary* Chief Magistrate.
>
> Were we to attempt a correct definition of a Republican Government, we should say, "That is a Republican Government in which both the Executive and Legislative organs are appointed by a popular Election, and hold their offices upon a responsible and defeasible tenure."[4]

This definition includes five elements, expressed or implied, that give form to Hamilton's republic: natural law and divisible sovereignty, no hereditary offices, partitioned powers, representation and popular elections, and accountable forms of responsibility. When Hamilton said republics vest "a large portion of the sovereignty" in the people, he really meant a portion as distinguished from total possession of sovereignty. The people are the source of the Constitution, but their sovereignty is not absolute. Other considerations pertain, especially natural law and the divisibility of sovereignty.

Natural Law and Divisible Sovereignty

Hamilton understood natural law to be rationally and intuitively apprehendable, with many of its insights discerned in the discourse of influential writers on the subject and manifested in large part through the law of nations. This law "embodied the deliberative experience [and scrutiny] of generations of human beings from different nations" and in the eighteenth century was expounded by such leading figures as Hugo Grotius, Richard Hooker, Samuel von Pufendorf, Jean-Jacques Burlamaqui, and Emmerich de Vattel.[5] Hamilton treated the natural law as "indispensably obligatory upon all mankind, prior to any human institution." Hence, all constitutions created by men are subject to the dictates of natural law. A positive (human-made) law that violates natural law is void. Hamilton stated as much in an early pamphlet titled *The Farmer Refuted*: "No human laws are of any validity, if contrary to this [natural law], and such of them as are valid, derive all their authority, mediately or immediately, from the original." He thus rejected Thomas Hobbes's assertion that there is no morality outside of civil society, as well as David Hume's reduction of morality to matters of social utility or expedience. His republican theory therefore rids sovereignty of some absolutist baggage.[6]

Natural law provides limits and structure for sovereign power that extend beyond the people of a specific regime to include, for example, treaties informed by standards drawn from the law of nations. Natural law thus limits and conditions sovereignty through a variety of sources and institutions. Sovereignty in its traditional sense (as expressed during the European renaissance) meant "independence and power which are *separately* or *transcendently* supreme and are exercised upon the body politic *from above*."[7] The sovereign is the source of law and is therefore above the law (i.e., absolute). Moreover, sovereignty as traditionally conceived must be indivisible, proceeding from one body— that of a prince or a king—and clothed with a majesty that is wholly separate from the governed.[8] The sovereign stands apart from the rest of society. Hamilton and his colleagues found this formulation untenable. They conceived of a sovereignty divided between the states and the national government and of sovereign power as flowing from the people who, with those chosen to govern, were themselves subject to the laws of the country and of the law of nations. No one should be above the law. Sovereignty clearly entailed a different meaning, one for which other terms seem more appropriate.[9]

The kind of power the founders spoke of as flowing from the people is better described as "plenary" or "requisite" power—terms they used often and seemingly interchangeably. This is power complete over a particular area or for a particular purpose. For example, when Hamilton spoke of executive power as plenary, he meant that the executive has all those powers deemed essential or requisite to the performance of executive duties, subject to prudent limits and exceptions. This state of power is distinguished from the state of having all conceivable power, which is more in the spirit of sovereignty's original meaning. Hamilton employed the terms "plenary" and "requisite" in the former sense, not in the latter. To illustrate, in his opinion on the constitutionality of the US Bank, he used "requisite" in direct reference to sovereignty: "Now it appears to the Secretary of the Treasury, that this *general principle* is *inherent* in the very *definition* of Government and *essential* to every step of the progress to be made by that of the United States; namely—that every power vested in a Government is in its nature *sovereign*, and includes by *force* of the *term*, a right to employ all the *means* requisite, and fairly *applicable* to the attainment of the *ends* of such power; and which are not precluded by restrictions & exceptions specified in the constitution; or not immoral, or not contrary to the essential ends of political society."[10] In Hamilton's mind, both the people and their governing officials are limited in their powers first by natural law and second by the positive laws and processes established or recognized under the Constitution. The people possess the power to change the Constitution through processes stipulated therein, but only in a way that coincides (as Hamilton stated in his *Phocion* letters) with the "dictates of natural justice," the "dictates of reason and equity," and "many other maxims, never to be forgotten in any but tyrannical governments."[11] So, when employing the term sovereignty in the republican context, it is more appropriate to say that the people are sovereign through their Constitution, and that the national and state governments participate in this sovereignty through the plenary powers assigned to them.

This formulation accords with Hamilton's treatment of the subject and is significant because Hamilton wanted to change what he believed was a fundamentally flawed relationship of the national government to the states as established under the Articles of Confederation.[12] The articles made the national government dependent upon the powers of the states, a relation he described in *Federalist* essay 15 as "the political monster of an *imperium in imperio*" in which "the concurrence of thirteen distinct sovereign wills is requisite . . . to the complete execution of every important measure that proceeds from the Union." In effect, the arrangement denied to the national government the plenary powers needed to perform its duties effectively in order to establish a true union. As a result, the arrangement "arrested all the wheels of the national government and brought them to an awful stand."[13] This was hardly a matter of abstract theory for Hamilton. He had experienced firsthand the terrible effects of this disparity of power during the Revolutionary War.

The Articles of Confederation established a weak and feckless national government. It could generate no independent revenues and had to rely instead upon requisitions from the states for everything. Furthermore, the few powers ceded to it were lodged entirely within the Continental Congress. All aspects of administration were conducted by congressional boards or committees, with predictable and debilitating results. The states often failed to comply with congressional requests for resources, and the congressional boards acted slowly, if at all, and entirely without consistency or system. Hamilton chronicled the effects in his *Continentalist* essays of 1781, stating that the "whole system is in disorder and unprovided with everything."[14]

As General Washington's chief aide-de-camp, Hamilton witnessed on a broad scale the failures of this arrangement. The country possessed willingness, resources, men, and foreign aid sufficient to quickly defeat the much smaller British forces. But instead, the war dragged on for years because of poor organization and management. "As in the explanation of our embarrassments nothing can be alleged to the disaffection of the people, we must have recourse to the other cause of IMPOLICY and MISMANAGEMENT in their RULERS."[15]

After the war, the confederation continued in the same fashion, perpetuating if not exacerbating the conditions established during the war. Lack of power and organization in the national government precipitated political and economic crises, and leading figures pressed for the establishment of a new government, one capable of stable and systematic public administration. Thus followed the Annapolis and Philadelphia conventions and the framing of the Constitution in 1787.

In Hamilton's view, the new constitution remedied the problem with a safely vested mix of independent and concurrent powers for both the states and the federal government, such that neither is "dependent on the other for the efficacy of its power."[16] However, as

Michael Federici observes, the remedy required some subtraction of the states' powers in order to establish independent federal powers, and it "was this very subtraction that bothered many anti-Federalists and caused them to oppose ratification, or to insist on the addition of a national bill of rights that clarified the distribution of sovereignty."[17] The Bill of Rights notwithstanding, Americans have been arguing and fighting over this distribution ever since. In the founding era, the Jeffersonian Republicans coalesced into a political party in large part to claw back some of the new federal prerogatives in favor of states' rights, while Hamiltonian Federalists endeavored to firmly establish a broad construction of requisite federal powers. Hamilton led the Federalist effort with legal opinions and new national administrative organs that would make the supremacy clause and other broad provisions of the new constitution a reality.

The connection of law to administration here is of crucial significance. The political battles of the day centered around the establishment of federal administrative agencies and quasi-public institutions such as the Bank of the United States, and Hamilton's legal opinions outlined an administratively empowering jurisprudence that Federalist judges such as John Marshall and Joseph Story would apply well into the nineteenth century. The more immediate point is that the disputes over political power were channeled or sublimated into the legal/administrative realm, which made the principle of rule by law the overarching standard in American governance. Ron Chernow described it this way: "Virtually every program that Hamilton put together raised fundamental constitutional issues, so that his legal training and work on *The Federalist* enabled him to craft the efficient machinery of government while expounding its theoretical underpinnings."[18]

The founders in general equated rule by law with liberty. As Hamilton put it, "Government is frequently and aptly classed unto two descriptions—a government of FORCE, and a government of LAWS; the first is the definition of despotism—the last, of liberty."[19] Republican governance thus requires reasoning and reasonableness regimented through forms and processes of law that can be publicly scrutinized and debated. In that context, Jeffersonian Republicans emphasized the limits and constraints they believed the Constitution imposed on federal administration, while Hamilton and the Federalists showed how many of the same clauses cited actually justified expansive, developmental powers. As Samuel Konefsky puts it, "The Constitution was launched both as a tool of statecraft and as a touchstone of permissible authority to govern."[20]

No Hereditary Offices

Though Hamilton proposed tenure during good behavior for the president and the Senate in his plan at the Constitutional Convention, he never advocated hereditary office. As Federici observes, "There is not a grain of support for hereditary government in the whole of Hamilton's writings."[21] Indeed, the idea of hereditary office went very much against his preoccupation with merit in appointments to office, whether for the office of president or for a mere clerkship. "I desire *above all things* to see equality of political rights exclusive of all *hereditary* distinctions firmly established by a practical demonstration of its being consistent with the order and happiness of society."[22] Given Hamilton's origins, considerations of birth likely held little sway over him in any matters, much less those concerning public office. He demonstrated his preoccupation with merit over birth and patronage early in his military career. As a young captain in charge of an artillery company, he proposed to the New York Congress that promotion to officer status from the lower ranks be instituted to bolster morale and confidence. He believed that highly capable men existed in those ranks and should be promoted quickly to seal their commitment to military service and to address the scarcity of effective leaders in the field. His proposal was accepted, and it contributed significantly to the democratization of the military.[23]

Hamilton's aversion to hereditary office was practical rather than ideological. He believed that hereditary office was appropriate in other kinds of regimes with histories and political cultures quite different from those that had emerged in the United States. For example, when asked in 1799 to recommend a form of government for Santo Domingo, he suggested that "a hereditary Chief would be best" and that "no regular system of Liberty will at present suit [it]. The government if independent must be military—partaking of the feodal system."[24] Writing to his good friend the Marquis de Lafayette earlier that year, he agreed with Montesquieu that forms of government "must be fitted to a nation, as much as a coat to the individual, and consequently that what may be good at Philadelphia may be bad at Paris and ridiculous at Petersburgh."[25] This aspect of his thought stemmed from the strong sense of moral realism and political contingency that pervaded his writings and actions in public service. It sometimes forced him into controversy for taking stands that went against the popular mood, such as when defending the property rights of Tory loyalists at the end of the Revolutionary War. The charge of "Monarchist!" with all its hereditary implications, stuck to him unfairly as a result, despite his careful treatment of executive power and the presidency as republican in letter and spirit.

Partitioned Powers

Hamilton's mention of "executive and legislative organs" in his definition of a republic refers to the partitioning of power, about which he and Madison had written extensively. Under the new constitution, the partitioning worked vertically as well as horizontally. Vertically, the division of sovereignty between state and federal governments made each level a check against the other. People were overwhelmingly preoccupied at the time with the ability of the states to resist a tyrannical federal government. Hamilton saw it differently. He believed the states would pose a more dangerous threat to liberty if they lacked a strong unifying power through the federal government. They would likely descend to a state of warring rivalries akin to those in Europe and thereby lock themselves into primitive conditions that would make durable liberty meaningless. He feared that even under the new constitution the states retained a clear advantage over the federal government due to the close affection and loyalty of their citizens. Writing in *Federalist* essay 17, he offered one distinguishing element that might give an advantage to the federal government—the prospect of a more effective administration: "It is a known fact in human nature that its affections are commonly weak in proportion to the distance or diffusiveness of the object. Upon the same principle that a man is more attached to his family than to his neighborhood, to his neighborhood than to the community at large, the people of each State would be apt to feel a stronger bias towards their local governments than towards the government of the Union; unless the force of that principle should be destroyed by a much better administration of the latter."[26] Hamilton believed that if the new national government could impress the people with sound administrative practices and policies, it might win their approval and perhaps even their loyalty.

It was thus imperative that the new national government take advantage of every constitutional means for improving its administrative capacities and quickly exercise the powers granted to it to avoid losing any of them through neglect. For Hamilton, the horizontal partition of powers (or separation of powers through checks and balances) played a vital role in that effort.

In the *Federalist* essays, Madison and Hamilton carefully explained the nature of the separation of powers as manifested in the three superintending branches: legislative, executive, and judicial. They focused primarily on how this separation could be sustained through carefully designed checks and balances that would prevent any one branch from usurping the powers of the other two. For rhetorical effect, they drew public attention mainly to how the design ensured representativeness and then to how it prevented the national government from exercising tyrannical power—defined as one branch usurping the whole powers of the others.

Fear of tyrannical government ran rampant among the founding generation, which had just overthrown its British masters through a bloody and protracted war. Many were suspicious of granting government any power at all in the aftermath. As Herbert Storing put it, the Federalists had to remind Americans "that the true principle of the Revolution was not hostility to government, but hostility to tyrannical government."[27] Both Hamilton and Madison committed themselves to explaining in detail how a powerful national government could protect individual rights and liberties more effectively than the Articles of Confederation could and how that power could also be controlled. The essays were long and thorough in discussing both limits and powers, but their rhetorical design drew most attention to limits. To this day, the essays are explained mainly for how the federal government's powers are constrained. It is easy to overlook the fact that the separation of powers also set in place a means to effective administration.

The *Federalist* treated the Constitution as a superstructure of safe yet powerful administration, and as will be shown in the next chapter, the framers accomplished this through the same features that prevented tyranny. Hamilton pushed this administrative capacity further than Madison in pursuit of his vision for an effective national republic, and this became their point of schism as political allies during the Washington administration.[28] Nevertheless, they both embraced the idea that a partitioning and sharing of power through *partial agency* also lends itself to degrees of specialization, cooperation, and integration of all three powers to facilitate energetic administration.

Popular Election and Representation

The fourth element in Hamilton's definition of a republic involved popular election and the root principle of representation. He deemed it essential in a republic that the "principal organs of the executive and legislative departments be elected directly or indirectly by the people."

A representative democracy is a republic with "representatives chosen by them [the people] either mediately or immediately and legally accountable to them."[29] As Flaumenhaft indicates, Hamilton wanted the national government based on the broadest possible representation because he believed that the multiplicity of interests and the extended geographical sphere of the American republic would make compromise necessary and lessen the inclinations of local prejudice and faction.[30] Contrary to the Anti-Federalists' desire for a government close to the people, Hamilton wanted to give representatives some distance, some breathing room from their constituents, to gain perspective on the needs of the nation. This did not mean that he wanted them to ignore local interests. By dint of their short terms, they would take care to return often to their home states and communities and stay in touch at least with local opinion leaders. In general, he believed that the "popular views and even prejudices" of local constituents would direct their actions.[31] What he hoped for, however, was that the distance from local constituents would help representatives channel local interests into broader interests and connect their own personal ambitions to the fortunes of the nation.

In the event that this dynamic failed in the House of Representatives, the Senate as well as the executive and judicial branches would be there to temper its impassioned fluctuations through various checks and balances. If the people are sovereign through their constitution, then the organs of that constitution must, as Federici explains, balance its *ephemeral* aspects with its more *permanent* features. "In this sense, then, political and social communities, like individuals, have centripetal and centrifugal forces working against one another at any given time. Hamilton was convinced that democratic impulse was part of the centrifugal aspect of politics; it was fleeting, ephemeral, and transitory. By contrast, the centripetal aspect of political life had a unifying effect. It harmonized disparate interests and pulled society toward an abiding and enduring standard that was, in Hamilton's words, *permanent*."[32] The constitutional system intendedly "serves as an expression of the society's permanent will"[33] and is thus "representative in all its parts." Hamilton made the crucial point that confining the representative principle to the legislative branch alone would necessarily make it the supreme body of the government, and that would inevitably lead right back to the enervating legislative vortex experienced under the Articles of Confederation. The Constitution provides a solution to this problem through successive layers of direct and indirect election in the legislative and executive branches and then through participation in appointments of judges and subordinate administrative officials by those elected officials. It is significant that the Constitution recognizes twenty-two different methods of appointment to federal offices, only one of which is through direct election by the people. The entire government, including the subordinate public administration, participates in the constitutional order of the republic and in varying degrees bolsters the representative principle.[34]

Judges and subordinate officials, who often enjoy career appointments (during good behavior), participate in representation by protecting and tempering it through the rule of law and by extending it through the administrative ranks. Leonard D. White noted that one of four main criteria for appointments to subordinate offices in the founding period emphasized geographical and state-by-state representation, and it has remained an important criterion ever since.[35] Hamilton favored long-term appointments for most federal offices. Representation in the administrative ranks would play a direct role in forming the expression of society's permanent will and would connect their interests and loyalties to national office.

Furthermore, in their representational roles, they should display a temperament appropriate to governing in a republic. As treasury secretary, Hamilton took great care in selecting street-level officials who "afforded the strongest assurance that their conduct will be that of good Officers & good Citizens" and that they would display a proper bearing as officers of a republic.[36] They were to be "embued with a sense of public service"[37] and to avoid any display of arrogance or officiousness with the public. His first instructions to new revenue-cutter employees illustrate the point:

> While I recommend in the strongest terms to the respective Officers, activity, vigilance & firmness, I feel no less solicitude that their deportment may be marked with prudence, moderation & good temper. . . . The charge with which they are entrusted is a delicate one, & that it is easy by mismanagement to produce serious & extensive clamour, disgust & odium.
>
> They will always keep in mind that their Countrymen are Freemen & as such are impatient of everything that bears the least mark of a domineering Spirit. They will therefore refrain with the most guarded circumspection from whatever has the semblance of haughtiness, rudeness or insult. . . . They will endeavor to overcome difficulties, if any are experienced, by a cool and temperate perseverance in their duty, by address & moderation rather than by vehemence or violence.[38]

Here is a temperament suitable for officials in a republic. It prescribes an attitude toward public service to which Hamilton then coupled his sense of proper responsibility and accountability in office.

Responsibility and Accountability

Lynton Caldwell described Hamilton as "the nation's foremost advocate of responsible administration."[39] Hamilton's writings are replete with references to the subject, and he held a rather nuanced view of it in the context of the Constitution. He shared with James Madison the conviction that in public office one must learn how to connect a person's interests and passions "with the constitutional rights of the place" (*Federalist* essay 51) and "to make them cooperate to the public good."[40] This modern liberal principle entails both internal and external dimensions that Hamilton derived from his sense of public morality. Drawing insights from Vattel and Hume, he developed a theory of administrative responsibility that viewed public office as a place to combine nobler passions for achieving great public things with a jealous regard for one's public reputation—matters treated at length in chapter 4. Suffice it to say here that the new Constitution conferred both the power to act and the checks necessary to ensure accountability in ways that even people with less-than-stellar private lives could become public-spirited in office. Hamilton regarded this prospect as essential to a republic where common people would seek office at every level and where minimum qualifications for most elected offices are constrained only by age and defeasible tenure.

To summarize, Hamilton's conception of republican government included the following: (1) the rule of law with dual sovereignty (plenary powers) emanating from the people and in accord with the dictates of natural law; (2) no hereditary offices, with a focus instead on merit, representativeness, and opportunity as leading criteria for holding office; (3) carefully partitioned powers that guard against abuse of office while contributing to effective governance; (4) popular elections where governance is carried out by representatives of many stripes who are appointed through direct and indirect elections and who oversee cadres of political and career appointees; and (5) a strong sense of public responsibility that requires substantial powers and requisite checks to ensure accountability.

Within this republican framework, Hamilton envisioned ample room for variation in organizational forms and administrative practices. The Constitution itself manifested a novel and innovative superstructure for a new government that he believed was conducive to an energetic and stable administration. His reports and proposals as secretary of the treasury will show that subordinate administrative organs could be structured permissively into a variety of forms to meet the ends entrusted to them. It made no sense to him to allow form to cripple the ability of government to achieve those ends for the sole purpose of limiting and checking power. He did not see these as mutually exclusive matters but rather as providing a productive tension through which to safely conduct ambitious and effective administration. He continually reminded his political rivals of this point. The dilemma, though, lay in the fact that the Anti-Federalists embraced a contrary view of the role of the new national government in American society, especially in relation to the states. Their views followed from their differing vision of what that society should look like and how it should evolve. Hamilton's vision stood in marked contrast to theirs, and both have contributed to the character of American public administration ever since. To appreciate the significance of Hamilton's administrative theory, one needs to explore these contrasts.

Founding Visions of the American Republic

The founders' arguments over the framing of a new republican constitution took place in the context of sweeping changes in Europe. The embrace of modern liberal political ideas led not only to innovations in political reform but also to liberalized economic theories and reforms that transformed markets and financial practices and accommodated the European Industrial Revolution. The American founders witnessed these changes with a mix of enthusiasm and horror. The Anti-Federalists drew upon those theories and practices that they believed would help them sustain a relatively sedate agrarian republic, while Hamilton and the Federalists embraced theories and practices that would promote development of a feverish and complex commercial republic. Each bore implications for what powers should be conferred through the new constitution and how the new government should be run.

The Anti-Federalist Republican Vision

While significant variation existed among the Anti-Federalists about their vision for the American republic, they were, as Herbert Storing characterized it, "on the whole defenders of the status quo." They strongly identified with their home states and "saw in the Framers' easy thrusting aside of old forms and principles [serious] threats to four cherished values: to law, to political stability, to principles of the Declaration of Independence, and to federalism."[41] Anti-Federalists were wedded to the federation of states established under the Articles of Confederation and could not accept the idea of dual sovereignty. One power or another must prevail in the relationship, and that should be the states. The national government must serve strictly as an instrument of the federation. They viewed the framers' attempt to set aside the Articles of Confederation at the Annapolis Convention as a brazen disregard of law and as a violation of their obligation as state delegates simply to improve on the existing order of things. An attempt to consolidate the union with a much stronger national government meant, to their way of thinking, the eventual abandonment of state preeminence and of local customs that embraced both ancient and modern aspects of their lives.

Anti-Federalists seemed more ambivalent about modern liberal trends, often looking aghast at the societal conditions established in Europe through the Industrial Revolution. They deplored the abuses of the coalescing nation-states of Europe and were hypersensitive to the abuses they personally suffered under British rule. They subscribed to an *exceptionalist* notion that the American states were offered a unique setting and God-given opportunity to establish small, peaceful republics that emphasized the virtues of moderation, vigilance, hard work, and thrift. America enjoyed the good fortune of being isolated by a long distance from the European empires, and this offered the prospect, they believed, of establishing separate state republics, (1) whose spirit was naturally pacific toward each other; (2) in which agrarian-based commerce would soften mores and thereby mute the inflammable passions for war; and (3) in which a modest commercial spirit would bind them together by "mutual interest, amity, and concord."[42] The confederation, therefore, needed neither a standing army nor a strong central government. These were, in Patrick Henry's words, the tools of empires seeking the blessings of "grandeur, power and splendor," at the sacrifice of the simple and modest end of protecting individual rights.[43]

For Anti-Federalists, then, the quality most vital to a small republic was the vigilant temperament thought to exist most prominently in those of middling circumstances, who "are inclined by habit, and the company with whom they associate, to set bounds to their passions and appetites." They believed that the substantial yeomanry of the country were "more temperate, of better morals, and less ambition, than the great."[44] Correspondingly, they subscribed to a governance model at state and local levels marked by very short terms of office, civic activism or engagement based largely on suspicion of those in power, immediate responsiveness to the community, low pay for public servants, open access to their jobs and their attention, and home-grown, intimate knowledge of the community and its local customs. The central government should operate under the same policies but must be subject to even more intense scrutiny and suspicion because of its distance from most states and the people. Representatives, they feared, would lose their local attachments if allowed to stay in national office much beyond a few years. Representation in their minds meant putting people in office who were just like them, retaining all their local prejudices and attachments.

Some Anti-Federalists also "deplored departures of the Constitution from 'the good old way' or 'the antient and established usage of the commonwealth,' and were nervous about '*the phrenzy of innovation* sweeping the country.'"[45] However, the vision and ideals they expressed in opposition to the Constitution also partook substantially of modern liberal ideas expressed by such luminaries as Montesquieu, Smith, and Hume, as well as by spokesmen for the English Opposition movement such as Trenchard, Gordon, and Bolingbrook. They heartily subscribed to individual liberty as an ascendant principle and reviled infringements on their property such as were listed in Jefferson's Declaration of Independence. They also embraced new political-economic ideas, found in works by Richard Cantillon, François Quesnay, Adam Smith, and David Hume, which they believed supported small agrarian republics.

McDonald explains that Anti-Federalists were especially drawn to Physiocratic theory with its claimed empirical justification for, and "insistence upon, the absoluteness of property rights, the uniqueness of land as the source of wealth, and the superiority of agriculture as a way of life."[46] The theory posited that "land alone could produce a surplus of greater value than that of the labor invested in it." Quesnay divided people into two classes, *productive* and *sterile*. Only farmers were productive, while merchants and landowners "produced nothing but consumed much through their rents and profits," and urban artisans "produced an amount equal to but never exceeding the value of their labor, which provided them a bare subsistence."[47]

Anti-Federalists seized upon these ideas as further justification for an agrarian republic and quickly embraced Adam Smith's liberal doctrine of laissez-faire (a term first employed by the Physiocrats), which advocated a hands-off approach to the economy. The doctrine espoused the very seductive idea that unregulated competition among individuals in the marketplace would automatically produce the greatest welfare for all, as opposed to merely benefiting the few who are in league with those who govern. The idea could hardly be more attractive to those wanting a weak national government that would stay out of their lives. Moreover, the automatically regulating assumption in Smith's doctrine would reinforce in many minds the idea, born during the revolution, that Americans would need very little government at all. The public interest is best served by simply letting individuals rationally pursue their own interests.

As McDonald explains, however, Adam Smith's laissez-faire doctrine owed much to an earlier work by Bernard Mandeville, "whose writings conveyed a message that was at once unwelcome and irresistibly attractive." It revealed a dark side to "letting nature takes its course" that some Anti-Federalists worried would "doom the republic in the long run."[48] Mandeville had written an allegory, *The Fable of the Bees*, in 1714 that was meant to shock and ridicule the puritanical fanatics of his day by showing how private vices such as lust, vanity, and greed could yield public benefits. But moral reformers, he asserted, "hypocritically feigning discontent at having their prosperity depend upon their vices, pray to be made virtuous, then bring an end to this natural course of things," and thereby destroy the beneficial economy they had wrought.

Mandeville's work was roundly condemned and became notorious, but it anticipated key aspects of subsequent economic theory made more palatable by Smith, who taught in *The Wealth of Nations* that "it is not from the benevolence of the butcher, the brewer, or the baker, that we expect our dinner, but from their regard to their own interest." They are "led by an invisible hand to promote an end which is no part of [their] intention."[49] This sounds more benign in moral terms, but its logic clearly led to a result that rural agrarians reviled: the transition to a thoroughly commercial society that embraces manufacturing as a key element of the economy. With it, they believed, would come all the attendant social ills witnessed in Europe. Moreover, it would elicit the desire for luxury among those gaining in wealth, and this would eventually corrupt the agrarian virtues that Anti-Federalists believed were essential to the life of a republic.

However, some in the founding generation, Jefferson and Madison among them, spied a way to forestall the advent of a full commercial stage of development. They believed that the vast western lands of the American continent provided an opportunity for retaining the agricultural base of the nation. McDonald nicely summarizes Madison's description of the theory: "The essence of it was that government should intervene to arrest the evolution of stages of progress at the commercial agricultural stage, so that America might enjoy the refinements but not be subject to the corruption. This would involve commercial regulations that would secure markets for American agricultural production, promote the household manufacture of simple objects, and keep America dependent upon Europe for the finer manufactures; and crucially, it would involve a policy of territorial expansion to ensure that there would be land enough to keep most of the people on farms and thus to prevent the growth of the *superfluity* of population which was thought to be necessary for the development of large-scale manufacturing industries."[50] Anti-Federalists quickly found Madison's theory attractive, to the point of acquiescing to his plan of national government and thereby making the new Constitution's eventual ratification possible in the middling and southern states. It was, however, a theory based upon seriously flawed assumptions and a lack of understanding of current political-economic realities in England and the rest of Europe. McDonald described it as "pie-in-the-sky political economy."[51] The founding father who most clearly understood the political-economic realities of the day was Alexander Hamilton, and his vision of the American republic differed accordingly.

Hamilton's Republican Vision

Hamilton found the Anti-Federalist vision shortsighted and unrealistic. He had read the sources that supported it and much more, especially the broader literature on political economy and the works of European statesmen who improvised the policies and laws that transformed the European political and economic landscape. He had also read history voraciously, and what he learned led him to very different conclusions about the nature and prospects of commercial republics.

He viewed as sheer utopian speculation the argument that commercial republics were by nature more peaceful and that the American setting far from Europe would enhance that peacefulness, especially if the states remained separate and merely federated republics. Rather, he argued in *Federalist* essay 6 that staying in that condition "would be to disregard the uniform course of human events, and to set at defiance the accumulated experience of ages." The states would inevitably be thrown into "frequent and violent contests with each other. To presume a want of motives for such contests as an argument against their existence would be to forget that men are ambitious, vindictive, and rapacious."[52] And then after reviewing "innumerable" causes of enmity and war among nations generally, he addressed commercial regimes specifically:

> Have republics in practice been less addicted to war than monarchies? Are not the former administered by *men* as well as the latter? Are there not aversions, predilections, rivalships, and desires of unjust acquisitions that affect nations as well as kings? Are not popular assemblies frequently subject to the impulses of rage, resentment, jealousy, avarice, and of other irregular and violent propensities? . . . Is not the love of wealth as domineering and enterprising a passion as that of power and glory? Have there not been as many wars founded upon commercial motives since that has become the prevailing system of nations, as were for territory and dominion? Has not the spirit of commerce, in many instances, administered new incentives to the appetite, both for the one and for the other?[53]

To demonstrate his point, he presented numerous examples from history, and then in *Federalist* essay 7 he detailed specific causes of strife germane to the American states as separate or federated republics. Jealous disputes were likely to arise over (1) the distribution of territorial lands; (2) the differences in commercial policies (import/export regulations, taxes/duties, etc.) favoring one or a few states over others by way of invidious "distinctions, preferences, and exclusions"; (3) the apportionment of war debt and its extinguishment afterward; (4) laws in violation of private contracts that work injury upon citizens of other states; and (5) the "probability of incompatible alliances between different states, or confederacies, and different foreign nations."[54] These problems were already evident, especially those arising from regional differences in commercial policies between southern states, whose economies were founded upon slavery, and northern states, whose economies were based in commerce. Hamilton averred, prophetically, that even with a more solidified union, such differences would be difficult at best to overcome. He expressed doubt that Madison's multiplicity of interests (à la *Federalist* essay 10), if spread through the extended republic, would effectively mute regional differences and prevent the emergence of dominating interests.

Hamilton believed the influences of western European commercialism were already sewn deep in the hearts of most Americans. Thus, despite its many dangers, he believed that only a complex political economy with its blend of manufacturing, commercial trade, and agriculture would be able to provide the range of opportunities needed for Americans to better themselves. Staving off manufacturing and constricting commercial trade for the sake of preserving a rural agrarian republic would favor only a small, elite portion of the population that would continue to bank its prosperity on the backs of slaves. He viewed Jefferson's yeoman farmer more as a romantic ideal than as a reflection of real agrarian conditions. He knew their frugality often stemmed from severe want, punctuated by long periods of indolence due to crop cycles. Local manufactories could productively fill their free time and improve their living conditions. These would complement the agrarian way of life and bring about a more mature and vibrant commercial and manufacturing base in northern states that lacked sufficient arable land. A mixed economy was therefore essential to sealing the union of the states into one nation. Furthermore, it could offer the prospect of establishing a republic marked at least in part by the virtue of liberality.

Michael Chan has explored the meaning of liberality through a comparison of Aristotle's and Hamilton's thought and finds that it played a significant, if understated, role in Hamilton's republican vision. In its classical sense, liberality is the mean between extravagance and stinginess. It inculcates generosity. Ancient regimes treated virtues in general as matters of "individual excellence of the soul," but with liberality there is "a political counterpart in such things as common messes, beautiful public works, religious sacrifices, and rewarding slaves (public and private) with their freedom."[55] Liberality was thus ennobling individually and collectively, and Hamilton clearly envisioned a noble republic in both senses. Leaders of the American republic would "undertake or execute liberal or enlarged plans of public good" that if implemented effectively would earn the public's trust and burnish its reputation abroad. These would contribute to an admirable and powerful national character that would win more favorable terms in treaty, trade, and financial negotiations and thereby improve the standard of living throughout the republic.

Chan sees in Hamilton's political economy an ordering of lower to higher ends: "security, prosperity, reputation of the commonwealth, keeping engagements (good faith/justice), [and] liberality." Hamilton believed that a properly funded government would "avoid a frequent sacrifice of its engagements to immediate necessity."[56] An effective and prosperous republic could thereby avoid the often immoral extreme of constant expedience and exigency and practice liberality in its domestic and foreign policies.

In his Camillus essays responding to challenges against the proposed Jay Treaty with Great Britain (1795), Hamilton referred to a recent treaty with Prussia as a *model of liberality* and criticized statements by Republican pamphleteers who tried to sway public opinion against such with Britain. "These particulars are stated as evidence of the temper of the day, and of a policy which then prevailed to bottom our system with regard to foreign nations upon those grounds of moderation and equity, by which reason, religion, and philosophy had tempered the harsh maxims of more early times. It is painful to observe an effort to make the public opinion in this respect retrograde, and to infect our Councils with a spirit contrary to these salutary advances towards improvement in true civilization and humanity."[57] The particulars mentioned by Hamilton were treaty provisions notable for their protection of "freedom of conscience and worship," for "extending protection to the persons as well as the goods of enemies," and even for paying for confiscated contraband articles "other than arms, ammunition and military stores."[58] These were indeed generous provisions even by modern standards, but the resentment against the British ran deep and fostered motives of revenge and stinginess that the Washington administration (and especially Hamilton) believed would betray American interests and sully the nation's reputation.

In Hamilton's mind, then, commerce would provide the equipment of liberal virtue for the republic, and this would, in Chan's words, stand in contrast to the liberality of the ancient republic, "which was grounded in slavery and plunder": "Modern public liberality would be *just* because it would be grounded in consent, something guaranteed by the Constitution's requirement of popular consent to all taxation (i.e., all revenue bills must originate in the most popular branch, the House of Representatives). Hamilton's great innovation in American Republicanism was to understand that consent served not only to limit but to invigorate the powers of government; that is, consent can provide the grounding for *energy* in government" (emphasis mine).[59] Here lay the critical disjuncture between Hamilton's and Madison's constitutional theory, and they parted company over it in the early 1790s, as Hamilton laid out his financial plans for the public good. Madison wanted a more powerful national government to stabilize and regulate the commercial affairs of the states, but he could not support the active involvement of the national government in developing a prosperous national economy. As a Virginian, he embraced the vision of an agrarian republic with limited manufactures. Thus, like Jefferson, he emphasized the limits imposed on the national government through the Constitution and refused to acknowledge that its provisions could also invigorate it for more ambitious and liberal plans. The dispute reveals how the broad language of the Constitution could be interpreted by eminently reasonable founders in widely different ways. We have been arguing over those differences ever since.

Hamilton's vision embraced active national leadership and governmental involvement in shaping a liberal commercial republic. His plans for the public good involved the establishment of a financial system that included a treasury department at its hub, a central bank for monetizing debt and stimulating credit on good terms, a sinking fund for managing public debt, a mint for standardizing the currency, a diverse system of taxation to be phased in over time, and an aggressive customs service and coast guard. Beyond that, he laid plans for stimulating and integrating manufactures with robust commercial and agricultural development, for employing policies of protection from unfair trade practices abroad, and for generous incentives as well as aggressive regulatory provisions for ensuring the quality of goods produced and traded. Hamilton envisioned the construction of roads, canals, public buildings, and military academies, and the promotion of mechanical arts, immigration of foreign artisans, and importation of capital in all its forms. These are addressed at length in the following chapters as matters integral to Hamilton's energetic public administration.

Conclusion

Hamilton's republican vision brings us back to his words at the start of this chapter: "There is something noble and magnificent in the perspective of a great Federal Republic, closely linked in the pursuit of a common interest, tranquil and prosperous at home, respectable abroad." He aimed to establish such a regime, and central to that project was erecting a constitutional republic based on popular consent, careful in its partition of powers, and conducive to a wise and effective public administration. Much of the focus of that administration should be directed to "liberal and enlarged plans for the public good," which multiply the opportunities of its people to better their lives through prosperous commerce and related pursuits and which cultivate public as well as private liberality. This would require active and responsible leadership, and the key to it lay in a high-toned administration and an energetic executive.

2
The Energetic Executive in Constitutional Context

> The administration of government, in its largest sense,
> comprehends all the operations of the body politic, whether
> legislative, executive, or judiciary; but in its most usual and
> perhaps in its most precise signification, it is limited to executive
> details, and falls peculiarly within the province of the executive
> department. The actual conduct of foreign negotiations, the
> preparatory plans of finance, the application and disbursement
> of the public moneys in conformity to the general appropriations
> of the legislature, the arrangement of the army and navy, the
> direction of the operations of war—these, and other matters of a
> like nature, constitute what seems to be most properly understood
> by the administration of government.
> —Alexander Hamilton, *Federalist* essay 72

Hamilton's definition of public administration includes two important meanings. First, public administration refers to the process or operation of the whole government. It comprehends all three branches.
Legislators and judges participate in the public administration, but
their powers and contributions differ in ways that distance them from
the locus of governmental action. They make vitally important decisions, but they must rely on agencies and independent boards and
commissions to bring them to fruition. Importantly, the dynamics that
ensue from this relationship guarantee a mixture of conflict, cooperation, and integration of their powers in subordinate agencies. This will
be illustrated in Hamilton's management of the Treasury Department
and related financial institutions. The experience of governing shaped
much of Hamilton's thought, so his public administrative theory must
be drawn from both his words and his actions.

The second and more usual meaning of public administration is
"limited to executive details." However, the *details* offered by Hamilton are hardly mundane or trivial. They are breathtaking in scope—
what could be more significant than conducting foreign relations,
stimulating public finance and credit, managing funds pursuant to
appropriations, organizing the military, and directing warfare? These

are governing activities that directly secure and enhance the liberties of the people—the chief ends of a liberal republic. They turn parchment laws and judicial decisions into lived reality. The executive and the subordinate administrators who oversee such matters play roles that are critical to the fate of the republic. They are no mere instruments. They govern in the fullest sense of the word, and in Hamilton's thinking, they exert a formative or *constitutive* influence on public policy and thence on the character of the people and the country.[1] In their pursuits, they must cultivate the "productive spirit of political economy," and through their tasks produce solid and durable results. Thus, as Harvey Flaumenhaft indicates, "When Hamilton spoke of *energy*, what he had in mind was not display: he meant business. The rejection of classical politics [with its focus on military glory and oratorical display] culminates in the politics of administration."[2] And it is the peculiar pedigree of the politics of administration to blend power with experience and expertise.

Energetic Government as Adequate Means to Republican Ends

Hamilton reasoned that if the ends of government are to be achieved, even to a modest degree, then governmental means must be granted in proportion to the ends, power must be made requisite with responsibility. This was one of the "most obvious rules of prudence and propriety," and he reiterated it throughout his writings and speeches and especially in the *Federalist*.[3] The advantage of *representative* democracy is that government can work *for* the people, freeing them from the complex burdens of governance to pursue their own interests and yet not stifling any honorable determination to strive for office or participate in the political process.[4] And if government is to work effectively for the people, it must exercise significant power. It was a principal argument of Publius (a favorite among his many nom de plumes) in the *Federalist* that the ends sought by the American people demanded union and sufficient concentration of power to achieve energetic government.

In the first *Federalist* essay, Hamilton wrote that a powerful government is "essential to the security of liberty" and that many people tend to forget this in their zeal for rights. He warned that "a dangerous ambition more often lurks behind the specious mask of zeal for the rights of the people than under the forbidding appearance of zeal for the firmness and efficiency of government. History will teach us that the former has been found a much more certain road to the introduction of despotism than the latter." As Flaumenhaft notes, "Hamilton finds ample concern for republican safety; the difficulty is in sufficiently providing the unity of power and the stability of policy necessary for energetic government. The Americans' habits and opinions in the situation impede the effort to protect their rights and promote their interests; they resist being governed because they fear to be oppressed."[5] The prudent framer must therefore accomplish a fusion of safety with power that helps to allay the fear.

A Safe yet Powerful Structure

If powerful government is necessary to preserve rights, then so are effective precautions against its abuse. Government must be "modeled in such a manner as to admit of its being safely vested with requisite powers."[6] Separation of powers and checks and balances, combined with the requisite powers of the state governments, provide the structural part of the solution.

In *Federalist* essay 51, Madison refers to the "double security" that arises from the separation of powers and the maintenance of "two distinct governments," national and state. They share concurrent taxing power and divide spheres of administration between general and particular objects. "The supreme legislature has only general powers, and the civil and domestic concerns of the people are regulated by the laws of the several states."[7] Furthermore, the partition between the national government and state governments creates competition for the affections of the people. As noted earlier, Hamilton argued that the nearness of state governments to the people provides the advantage of natural affection and local bias. On the other hand, such bias is counterbalanced by confidence in the national government if it provides "a much better administration." Thus, the quality of administration may determine the political superiority of one government or another, but neither is threatened with extinction. That Hamilton hoped and believed the national government would gain political superiority by better administration is clear, yet he also stated unequivocally that the states would provide "indispensable support, a necessary aid in executing the laws, and conveying the influence of government to the doors of the people." His attentiveness to the requisites of street-level bureaucracy made their existence "absolutely necessary to the system."[8]

The competition between the national government and state governments enables a suspicious populace to be vigilant against unjust and illegal usurpations of power and jurisdiction. Moreover, the ultimate power and right of the people to unite as a whole in revolt against an oppressive national government is maintained in the combined bulwark of administrations and militias of the several states.[9] In such manner, federalism provides one part of the "double security" alluded to by Madison. The separation of powers and its attendant principle of checks and balances provide the second part and, with it, a novel framework for energetic government.

In forming a Constitution with institutionally separated powers, the framers aimed to strengthen the national government's capacity for "*a more faithful and regular administration,* and to prevent a union of governmental power, with all its dangers for the people" (emphasis mine).[10] Given the disposition of the American people and extent of their country, this required a unique and complex structure. The proposed model was difficult to explain and justify because the dominant model on their minds was the British system of mixed government.[11] The proposed constitution differed from the complex British model in confusing ways. The British constitution is unwritten, subject to centuries-long evolution in its institutions, and bases representation upon certain long-standing class divisions, or estates—King, Lords, and Commons. At the time of the American founding, the estates were integrated and their powers roughly balanced in a parliamentary body.

By contrast, the American Constitution is a written document that arranges powers of governance, rather than estates, in an abstract and entirely republican design. It confers limited powers by consent through a formal ratification process and loosely separates and balances those powers among three institutional branches. In theory, legislators directly or indirectly represent people (or their state or nation as a whole) regardless of social divisions. The executive and judicial branches do not reside in or under the legislature but as roughly equal and jealous partners in governance.[12] The arrangement prevents a legislative vortex that could swallow up all powers in the manner experienced under the Articles of Confederation. The framers intended to establish a balance of institutional powers wherein any one branch could stave off the encroachments of the others, thereby enabling government to control itself while governing the people. The mechanism by which checks and balances are made truly effective is called "partial agency." It entails a confusing paradox in that it is necessary to partially blend those powers in order to maintain their meaningful separation. At the same time, the blending enables government to function effectively.

Partial Agency

James Madison articulated and defended the principle of partial agency in *Federalist* essays 47–49. It is only "where the *whole* power of one department is exercised by the same hands which possess the *whole* power of another department [that] the fundamental principles of a free constitution are subverted." Some blending of power is indeed necessary if government is to work at all. A pure separation is impossible, and Madison showed in detail how many of the state constitutions already accommodated some blending, but without adequate refinement and balance.[13]

Therefore, to protect themselves as well as the people, each branch of the national government required a partial share in the powers of the others. In *Federalist* essay 66, Hamilton impatiently reiterated the necessity of this partial intermixture as "not only proper but necessary to the mutual defense of the several members of the government against each other."[14] The executive, for example, has a qualified veto (a legislative power) over acts of the legislative branch, while the House and Senate share the power to impeach executive and judicial officials. In the case of presidential impeachment, the chief justice presides over the Senate impeachment trial—a forum in which the Senate is exercising judicial power. These shared powers make very real the threat of open and effective political conflict, but more often than not they induce cooperation and permit specialization and integration of their powers.

Publius was concerned that each branch remain essentially independent.[15] Doing so enhances the branch's ability to do the work it is most fit to do. Effective governance requires some degree of specialization. Partial agency provides that and much more. First, it allowed the framers to give more permanence and stability to the government as a whole through an array of blended powers that buttresses the operations of the executive. The dominant tendency in republics is to give too much power to the legislative branch, so the framers remedied this by dividing the legislature into two houses and enhancing the shared powers of the executive. Second, it allowed the framers to coordinate each branch's specialized competence and power in the practice of administration. Third, it allowed them to integrate a nar-

rower portion of all three powers into individual governmental institutions for specific purposes. Hamilton viewed these factors as critical
to achieving "a more faithful and regular administration" marked by
efficiency, consistency, firmness, and wisdom. Hamilton and his Federalist colleagues referred to the combination of these qualities as lending high tone to the proposed national government.[16]

In the debates at the Philadelphia Convention and then at the
state ratifying conventions, delegates argued at length over the degree to which various mixes of the three powers would provide high
tone while providing safety. The right mix would induce cooperation
wherein the branches must coordinate their shared powers over such
matters as foreign affairs, war, public finance, and appointments to office. Hamilton wanted "close, direct working relationships" among the
branches for these purposes and was satisfied that the proposed document provided the needed types of blending and duration. The framers settled on a design in which the Senate and the judiciary could
lend temper and wisdom to the operation of the executive branch and
check intemperate measures in the House of Representatives.

The blending of power in the Senate provides an excellent example of how tone, cooperation, and integration were encouraged
and how they operated with safety as different sides of the same coin.
Contrary to our current view of the Senate as simply another legislative body of Congress, most framers viewed it as one of the more permanent branches[17] designed to moderate the "sudden impulses and
fluctuations" of the popular assembly *and* to work closely with the executive, particularly on matters of appointment to office and foreign
affairs. Though the Senate has the ability to check the executive, ultimately through impeachment trial, much more attention was given to
its contribution to wisdom and stability in routine administration. It
was viewed primarily as a cooperative partner to the executive.[18] The
Senate, therefore, required a complex integration of all three powers
that emphasized its close relation to the executive, as well as its role in
checking the House. At the New York Ratifying Convention (1788),
Hamilton addressed the proper role of the Senate in relation to its
congressional partner:

> There are few positions more demonstrable than that there
> should be in every republic, some permanent body to correct
> the prejudices, check the intemperate passions, and regulate the
> fluctuations of a popular assembly. It is evident that a body in-
> stituted for these purposes must be so formed as to exclude as

much as possible from its own character, those infirmities, and that mutability which it is designed to remedy. It is therefore necessary that it should be small, that it should hold its authority during a considerable period, and that it should have such an independence in the exercise of its powers, as will divest it as much as possible of local prejudices. It should be so formed as to be the center of political knowledge, to pursue always a steady line of conduct, and to reduce every irregular propensity to system. Without this establishment, we make experiments without end, but shall never have an efficient government.[19]

The Senate, though a part of Congress, was intended to operate by an *opposite and rival principle* to mute the fluctuations of the popular assembly by possessing qualities that simultaneously enhance executive power. Giving advice and consent in the appointments of high officials, as well as to treaties, means participating in executive power. John Rohr's careful analysis of the constitutional debates provides convincing evidence that the Senate was "intended to be part of an executive establishment." It should "possess aspects of all three powers, serve for a long period, exercise a wisdom and expertise not found in the House of Representatives," acquire institutional support "to resist popular whims of the moment, be able to conduct executive affairs outside the legislative chamber, exercise supervisory power over federal personnel matters, and express a permanent will and national character."[20] Hamilton spoke to all of these matters, and especially (in *Federalist* essays 65 and 75) to the notion that the Senate should possess a permanent will and a "due sense of national character." Senators would represent the nation rather than the states and thereby serve a vital role as the president's counselors on national issues and interests.

In subsequent practice, Hamilton emphasized the cooperative role of the Senate by advising President Washington to extend to it a "right of individual access on matters relative to the public administration" because it shared "certain executive functions" and made them "his constitutional counsellors."[21] This did not, however, imply a general grant of power to the Senate in all matters executive. The relationship required careful discrimination to preserve the balance of roles and powers. Most significantly, Hamilton stipulated that although the Senate must ratify treaties, this did not mean that they should participate in negotiating them. Here Hamilton plied a vital distinction relating to the status of treaties and the *federative power*—a power conceived in Europe and elaborated upon by John Locke.

Treaties, Hamilton argued, are contracts rather than legislation in the proper sense, and thus fall to the executive branch. The executive can more effectively protect diplomatic confidences and maneuver freely during the formation as well as administration of treaty agreements. This "is essential to the conduct of foreign negotiations and is essential to preserve the limits between the Legislative and Executive Departments."[22] This line of reasoning flowed from an understanding of *federative* or foreign affairs powers, which in Europe were ceded to kings. It was understood that federative power included an amalgam of legislative and executive powers to be exercised by monarchs. The US Constitution, however, accords a portion of the federative power to Congress in order to limit the discretion of the president. Thus, Congress has the power to declare war, grant letters of marque, and ratify treaties to give them the force and effect of law, even though they are contractual in nature. However, the greater proportion of federative power must reside with the executive, who can exercise the prudence required to negotiate and manage treaty terms made in good faith between nations.

In his Pacificus essays, Hamilton argued that the general vesting of executive power in Article II gave the bulk of federative power to the president, whereas comparatively, Congress enjoyed only specified powers in Article I. As Karl-Friedrich Walling indicates, this argument has often been misconstrued as Hamilton claiming *prerogative power*, which in Europe was a general power beyond law enjoyed by sovereign monarchs. Hamilton made no such claim. The extent of such kingly power would collapse the constitutional framework of responsibility. "His [only] point was that an effective constitutional division of labor required the executive to maintain control of most of the federative power" in order to "steer between the Scylla of weakness and the Charybdis of prerogative."[23] In the arena of foreign affairs, then, the executive enjoys a greater measure of flexibility and power but not absolute power.

In more general matters, Hamilton emphasized cooperation between the executive and the Senate to bolster counsel, consistency, and system in administration, and this went beyond the tenure of specific presidents. In *Federalist* essay 77, he asserted that "the cooperation of the Senate" lent itself to "stability in the administration" because its consent "would be necessary to *displace* as well as to appoint" subordinate officers (emphasis added). The power to displace subsequently fell to the president alone because of the momentous *Decision of 1789* (hereafter, *Decision*) in which the first Congress ceded power to the president to remove the secretary of foreign affairs. Congress argued the matter at length and, in a close vote, settled on it primarily because of the executive's broad role in foreign affairs. The complexity of the debate, however, made it easy to conflate the grant of removal power with the power to remove department heads generally, given that Congress's agenda at that point addressed the establishment of the three great departments, with Foreign Affairs considered first. What is often overlooked is that the debate over the design of the Treasury Department took on a very different character, focusing in a much more detailed way on how it could be controlled by both Congress and the executive (a matter further addressed later). And the heated debate overall on the removal power resulted in a vote so close that it required tie-breaking votes. Despite that, the *Decision* set the stage, as Brian Cook argues, for a progressively instrumental conception of administration across two centuries of expansive presidential claims and some fascinating court cases.[24]

Significantly, Hamilton did not mention the *Decision* in writing until 1793 and then acceded to it only in passing references to the neutrality proclamation—clearly a foreign affairs matter. But did he *endorse* the *Decision* or merely *acquiesce* to it? Many writers on this subject believe Hamilton simply mused about the removal power in *Federalist* essay 77 and that he easily endorsed the *Decision*, if for no other reason than for the sake of expedience in supporting President Washington's power to issue the neutrality proclamation. Jeremy Bailey, however, observes that Hamilton had ample occasion throughout his career to firmly employ the *Decision* in his public arguments, but he never did. He argues instead that Hamilton remained consistently "less than enthusiastic about strong presidential removal powers" and that expansive claims for his support of it ignore the way he balanced the principle of unity in the executive with his extensive writing on duration in office, even to the street level of the administration. My own sense of Hamilton's writing on duration fully concurs with this argument. Indeed, the balance of duration with unity in the executive forms an integral part of his theory of administrative responsibility, the subject of chapter 4.[25] The *Decision* did not deter him and others (including some of his opponents) from the expectation that subordinate officers, including department heads, would retain their posts well beyond the appointing president's term.[26] Federalist appointees from upper middle to lower ranks held their offices for decades beyond Washington's two terms, contributing mightily to the stability Hamilton sought for the national administration.

The founders also considered the judiciary a more permanent and specialized branch of administration. It would lend tone through independence born of permanent tenure and dampen the effects of change and innovation by "invalidat[ing] new laws which violate the oldest law."[27] It should mitigate the severity and confine the operation of "unjust and partial laws."[28] The fluctuations of the popular assembly are thus further muted and their authority confined within constitutional limits. The operations of the executive are held to the law, and individual rights are protected by appeal and impartial judgment.

Here too Hamilton and his Federalist colleagues pressed their relaxed view of the separation of powers by intending that the judiciary cooperate with the executive in matters of law and policy. In the Philadelphia Convention, Madison proposed a Council of Revision consisting of "a convenient number" of the judiciary and the president. The council would participate in the review of all proposed laws and would possess the power of rejecting them if required.[29] Though this measure failed in the end, the idea of judicial cooperation in executive matters was vindicated in practice during the Washington administration. President Washington formally requested their insight and advice, and Hamilton, as secretary of the treasury, proposed and won the chief justice's formal participation on the board of the sinking fund, which he designed to gradually retire public debt.[30] Supreme Court justices who rode circuits in that era were also asked to assist in executive matters while in the field. The judiciary's powers were intended to enhance executive power via cooperation with, and integration in, administration for specific and limited purposes. Though the court eventually rejected some of these roles, close mutual cooperation and coordination continues between executive and trial-level courts in the administration of justice, as do relations with judicial officials who participate on specialized courts and supervise agencies carrying out remedial orders.

Hamilton viewed the House of Representatives as the body most fit for deliberation and investigative oversight of the administration. It should "inspect the conduct of their ministers, deliberate upon their plans, originate others for the public good." It should "consult their ministers, and get all the information and advice they could from them, before they entered into any new measures or made changes in the old."[31] The House should display *sensibility* to the interaction of broad classes of interests in society, such as agriculture, manufacturing, commercial trade, and science,[32] and deliberate on the plans of the executive branch relative to those interests and the public good.

Where executive plans were needed but lacking, the representatives should initiate them for the public good, subject of course to the input of the Senate and the executive branch. In all cases, the executive branch should play a leading role in policy formulation as well as implementation. In this regard, Hamilton expected that the administration would be able to defend its policies "directly in the legislative chambers by the ministers who possessed the fullest knowledge of proposed measures." Those in opposition would have ample opportunity for "pointed and constructive criticism and questioning."[33] So, more often than not, even the House would cooperate and lend tone to the administration.

For Hamilton, the framework described above constituted the superstructure of the public administration. All three branches, with their attendant specializations, interact in the conduct of administration. Public administration is therefore equated with governance as a whole and is not exclusively an executive power. He was neither doctrinaire nor formulaic about the nature or definition of the three powers. He knew full well that functions such as treaty making and public finance necessarily included both legislative and executive powers and that some activities would confound these classifications altogether. Thus, a fusion of powers will likely occur as one descends the ladder of administrative practice, and it is the nature of the fusion to require tailoring to particular policy and institutional needs. This applied as well to the integration of quasi-judicial power and legal interpretation, which Hamilton and some subordinates employed routinely in their Treasury work. Hamilton's Treasury circulars are replete with discussions of legal interpretation and with adjudication of disputes pertaining especially to decisions by customs officials that affected citizens and noncitizens alike. The comptroller of the treasury exercised quasi-judicial authority independently of Hamilton, at the insistence of Congress.[34]

Furthermore, as Flaumenhaft notes, Hamilton "was equally emphatic about the need to recognize that the business of administration cannot be fully subordinated to rule as some would wish; the machinery cannot work without latitude in interpreting the rules for the expenditure of public money." Hamilton illustrated this point in a letter to Otho Williams, the collector of the customs at Baltimore: "As Inspector of the Customs his duties are not specifically defined by law—he is to be employed generally *in aid of the Customs.*" At best, they could rely only on "certain intimations in the law, and from practice, the prominent features of his duties." Implicit here is a gradual process of forming standards and defining duties as a practice develops. Only at some future point might aspects of the position become amenable to consistent policy and then perhaps codification. Administrative discretion is also necessary to "take into account the actions of men not subject to the authority of that government's laws," such as in matters of foreign negotiations and war.[35] Administrators must often exercise judgment in accommodating governance to the fluidity of events and in the process apply all three powers of governance in focused and limited ways.

Hamilton's theory of public administration, then, comprehends differing levels and foci of administration with an increasing integration of powers made possible through partial agency. It proceeds from the level of general governance, where the three branches remain independent of each other but have partially blended powers, to levels of administrative detail, where the three powers necessarily integrate but are limited in scope to specific policies and practices. In such manner, all branches participate in distinctive ways in the controlled improvement of public administration. This was especially evident in the administration of the Treasury.

Partial Agency in Hamilton's Treasury

Because Congress held the power of the purse, it exercised jealous scrutiny over the operations of the Treasury Department, and so in framing its organic act, it made special reporting provisions for specific officers and argued over the degree of managerial and planning control they should accord to the secretary or hold for themselves. In comparing the organic acts establishing the first three executive departments, one finds much greater detail concerning congressional control over Treasury than over War or Foreign Affairs. In fact, the Treasury Department was not designated as an executive department in the law as the others were. In a subsequent law fixing salaries, though, Congress designated the secretary of the treasury as an executive officer. The Treasury Act imposed many more specific duties on the new department and more carefully structured key positions to reflect significant ambiguity about the extent of control by one branch or the other. Notably, the comptroller of the treasury did not even fall directly under the control of the president, reporting primarily to Congress instead.[36]

Hamilton took full advantage of the ambiguity to make use of both legislative and executive power. Tellingly, Jefferson judged that Hamilton "endeavored to place himself subject to the house when the Executive should propose what he did not like, and subject to the Executive when the house should propose anything disagreeable." Hamilton knew intuitively that public administrators would encounter the necessity of choosing which constitutional master to follow in disputes over policy and that it could enhance their own powers in the process.[37] Leonard D. White recounts that members of Congress became acutely aware of this, and as Hamilton's tenure progressed, some of them pressed the use of itemized appropriations—the beginning of line-item budgeting—as a way of constraining his actions. However, even his critics conceded that in matters of "urgent and unexpected necessity, [the secretary] may be induced to depart from the authorized path of duty, and have great merit in so doing." More generally they asserted their "share in the conduct of administration," sometimes through legislation mandating specific decisions, more often through their power to investigate and compel reports, and of course through specific appointments to offices.[38] Hamilton's allies in Congress successfully rebuffed some of these efforts, which Hamilton thought overreached to curtail his powers. The early developmental years of the new government necessitated broader discretion in the agencies in large part because Congress had little idea of the specific demands of the work. Nor were they about to embarrass the distinguished men in charge of the agencies with petty restrictions, though this began to change as the balance of party power changed in Washington's second administration.

An interesting example of how members of the three branches would participate directly in the controlled improvement of executive administration involved the design and management of the sinking fund (established in 1790) for the reduction of public debt. Hamilton proposed that it be directed by a board of commissioners consisting of the vice president, the chief justice, the Speaker of the House, the attorney general, and the secretary of the treasury: "Any three of them [could] discharge the existing debt, either by purchases of stock in the market, or by payments on account of the principal, as shall appear to them advisable, in conformity to the public engagements; to continue so vested, until the whole of the debt shall be discharged."[39] Their stature would bring real visibility to debt reduction and management functions while immersing them in very technical administrative work.

In other instances, administrators would exercise executive, legislative, and/or judicial powers that were if not explicit, then implied in statutory authority but confined to a narrow field of policy. Hamilton exercised extensive rulemaking and some adjudicative authority over the many financial and customs operations of the Treasury. The comptroller of the treasury exercised discretion and quasi-judicial authority over the drawing of funds pursuant to law. Leonard D. White notes that some congressmen strongly opposed giving so much power to the secretary and his subordinates, arguing that his rules of office would take precedence over and eventually contravene statutory laws.[40] The arrangements foreshadowed the emergence of administrative law in the twentieth century, with the same disputes occurring over administrative power through legal interpretation on a much broader scale.

These examples illustrate the very flexible and pragmatic approach Hamilton and his colleagues took to the separation of powers via partial agency. One could argue that because they were creating a new government, such flexibility was unavoidable while the implications of their respective powers were being worked out. There is some merit to this point. The Supreme Court, for example, would eventually refrain from offering advisory opinions, and congressional governance would become more rigid and even obstructive in its relations with the executive branch, especially in its drive to achieve dominance among the branches in the nineteenth century. However, the framers argued these matters on the basis of constitutional principles, and many of them tried earnestly to bring their intentions to fruition despite the divisive issues they faced. The stakes, though, were very high, and many of the framers grasped immediately at almost every clause of the document for their own advantage. The first Congress quickly became a hotbed of contention over regional and partisan issues. The Senate delayed and fussed over how much and in what ways it should informally cooperate with the president, so much so that Washington eventually gave up consulting with them on most matters.[41] The Constitution engendered jealous conflict almost immediately over new governmental policies and administrative institutions, most of them formulated by Hamilton. He feared that unless executive leadership could hold the government together, the conflict inherent to the constitutional design might overwhelm its coordinative and integrative tendencies.

Centripetal Leadership in the Executive

Hamilton's achievements during his six years as secretary of the treasury were astounding, and he would have been the first to admit that he could not have succeeded without the judgment and reputation of President Washington. Washington enjoyed near universal acclaim among the founding generation. As a war hero and a man with an unassailable public character, he had acquired a stature and a level of respect that placed him above the political fray during much of his two terms. He was a rare figure among a host of impressive figures. As the preeminent national statesman, he came to the presidency reluctantly but was wooed and enticed by several colleagues, among them Hamilton, who appealed to his public reputation and passion for fame. Washington was the only president elected without need of a campaign, and his wide acclaim enabled him to unite the country under a new national government. Throughout his terms of office, he endeavored to exercise *centripetal leadership*.[42]

As a leader, Washington was reserved and stoical, acting in a hands-off manner typical of the era's patrician style. As the first president, he had to determine, in consultation with colleagues, a style of demeanor and leadership appropriate to a republican chief executive. He selected some of the most prominent public figures to run the new departments and gave them wide latitude, allowing them to push with his general support those of their agendas that were in line with his broad priorities. He seldom meddled and preferred stepping in to settle disputes only when compromises continually eluded the players. Maintaining distance and circumspectness increased the gravity of his words when he finally spoke. It also demonstrated restraint, which Washington thought necessary to avoid the "monarchical cloud of suspicion" about executive power that persisted after the revolution.[43]

Washington cultivated close relations with members of Congress, especially with Madison, a fellow Virginian, whose leadership in the House of Representatives he found indispensable. He disliked the increasingly heated political infighting in Congress and among his distinguished subordinates, and he liked even less the public disputes that arose as political parties coalesced around these leading figures. For most of his administration, though, his presence, his carefully timed remarks, and his astute judgment commanded a level of respect that induced effective compromises on some of the most contentious issues.[44] Washington personified the kind of leader the framers could endorse because he set a calming tone and a firm resolve to establish a national government that would promote accountability while unifying the new nation. He was the polar opposite of leaders who stir up strong passions in people and manipulate them for the sake of accruing more power. These were the demagogues that Hamilton and Madison ridiculed throughout the *Federalist* as most dangerous to republics.[45]

As Washington's administration progressed, his support for Hamilton's agenda grew, and his support for Jefferson's policies gradually diminished. As Joseph Ellis noted, Washington too was "a thoroughgoing realist" who "believed that the behavior of nations was not driven by ideals but interests," and "this put him at odds ideologically and temperamentally with his secretary of state, since Jefferson was one of the most eloquent spokesmen for the belief that American ideals *were* American interests."[46] Washington gradually found Hamilton's assessments of the problems more compelling, his judgments and arguments about how to deal with them more convincing, and his exhaustive research more determining of the proper course of action. He also shared Hamilton's strong affinity for the new union and became much less enthused with Jefferson and Madison as their provincialism became more evident. He had staked his reputation on the success of the national republican experiment, and so he endeavored to hold the new government together amid forces that would otherwise have torn it apart. He exercised the centripetal leadership that Hamilton believed to be an essential complement to the institutional checks and balances of the Constitution. Many subsequent presidents would have to find their way to doing so as well, though in styles more attuned to their own eras.

Federici argues that centripetal leadership flowed logically from Hamilton's conviction that American politics would be plagued by factions and that some, such as political parties and wealthy business interests, were likely to become more dominant than others. He was less convinced than Madison of the effectiveness of the extended republic in muting and balancing these contending interests, though more attuned with him to the need for channeling those interests toward a public good. The stability and permanence gained through constitutional provisions for longer terms and partial agency had to be matched with public officials who were public-spirited. This meant these officials would, as Michael Federici describes it, "subordinate self-interest and ideological passion to the common good, and conduct public affairs with energy and prudence."[47] They require degrees of institutional protection from the popular passions of the moment, as well as from continual partisan pressure, so that they can discern and pursue the *permanent will* or longer-term interests of the people. Hamilton stressed the point in *Federalist* essay 71: "The republican principle demands that the deliberate sense of the community should govern the conduct of those to whom they intrust the management of their affairs; but it does not require an unqualified complaisance to every sudden breeze of passion, to every transient impulse which the people may receive from the arts of men, who flatter their prejudices to betray their interests. . . . When occasions present themselves in which the interests of the people are at variance with their inclinations, it is the duty of the persons whom they have appointed to be guardians of those interests to withstand the temporary delusion in order to give them time and opportunity for more cool and sedate reflection."[48] Contrary to the way Hamilton is sometimes characterized, he did not express disdain for popular will in general. He distinguished between impassioned whims and durable interests. Leaders in the republic, joined by ranks of professional administrators and experts, should restrain the former and promote the latter. It was vital in this regard that the chief executive be shielded somewhat from the direct effects of an impassioned populace. President Washington was able to maintain his aloof style of leadership in part because the Constitution interposed an electoral college between the office and the populace. This Hamilton addressed at length in *Federalist* essay 68.

"It is desirable," he said, "that the sense of the people should operate in the choice of the person to whom so important a trust was to be confided," but he felt that this choice should be made by an "intermediate body" of people, "selected by their fellow-citizens from the general mass," who will be "most likely to possess the information and discernment" needed to best judge the competence and character of candidates. The college would come from the states with but a single purpose and not be pre-established so it could not be manipulated or corrupted by undue influence from the candidates or others, especially foreigners. It would be above any "cabal, intrigue, and corruption" and would prevent those with "talents for low intrigue, and the little arts of popularity" in particular states from commandeering "the esteem and confidence of the whole Union." It would make the president "independent for his continuance in office on all but the people themselves," yet shielded from the tumults among them. That independence is critical to the "share which the executive in every government must necessarily have in its good or ill administration."[49] It forms a leading characteristic of effective administration, and the role demands centripetal leadership. Furthermore, in Hamilton's formulation of it, centripetal leadership required a combination of qualities that necessarily reside in more than one person. The president thus inspires and presides over other leaders in administration, and Washington took that role seriously.

At its root, the term "president" refers to one who *presides* over an administration of subordinate officials who will pursue a variety of active duties and agendas. The president is not a manager per se; he superintends those who will see to the management of departmental affairs, and those who do so should be distinguished leaders in their own right. The president is the commander in *chief*, not the sole commander. He should consult with his subordinates and, as stated in Article II, Section 2 of the Constitution, "may require their opinion in writing upon any subject relating to the duties of their respective offices." He may also recommend to Congress (Sec. 3) "such measures as he shall judge necessary and expedient." The recommended measures are developed mainly by his subordinates, who have grand plans of their own, and by their respective departments or agencies, and he exercises critical judgment about the measures' general direction and fit with his priorities. He and his subordinates work closely with members of Congress to craft their measures into law.

Congress may, as in the case of the Treasury Department, work as ordered by law with subordinate officials on a routine basis and require reports from them at their convenience. This underscores the important points that the president's subordinates are constitutional officers and leaders in their own right and that the president is not the sole conduit between Congress and public agencies. No department head, much less Hamilton, could have carried out his duties under such a narrow conception of interbranch relations. President Andrew Jackson would try to assert himself as the sole conduit between Congress and his administration and was thoroughly rebuffed by a unanimous Supreme Court.[50] Hamilton envisioned a rich variety of ties between the administration and members of Congress, as well as with the courts, that would knit them into an administration marked more by harmony than by conflict.

The president, then, presides over subordinate officials who manage a wide variety of duties for the country and who therefore must possess experience and expertise appropriate to their functions. They are ambitious in their own right, anxious about their reputations, mindful of the general obligations to protect rights, and ready to promote their plans for the public good.[51] Hamilton noted, however, that the more specialized competencies of these officials might work at cross-purposes with other agencies and that all three branches would need to cooperate in order to harmonize or balance these inherent tensions through joint administrative organs such as advisory boards and governing commissions.[52]

Agency leaders must also harmonize their plans with the president's priorities and, in those plans, harmonize the interests of the people. Federici observes that "Hamilton tried to harmonize various interests to serve the public good." For example, in his *Report on Manufactures*, he illustrated how the diverse interests among southern agricultural and northern commercial states could be harmonized through the introduction of manufactures that could transform raw agricultural goods into many useful products for domestic consumption. Market interdependence could knit the country's regional interests together.[53] Promoting this kind of harmony among durable interests becomes a primary concern for centripetal leaders, and the prospects for success are considerably enhanced by an *energetic executive*.

Energy in the Executive

Hamilton thought it necessary to structure the government in such a manner that persons with a "particular taste or disposition" to govern a nation "with justice and ability" would be appointed to office. In particular, those who seek office and "love the fame of laudable actions" could be entrusted with power for longer periods of time because their most passionate interests connect with the duties of office. Thus, he argued, the executive branch could be made powerful and yet safe. Insufficient power in the executive branch would frustrate such ambition and encourage irresponsibility by enticing officials to instead pursue their private interests through their offices. They must see real prospects for bringing their public plans to fruition. We can, Hamilton said, "prompt him to plan and undertake extensive and arduous enterprises for public benefit" if he is given "considerable time to mature and perfect them, if he could flatter himself with the prospect of being allowed to finish what he had begun." Moreover, "it is certainly desirable that the executive should be in a situation to dare to act on his own opinion with vigor and decision," and *energy* provides the impetus.[54]

Hamilton's concept of energy in the executive is justly famous. He explains it at length in *Federalist* essays 70–77. If its conditions are met, the executive can become the centripetal force in partitioned government. "Energy in the executive is a leading character in the definition of good government. It is essential to the protection of the community against foreign attacks; it is not less essential to the steady administration of the laws; to the protection of property against those irregular and high-handed combinations which sometimes interrupt the ordinary course of justice; to the security of liberty against the enterprises and assaults of ambition, of faction, and of anarchy."[55] Energy consists of four elements: unity, duration, adequate provision for support, and competent powers. In combination, they promote vigor as well as responsibility. Unity refers to the "exercise of power by a single hand." It implies unified command and centralized organization as a general operating principle. It is conducive to "decision, activity, secrecy, and dispatch." It focuses broad responsibilities in a single person, thereby avoiding confusion and obfuscation. Whereas the legislative body benefits from its numbers in the promotion of deliberation and wisdom, the executive is most effective when run by a single person. Hamilton defended this arrangement against proposals to establish a plural executive, or an executive "subject in whole or in part to the control and cooperation of others, in the capacity of counselors to him."[56] In either case, power and planning would be frustrated and responsibility diffused, and that would enervate rather than energize. A plural executive would also invite rather than impede faction. He employed a bit of political psychology to illustrate his point: "Men often oppose a thing merely because they have had no agency in planning it, or because it may have been planned by those whom they dislike. But if they have been consulted, and have happened to disapprove, opposition then becomes, in their estimation, an indispensable duty of self-love. They seem to think themselves bound in honor, and by all the motives of personal infallibility, to defeat the success of what has been resolved upon contrary to their sentiments."[57] This "despicable frailty" of human character must be guarded against in designing the executive branch. Its presence would already be manifest in the broader play of partitioned powers and contending interests, so the executive needs some internal respite from its effects in order to act with "vigor and expedition." The "weightiest objection to plurality in the executive," however, is that it "tends to conceal faults and destroy responsibility." Plurality enables officials to hide their betrayal of public trust "with so much dexterity and under such plausible appearances, that the public opinion is left in suspense about the real author [of] pernicious measures." Unity in the executive focuses responsibility and enhances transparency.[58]

This did not mean, however, that all executive institutions must conform to the single-head model. Hamilton readily admitted of exceptions, such as in the design of the Bank of the United States and the sinking fund and in regulatory institutions that "require prudence and experience to grow slowly and gradually, for which boards are very well adapted."[59] Moreover, he was readily disposed to establish quasi-public bodies that blended private ventures and/or charitable causes with public leadership over the publicly interested aspects of such operations. He thus endorsed and practiced a version of public entrepreneurship that pursues public purposes through public/private partnerships. The Bank of the United States is a classic example, and its governance is examined more closely in chapter 5. It is clear that Hamilton was far more pragmatic than doctrinaire about organizational principles, and he clearly believed the Constitution to be permissive as to organizational and quasi-organizational forms.

The second element, duration in office, is necessary to "give the officer an inclination and resolution to act his part well, and to the community time and leisure to observe the tendency of his measures, and thence to form an experimental estimate of their merits." The psychology of ownership figured into his reasoning: "It is a general principle of human nature that a man will be interested in whatever he possesses, in proportion to the firmness or precariousness of the tenure by which he holds it; will be less attached to what he holds by a momentary or uncertain title, than to what he enjoys by a durable or certain title; and, of course, will be willing to risk more for the sake of the one than for the sake of the other. This remark is not less applicable to a political privilege, or honor, or trust, than to any article of ordinary property."[60] Thus, an executive faced with a short tenure "will be apt to feel himself too little interested in it to hazard any material censure or perplexity from the independent exertion of his power," and worse, would tend to "corrupt his integrity, or debase his fortitude" in the worst of circumstances. Substantial duration thus encourages risk-taking and allows steady effort and adequate time for preparation of complex plans and activities. It affords "the prospect of being allowed to finish what he had begun." It also gives the public the benefit of the executive's experience, "the parent of wisdom," and his ready availability in times of national emergency. Though Hamilton would have preferred that the president enjoy a longer term than four years, he deemed the prospect of reeligibility adequate to the purpose and that it would do more to allay "any alarm for the public safety." Energy and safety remain in balance.[61] Moreover, as will be explained in chapter 4, the element of duration should extend to the deepest levels of the public administration not only for the sake of energy but also as a hedge against irresponsible leadership.

Without "adequate provision for support," the third element of energy, the president is vulnerable to legislative encroachment by manipulating his compensation. "In the main it will be found that a power over a man's support is a power over his will." Hamilton admitted that there were individuals of "stern virtue" who would not be swayed by such pressures, but such virtue is too rare to be consistently relied upon. Thus, the Constitution prohibits Congress from changing his compensation during a term in office so "they can neither weaken his fortitude by operating on his necessities, nor corrupt his integrity by appealing to his avarice." The remark bore further significance to Hamilton's republican theory because it anticipates that persons lacking independent wealth could successfully hold the office. He wanted persons of merit regardless of circumstances to be able to occupy the highest offices in the new republic.

Finally, Hamilton devoted much of *Federalist* essay 73 and all of essays 74–77 to giving a detailed analysis of the powers vested in the president in Article II of the Constitution. He refers first to the veto (essay 73), which is a legislative power. It enables him to resist the legislative body by guarding "against the enaction of improper laws." It would protect against "undue haste, inadvertence, or bad design," as well as against mutability in the laws. However, it is a *qualified* negative, which again makes its "efficacy to depend on the sense of a considerable part of the legislative body." This guards against outlandish vetoes, or those that frustrate too much the sensibilities of two-thirds or more of both houses. The general intention of such checks is to moderate the impulsiveness of officials in both branches.

Next, the executive's role as commander in chief of the army, navy, and state militias when called into service (*Federalist* essay 74) gives him the power of "directing and employing the common strength . . . which forms a usual and essential part in the definition of executive authority. Of all the cares and concerns of government, the direction of war most peculiarly demands those qualities which distinguish the exercise of power by a single hand." Though Congress retains the power to declare war, the executive's war powers remain quite substantial because it possesses the power and means to respond immediately to hostilities commenced against the United States and its territories (see chapter 6).

The Constitution also anticipates that the president will consult with his principal officers and require their opinions in writing and empowers him to "grant reprieves and pardons," in the spirit of "humanity and good policy," without which at times "justice would wear a countenance too sanguinary and cruel" or work against the restoration of "the tranquility of the common wealth" during "seasons of insurrection or rebellion." These and other enumerated powers give the executive the ability to act swiftly in emergencies, to formulate elaborate and systematic policies for recommendation to Congress, and to heal defects in them by granting exceptions and pardons where consistency would wreak injustice.[62]

Other than the power as commander in chief, the two most significant powers the executive possesses are in the making of treaties and in appointments of principal officers and judges. As already discussed, these are so significant that they "would be utterly unsafe and improper to intrust to an elective magistrate of four years' duration" and so require the advice and consent of the Senate. Their concurrence "would have a powerful, though, in general, a silent operation" as a check on any temptation to sacrifice the public interest for the sake of private advantage in foreign affairs and against any "spirit of favoritism" in presidential appointments. Simply knowing that treaties and appointments of principal officers will be subject to senatorial consent will likely keep the executive on a proper bearing in such matters. Within those bounds, the single executive can "investigate with care the qualities requisite to the stations to be filled, and to prefer with impartiality the persons who may have fewer personal attachments to gratify."

Hamilton was quite aware of the "private and party likings and dislikes, partialities and antipathies, attachments and animosities" prevalent in appointments to office, especially when overseen by a group or party rather than by a single head. They will inevitably engage in bargained selections: "Give us the man we wish for this office, and you shall have the one you wish for that." In such practices, "it will rarely happen that the advancement of the public service will be the primary object either of party victories or of party negotiations."[63] This anticipates much of the abuse to public service that would occur during the nineteenth-century patronage era, when presidents (beginning in earnest with Andrew Jackson) embraced partisan appointments for the sake of "rotation in office." Hamilton would likely have heartily supported the civil service reforms passed in reaction to those abuses.

The foregoing analysis makes it quite clear that Hamilton expected the elements of energy to percolate through levels of the subordinate public administration. In general, subordinate agencies should follow the same hierarchical structure unless political or technical exigencies dictated the use of boards, commissions, teams, or other independent authorities. It is also clear that he avoided a strictly instrumental or servile view of the working relations in this model. Lynton Caldwell aptly characterizes Hamilton's view of superior/subordinate relations as "a working unanimity among the members of the administrative family," but one that forbids blind obedience or loyalty to a specific head to the "sacrifice of conscience and judgment" and "of higher duty to the community."[64] This relationship forms a vital element in Hamilton's theory of administrative responsibility. It remains here to examine the energy and reach of the Treasury administration under his leadership.

Energy and Reach in Hamilton's Treasury

During the first decade of the new government, the Treasury was the only Federal department of any size and complexity, and the scope of its operations was breathtaking by any standard of organization known at the time. It started with a central office staffed by thirty-nine positions (compared with five in the State Department, and just two at the War Department headquarters) and more than doubled in size in its first two years. The customs officers and surveyors numbered 122 at first, but quickly ballooned to nearly 500 (including new Coast Guard employees) at the end of Hamilton's service in 1795. By the end of the century, they had swelled to almost 1,700, and total Treasury employment was close to 2,500 if postal employees, who fell at least nominally under Treasury's arm, are counted.[65]

Hamilton started from scratch in bringing system and management information to bear and in creating whole new organs of the department—with the Customs service demanding by far the bulk of his time in the first couple of years. With constant urging and many circulars of instruction, he made it imperative that customs officers firmly enforce the new import tariff act (the new government's chief source of revenue) and regularize collections, practices only haphazardly maintained in previous years. This did more in one year to change the reputation and bearing of the service in the eyes of the public than any other measure while significantly increasing the national government's revenue stream.

Leonard D. White details the scope of responsibilities falling to Treasury in his definitive work on Federalist administration, noting the department's importance "not merely on account of the intrinsic quality of the duties performed, but also because it was the one department that had an extensive field service located in every large town and every section of the country." Its Customs Service, new Coast Guard, Bank of the United States and its branches, excise officers and land agents, purveyors of public supplies, and post offices "affected the 'small people' throughout the country," and dealt routinely with every business and professional group of any note. Through the Customs Service alone, "it dealt with the whole mercantile, fishing, and ship-owning interests along the eastern and southern coasts."[66] The employees of these agencies constituted the entire population of the federal government's street-level bureaucracy, so Hamilton knew full well the impact his organization could have in making a strong and trustworthy impression on the public.

White also noted that the seriousness and extent of these officials' duties not only gave them an impact on new governing routines but also made them indispensable in seeing the new government through "some of the most vital issues and problems of the decade, notably the embargo and foreign trade regulation and the Whiskey Rebellion." When war seemed imminent during the mid-1790s, "Treasury Collectors and naval officers stood at the front line of efforts to enforce the neutrality proclamation, the brief embargo of 1794 and the subsequent shipping regulations."[67]

Though Congress at first wanted more direct control over Treasury operations, it soon realized that it must rely extensively on the discretion of Treasury officials. The delegation process began even before the Treasury Act itself was passed. As White indicated, it vested powers through the Collection Act, which set up the Customs Service, as well as through a lighthouse act and a vessel registering act.[68] The Treasury Act contained a range of delegations so broad as to make Congress and Treasury a more significant administrative bulwark than anything possessed by the broader executive branch. Hamilton, however, would quickly assert the new delegations in executive terms, setting off institutional jealousies that would eventually force him to leave the position, but not before establishing executive reach into almost all aspects of Treasury administration.

The most significant powers under the Treasury Act included digesting, preparing, and reporting "plans for the improvement and management of the revenue and for support of the public credit"; estimating public revenues and expenditures; superintending revenue collection; "granting all warrants for monies to be issued from the treasury"; executing the sale of public lands as required by law; directing prosecutions for delinquencies of officers of the revenue; managing authorized loans (some of which were huge); and conducting land surveys. To these were added the superintendence of a new Coast Guard, nominal control of the Postal Service, oversight of the new Bank of the United States, purchasing army supplies, and overseeing and participating on the sinking fund board of commissioners. Because Treasury's reach extended into every significant local venue of the country, it also became necessary for Congress to mandate its assistance to other new departments until they could employ a sufficient number of their own street-level bureaucrats. Thus, Treasury employees were directed to assist with implementing quarantine laws, paying military pensions, and assuring the provision of medical services to naval employees. White details how collectors of the customs "appear to have become directors of [naval] hospitals ex officio, . . . prompting the beginning of the Marine Hospital Service, which eventually was to become the United States Public Health Service."[69]

Finally, Hamilton's administrative prowess and energy so far exceeded the abilities of his counterparts in the other departments that President Washington relied on him to assist them with organization, management, and policy. This was cut short at Foreign Affairs when Jefferson finally arrived from France to take over the reins, but that did not stop Washington and many other officials from calling on Hamilton for advice about foreign policy and war (see chapter 6). Because of the weak administrative abilities of leaders in the Department of War, Hamilton played a key role in its administration well into the Adams administration, serving formally as its inspector general but in many respects acting as its secretary. President Adams and Hamilton despised each other, mostly due to electoral politics but also because of their vastly different dispositions: Hamilton was more brash, assertive, and meddling; Adams was more reserved and retiring, preferring to preside at his home in Massachusetts than at the seat of power in Philadelphia. This irked Hamilton to no end, yet it gave him ample opportunity to exert powerful influence over military affairs.[70] For ten years, Hamilton exerted influence over the direction of the new national government. He set it upon a firm administrative foundation, one that subsequent Republican administrations found exceedingly difficult to undo and, in fact, ended up rejuvenating much of because the events of war and economic crises demanded it. This pattern of administrative development would eventually bring the executive branch into a prominence only Hamilton could foresee.

Conclusion

The analysis presented here illustrates how Hamilton's constitutional theory serves as a framework or superstructure of US public administration. That superstructure starts with powers partitioned among three branches that maintain their independence through institutional checks and balances made effective by partial agency. Simultaneously, these shared powers are arrayed in a manner intended to enhance and support executive administration as the locus of governmental action. In that context, the executive is made *energetic* through the elements of unity, duration, adequate compensation, and competent powers, which enable the chief executive to exercise centripetal leadership. Such leadership is necessary in Hamilton's theory for ensuring more harmony than discord in the conduct of public affairs.

In like fashion, the elements of energy percolate through the subordinate ranks of the public administration, providing the same advantages of enhanced planning, decisiveness, system, secrecy where necessary, and immediate action. Hamilton's constitutional superstructure comprehends differing levels and foci of administration marked by the increasing integration of powers in the agencies and institutions that bring policy to the street. Subordinate officials are constitutional officers in their own right and are often obliged to knit operational relationships together with the legislative and judicial branches and exercise their powers for specific institutional purposes. All three branches participate in their varying capacities to control and improve the public administration.

Today, one can see ample evidence of Hamilton's theory in practice throughout the federal and state governments. Governors, as well as the president, are expected to take the initiative in shaping public policy and brokering compromises among legislators and interest groups. Public agencies reside mainly (though not exclusively) in executive branches but also exhibit close, routine ties with their legislatures and in many cases with the courts. They also exercise quasi-legislative and quasi-judicial powers through rulemaking and administrative adjudication. That so much of this activity is routine tells us that administration is more often harmonious than discordant. Even much of the conflict that occurs is channeled and routinized among the branches and within the agencies. We also know intuitively at this point in history that the constitutional system copes fairly well with polarizing conflicts that result periodically in interbranch gridlock. The push and pull among the governing branches for an upper hand in shaping vision, in conducting elections, and in determining public policy sometimes erupts into full-fledged political conflict. Remarkably, even at such intense moments (the Civil War aside), the conflict is channeled through our institutions with minimal violence. The written Constitution has to a significant degree become an institutional reality because its checks and balances induce officials to ensure adherence to the rule of law. Of that Hamilton would heartily approve. He shaped much of the jurisprudence that would make this possible, and his theory of public administration cannot be fully understood without it.

3
Administrative Jurisprudence

> The powers contained in a constitution of government, especially
> those which concern the general administration of the affairs of
> the country . . . ought to be construed liberally in advancement of
> the public good.
> —Hamilton to George Washington, 1791

> Under the jurisprudence of John Marshall, Hamilton's admin-
> istrative theory was in large measure embodied in American
> constitutional law.
> —Lynton Caldwell

In the United States, new public servants at all levels soon learn the
importance of rule by law because the Constitution establishes it as
a primary standard in public decision-making. For some, just following specific rules will get them through their day, but most will have
to acquire substantial legal acumen in order to perform their jobs or
run their agencies and programs effectively. For the latter, politics,
law, and the administrative process run together in an almost seam-
less fashion, and law will alternately enable and restrict their discretion. Some public servants will emphasize the restrictions in the law
and become more legalistic as a result. Others will learn to capitalize
on the opportunities and ambiguities in the law in order to achieve
its articulable purposes. For the latter, Alexander Hamilton is the ultimate exemplar.

Hamilton stands out as both the premier bureaucrat and the dominant legal mind of his era, and his legacy on both counts remains
highly significant. His commentary, with Madison and Jay, in the *Federalist* stands on its own as the most authoritative and cited treatise on
the Constitution's meaning. In that work he also provided the rationale for judicial review (essay 78), a power not specifically mentioned
in the Constitution but that is inherent to the constitutional design.
The courts must serve as an "intermediate body between the people
and the legislature in order, among other things, to keep the latter
within the limits assigned to their authority." This keeps the legislature from "substituting their *will* to that of their constituents." It is the

"proper and peculiar province of the courts" to interpret the meaning of the laws.[1]

We now take judicial review for granted, but that was hardly the case in the founding era. It posed a threat to state power that Anti-Federalist Republicans fought at every turn. Hamilton began laying the foundation for judicial review early in his legal career with the Tory cases, well before the new Constitution had even been conceived. Beyond that, he developed both a philosophy and a practice of law that would influence the course of the developing nation and its legal profession long after his time. In his usual manner he was largely self-taught, with a little tutoring along the way by close friends, and he learned at lightning speed.

Law schools did not exist in that era, and the usual manner for preparation involved "reading law" as a clerk to practicing lawyers. The period of study typically lasted five years with a lot of office gofer work thrown in. In 1778, the New York Supreme Court reduced the clerkship to three years in order to redress a shortage of attorneys in the postwar period. Hamilton had begun reading legal classics by Edward Coke, William Blackstone, Wyndam Beawes, and others while at King's College, but he did not prepare in earnest until 1782, shortly after leaving the Continental army.[2] As McDonald indicates, he could not afford to endure a three-year apprenticeship given his intense involvement in public affairs and his having just married and begun a family. Fortunately, he was able to take advantage of a loophole offered by the state supreme court that suspended the three-year clerkship for those whose legal studies were interrupted by the war. They would be required to pass a rigorous bar examination by the end of the court's April term that year. Effectively, he had only three months to prepare, which clearly was not enough. He embarked on his studies anyway and then in April applied for and received a six-month extension from the New York Supreme Court. Remarkably, in July, he successfully gained admission to the bar as a practicing attorney, and in October he was admitted as counsel to practice before the state supreme court. Says McDonald, "In nine months, starting essentially from scratch, Hamilton had qualified himself for both roles"—office lawyer and litigator.[3]

He attacked the study of law with rigorous discipline and attention to detail. The objects of his studies ranged from classic legal commentators and natural law theorists to English case reporters, practice manuals, and detailed reference works. He also read more widely in ancient and comparative sources. Because American law was in its infancy, lawyers relied principally on English and some French sources of substantive law, and for purposes of legal process they relied almost entirely on English common law practices. The grafting of English common law onto American law was gradual and subject to experimentation. The adaptation process remains somewhat unclear for lack of adequate sources and documentation.[4] Each state took its own route, which led to significant variation. New York lawyers and judges adhered more closely to English common law practices, but of course they had to rethink many of them as the revolution progressed. Hamilton found himself at the crossroads of this transition, with little in the way of study guides. He therefore constructed his own practice manual of some forty thousand words as part of his legal preparation. It laid forth in grinding detail the substantive categories of law (damages, pleas, venue, judgments and execution, etc.), and its legal forms and practices in law offices and before the courts. Other law students often copied the manual, and as McDonald indicates, "it formed the basis of a published work that became the standard manual for New York lawyers" in the 1790s.[5]

As a New York attorney with knowledge of and experience in commercial trade, Hamilton had ample opportunity to build a lucrative law practice, but he preferred instead to defer his practice for the sake of public office. Moreover, when he did practice law, he tended to take on cases with broader political and legal significance, as well as pro bono cases for indigents brought to his attention. As already indicated, some of the highly significant cases mired him in controversy early in his career (in the 1780s). His defense of Tory loyalists' property rights against attempts by zealous patriots to take their property under the authority of newly passed confiscation and trespass acts raised a furor, with the press labeling him a monarchist. He participated in about fifty such cases over the next several years, and in his first, *Rutgers v. Waddington* (1784), he laid the groundwork for establishing judicial review and the supremacy of federal law, the law of nations, treaty law, and natural law over the laws of the states.[6] Though vitally important to the nation, these cases were not especially lucrative for him.

Hamilton's immersion in the complexities and details of legal practice led him to some important insights that Forrest McDonald succinctly describes. First, "he learned that liberty and compliance with prescribed rules of behavior are not opposites that must somehow be balanced, as they had seemed earlier, but are complementary and inseparable."[7] Blackstone's *Commentaries* had taught him that "laws, when prudently framed, are by no means subversive but rather introductive of liberty." They provide an ordered liberty that is "infinitely more desirable than that wild and savage liberty which is sacrificed to obtain it." Under the latter condition, "there would be no security to individuals in any of the enjoyments of life."[8] This is a lesson still not accepted by some Americans, and yet it is a profound insight that underpinned Publius's argument that a powerful government is necessary to protect rights. Moreover, those rights are hardly meaningful unless a variety of opportunities exist for their exercise. A robust legal system provides not only protections but also myriad, orderly processes for conducting all types of human affairs. The law may restrict some kinds of behaviors, but it also enables and empowers many others. This insight led in Hamilton's mind to the idea of a procedural republic. MacDonald nicely captures the point:

> Most importantly, he learned an elementary fact about the law which, applied on a larger scale, would constitute a new idea in the art of government. Blackstone had defined the law as "a rule of civil conduct prescribed by the supreme power in a state, commanding what is right and prohibiting what is wrong"; but every practicing attorney knew that in operation the law was less a matter of commands and prohibitions than of procedures. Hamilton was the first statesman to perceive that this characteristic of the law could be consciously applied not merely to bringing government under law through a constitution but to the grander goal of transforming society. He saw that one could best combine freedom and energy in a people, and infuse them with industry and love of country, by establishing the *ways* that things be done rather than trying to order *what* was to be done.[9]

Readers today might easily mistake this procedural republic as an entirely neutral framework for merely reconciling clashes of individual rights and interests. That is not the case. As McDonald indicates, Hamilton was strongly influenced by Vattel's natural law orientation to the overarching purposes of law and government. While Locke and other natural-rights theorists believed government "existed only to preserve the individual's natural rights to life, liberty, and property," Vattel saw three "principal objects of a good government" that were born out by centuries of experience: (1) "to provide for the nation's necessities," (2) to "procure the true happiness" of the nation, and (3) to "fortify itself against external attacks."[10]

For Hamilton, a republic that in principle rejects the conquest and plunder characteristic of ancient regimes must seek material necessities through the inducements and props required to establish a robust political economy where people can find a wide variety of private and public opportunities to secure their livelihoods. This included vigorous regulation against avarice and unjust combinations that "threw trade in channels inimical to the public interest, when desirable enterprises might otherwise not be undertaken for want of sufficient capital, or when unexpected causes thwarted a prosperous flow of commerce." Governmental support and intervention are required to ensure that markets are developed and then remain open and competitive.[11]

As for "procuring true happiness," Hamilton, like Vattel, viewed this as socially derived and obligating rather than springing solely from the individual. The idea that happiness is simply a matter of personal choices and self-determination was foreign to Hamilton's thinking. He viewed human beings as social animals by nature. He thus embraced Vattel's view that a society's "great end is the common advantage of all its members; and the means of attaining that end constitute the rules that each individual is bound to observe in his whole conduct."[12] The nurturing and preservation of a common civic ethic with attendant manners and protocols therefore becomes a matter of both public and private obligation. Hamilton believed that the state plays a role, though not an exclusive one, in fostering civic mindedness, promoting arts and sciences, and even cultivating "religious piety within the limits of liberty of conscience," though this last one should fall more to the purview of civic and religious institutions.

The government should at least indirectly support such efforts and avoid policies that tend strongly toward a corruption of morals. Here again ancient ideas influenced Hamilton's thought, especially Aristotle's virtue of moderation, which, with justice, "are the surest supports of every government."[13] This did not mean that Hamilton was unfazed by contrasting modern liberal ideas such as Hume's view that morality is based upon expedience or utility. As McDonald observed, he possessed a "keen awareness of the distinction between what was right and what was expedient [and this] marked his appraisal of all questions of public concern; his warmest endorsement of any course of conduct was that it was both intrinsically proper and good policy."[14] As indicated earlier, he did not accept Hume's stark equation of morality with expedience, but his realism dictated that one could not ignore expedience altogether.

Finally, fortifying the nation against foreign attacks may seem an obvious purpose of government, but in Hamilton's day one could not take that for granted. Many Americans held that standing armies "were incompatible with public safety and popular liberty" and that the vast distances that isolated the American continent greatly diminished need of them. To the contrary, Hamilton saw a direct connection between a well-armed and trained military and establishing a respected reputation abroad. This would be critical to its commerce as well as to its defense, and if built and executed effectively, such a military could provide an essential deterrence against frequent wars and bring respect and even glory to the American image abroad. On this view Hamilton stood clearly in the minority among his peers.[15]

Hamilton's procedural republic is ensconced within this moral framework, which means, first, that the laws proceed from broader moral purposes and, second, that they possess their own internal procedural norms. These include norms such as fairness of process and in some cases the results or equity of process. In a republic, fairness demands a significant element of transparency and consistency, which breeds public trust and cultivates an ongoing sense of legitimate consent. Furthermore, the entire legal edifice is based on the moral expectation that reasoned inquiry and debate will be brought to bear on the political process, this being the element distinguishing *free* governments from *tyrannical* ones. Rule by law engenders persuasion and expertise in decision-making because of the intrinsic norm that these should prevail over arbitrary will. That is what makes public accountability possible. As Clinton Rossiter notes, Hamilton was "a firm advocate of the double-barreled principle that the governors of men should think, explain, and bargain in making, administering, and enforcing public policy. The government . . . was to be decisive but not arbitrary, energetic but not oppressive."[16]

In this context, the Constitution and subsequent development of US law would yield an impressive array of legal mechanisms, such as liberal contract provisions, patents and copyrights, bankruptcy procedures, public credit, and inferior tribunals, along with a variety of public agencies to help accomplish the political-economic transformation Hamilton envisioned. It remained, however, to put these into effect with a jurisprudential perspective oriented to such development. A wooden or legalistic approach to interpreting the Constitution and laws could stymie the transformation. So Hamilton brought his jurisprudential reasoning to bear before and during the first national administration in order to establish institutions and administrative precedents that would support rather than impede the transformation.

Liberal Construction of Law

Hamilton viewed law as the principal enabling medium through which people achieve the ends set for government. Law prescribes limited purposes and confers powers to achieve them. It made no sense in his mind to deny or unduly restrict powers that are "necessary and proper" (Art. I, Sec. 8) to achieving those ends. Furthermore, it made no sense to adopt a restrictive definition of these terms, as in Jefferson's "absolutely" or "indispensably" necessary, and "strictly" or "narrowly" proper, or in a manner calculated to prohibit usual and efficacious means such as incorporation for carrying out proper governmental functions. Jefferson and his Virginia colleagues (Edmund Randolph and James Madison chief among them) set out to do just that in early 1791 with their opposition to the incorporation of a national bank. Hamilton responded to their opinions (at Washington's request) with a roughly fifteen-thousand-word opinion that remains the most comprehensive and lucid statement ever written on implied powers and liberal construction.

Ironically, Madison had provided solid support for Hamilton's opinion with his *Federalist* essay 44 on implied powers, but he reversed his position ostensibly out of fear that Hamilton was taking those powers too far and in ways that would favor northern commercial interests over southern agricultural interests. As McDonald observes, however, more immediate pecuniary and Virginia state interests likely figured into his reversal. These involved a compromise with Pennsylvania colleagues in Congress over the future location of the nation's capital on Virginia's northern border—land in which Madison had invested. Jefferson, like many other southern plantation owners, hated banks in general. However, at that point he likely adopted strict construction more as a matter of political tactics than of high principle, because he too "was on record in support of loose construction almost as definitely as Madison was."[17] Hamilton responded with a barrage of arguments and precedents, along with close textual analysis, in favor of liberal construction and its doctrine of implied powers. He inveighed against Jefferson's strict construction as a thinly veiled attempt to cripple the new government.

Moreover, tying the hands of the national government in such matters would have an ironic effect of driving politicians to act out of "extreme necessity; which is rather a rule to justify the overleaping of the bounds of constitutional authority, than to govern the ordinary exercise of it."[18] This was prophetic, because Jefferson as president in 1803 would do exactly as described to purchase the Louisiana Territory from Napoleon.[19] Alternatively, the doctrine of implied powers provides the necessary and proper means for making such decisions within the bounds of law and adapting the needs of governance to an uncertain future. John C. Miller concludes that "had it not been for the doctrine of implied powers, that government could not have preserved the people of the United States against the storms and stresses that they were called upon to endure."[20]

For Hamilton, the Constitution conferred a set of powers granted in general terms and subject to interpretation to accommodate changing times and conditions. Whereas Jefferson believed constitutions should be remade every generation, Hamilton (with Madison) wanted one that would endure the test of time and provide an orderly and stable means of adapting to the vicissitudes of national life. The opposing views of these great figures exposes the ambiguities in the Constitution's general terms and illustrates how one's view of the ends or purposes of the document helps determine the meaning of those terms. Hamilton believed that the national government could, with constitutional propriety, set a course that would transform a primitive, developing nation into a diverse and prosperous republic. As Rossiter describes it, Hamilton's "overriding purpose was to build the foundations of a new empire rather than to tend the campfires of an old confederation." Thus, he "looked upon the fundamental law as a launching pad rather than a roadblock,"[21] and liberal construction made that possible. Said Hamilton (echoing Vattel),

> the powers contained in a constitution of government, especially those which concern the general administration of the affairs of a country, its finances, trade, defence, etc. ought to be construed liberally, in advancement of the public good. This rule does not depend on the particular form of a government or on the particular demarkation of the boundaries of its powers, but on the nature and objects of government itself. The means by which national exigencies are to be provided for, national inconveniences obviated, national prosperity promoted, are of such infinite variety, extent and complexity, that there must, of necessity, be great latitude of discretion in the selection and application of those means. Hence consequently, the necessity & pro-

priety of exercising the authorities intrusted to a government on principles of liberal construction.[22]

With this language, Hamilton articulated the enabling rationale for discretionary, ambitious public administration. The subordinate administration shares in the express and implied powers of the whole. To be effective, the government must have the "right to employ all the means requisite, and fairly applicable to the attainment of the ends of such power; and which are not precluded by restrictions & exceptions specified in the constitution; or not immoral, or not contrary to the essential ends of political society." The guides to the use of such discretion are "the general principles and general ends of government." Therefore, "the only question must be, . . . whether the mean to be employed, . . . has a natural relation to any of the acknowledged objects or lawful ends of the government."[23]

It is significant that Hamilton wrote this opinion as secretary of the treasury because it illustrates the very active role he envisioned for at least higher-level administrators. They would participate in interpreting the Constitution and laws as they relate to their particular functions. He readily conceded that "the moment the literal meaning is departed from, there is a chance of error and abuse," but strict adherence to the letter of the law "would at once arrest the motions of the government." He argued that the passage of statutory laws in pursuance of constitutional ends admits to the necessity of *constructive powers*. They exemplify it. Statutes are derived more by implication than by literal interpretation of the Constitution.[24] He illustrated how this was true of state constitutions as well, wherein legislators construed state powers of incorporation as an implied power.[25]

This did not mean that Hamilton made whatever he wanted of the document. He based his interpretations and policies on clear relations to the language and values of the Constitution. Though neither a literalist nor a fundamentalist, he reasoned closely from the text of the law and seldom departed from what he believed were the usual or conventional senses of crucial terms. But he was also careful in construing their meaning in the context of articulable purposes behind a given term or clause. His interpretation of "necessary" in the necessary and proper clause adhered closely to this form. He showed how the opposing argument by Jefferson had in fact "departed from its obvious and popular sense" and given it an unprecedented, restrictive operation. Rather, "the *relation* between the *measure* and the *end*, between the *nature* of the *mean* employed towards the execution of a power and the object of that power, must be the criterion of consti-tutionality, not the more or less of *necessity* or *utility*." The necessary and proper clause simply spelled out a power that is plenary or requi-site for all governments. Without it, constitutional sovereignty would be nugatory.[26] It followed that "the power to erect corporations is not to be considered as an *independent & substantive* power but as an *inci-dental & auxiliary* one; and was therefore more properly left to impli-cation, than expressly granted." This was exactly as practiced by state governments and just as essential to the efficacy of the national gov-ernment.[27]

Hamilton then panned reliance on framers' intent in favor of the textual approach. If their intent is to matter at all, it "is to be sought for in the instrument itself, according to the usual & established rules of construction." He then observed the following: "Nothing is more common than for laws to *express* and *effect*, more or less than was in-tended. If then a power to erect a corporation, in any case, be deduc-ible by fair inference from the whole or any part of the numerous provisions of the constitution of the United States, arguments drawn from extrinsic circumstances, regarding the intention of the conven-tion, must be rejected."[28] The intentions of any given framer or group of framers may differ substantially, and Hamilton knew that indeed they had. The finished document, in its flow and array of articles and clauses, provides by far a more coherent foundation for fair and rea-sonable construction and is based more on consent through ratifica-tion than on the deliberations of a constitutional convention or of the separate ratifying conventions. Hamilton did occasionally invoke fram-ers' intent in arguments with his opponents, but he used it to supple-ment his textual analysis, not to determine the issue.

Hamilton as Judicial Activist?

Hamilton's advocacy of liberal construction has at times been treated as a justification for judicial activism as well as a roving brief for un-limited administrative discretion. The analysis above indicates other-wise, and other scholarly analyses of Hamilton's thought agree that he articulated a standard of *reasonable construction* that would leave ample room for discretion but would also avoid subverting or transcending the articulable purposes in law. He stated his opinion unequivocally that "no government has a right to do *merely what it pleases*," and he was certainly not a cynic who believed words could be made to mean whatever one wants.[29] A term such as "liberty" is ambiguous and con-

testable, but it is also rooted in a cultural, political, and legal context that bounds its meaning. Federici aptly characterized Hamilton
as "search[ing] for the mean between unlimited license and paralyz-
ing legalism."[30] Appropriate means must be drawn from ends stipulated in law and, with discretion, adapted to different sets of circumstances. This requires a wise and powerful administration but not an
unbounded one.

Despite these points, the issue over judicial activism in Hamilton's
jurisprudence requires a more nuanced analysis. In the founding era,
the public paid little regard to the new Supreme Court, and many of
the leading politicians avoided appointments to its bench. President
Washington wanted Hamilton to succeed John Jay on the court in
1796, but Hamilton refused, claiming he needed to reactivate his law
practice and earn a livable income. Judges' salaries were quite low, and
sitting on the court was especially burdensome at the time because the
justices were required to ride circuits twice a year to hear cases around
the country. In short, a Supreme Court appointment entailed a good
deal of legal drudgery and appeared to offer little chance for fame
because of the general belief that it would make few if any significant
decisions, at least in the early years of the republic. It was viewed as a
political backwater. John Marshall would eventually disabuse his generation of that impression, but not until 1803.

Hamilton envisaged a highly significant role for the court in exercising its power of review and interpretation of the laws. It would serve
as an essential balance wheel of the constitutional system. And yet, the
whole tenor of his defense of judicial review is passive. It has the power
neither of the purse nor of the sword. Its only power is judgment, and
most of that only on appeal for the Supreme Court. It suffers from a
"natural feebleness" that must be overcome with the protection of permanent tenure and adequate support. This "least dangerous branch"
will primarily pursue justice and protect rights for individuals, and on
occasion this means declaring null and void those legislative acts that
trample those rights. To deny this power to the court would, in effect,
"affirm that the deputy [the legislative body] is greater than his principal [the people]," for it would enjoy the power of final interpretation of its own acts. The court is thus acting as an intermediate body
between them, and not as one that substitutes its will for the legislative will.[31]

It can be argued that Hamilton was simply playing to his audience
in *Federalist* essay 78 and that he would support a much more aggressive supreme court in the wake of ratification. There is, however, no

evidence in any of his writings that would support this contention. His early arguments for judicial review in the Tory cases were much in line with his arguments in the *Federalist*, and so were his arguments in extant essays on the judiciary in *The Examination* in 1801–2. In the latter essays, he states unequivocally that the "main province [of the judiciary] is to declare the meaning of the laws," but the statement was couched in the context of the judiciary's weakness relative to the other branches. He went on to suggest that should the judges become more aggressive and "annoy" the other branches, or unduly curb the rights of citizens, the other branches "could quickly arrest its arm, and punish its temerity."[32]

On this basis, many scholarly analyses conclude that Hamilton would have rejected the judicial activism exercised in subsequent centuries. Federici, for example, argues that Hamilton's implied powers (which enable flexibility of means) "are tethered to the limits of their antecedent enumerated powers," which are fixed. He contrasts this with the *living constitutionalism* of twentieth-century progressives who "sought to change the nature of constitutional powers and rights." This is a different variety of discretion untethered from "any sense of originalism, or to the text of the Constitution for that matter."[33]

Peter McNamara accepts much the same formulation but goes further by tying Hamilton's conception of constitutional rights and powers to the classical liberal ideology of the era. "Hamilton, Smith, and the Constitution seem to agree that individuals are responsible for making their own way in the world. One need only look at the rights mentioned in the Constitution and Bill of Rights to see that there is no suggestion that the national government is responsible for the material welfare of individuals. In other words, there is no opening for an *entitlement* state."[34]

These arguments are not entirely convincing. While Federici and McNamara have accurately captured Hamilton's statements on judicial review, they are also projecting them into the milieu of twentieth-century jurisprudence and politics and skipping over a whole train of nineteenth-century dynamics (the dominance of strict constructionism being just one) that would have alarmed Hamilton as much as it did the Progressive and New Deal reformers. I am not saying that Hamilton would have adopted *living constitutionalism* as defined but rather that he may well have found sufficient room within the broad, enumerated powers of the Constitution to justify many of the same reforms and initiatives advocated by the Progressives and New Dealers.[35] And we can only surmise how he would treat federal powers granted through the fourteenth amendment, but it likely would not be in the manner treated by the conservative Supreme Court of the late nineteenth and early twentieth centuries. The effect of these dynamics on Hamilton's sense of reasonable construction of the constitutional text are impossible to nail down with any confidence, but there is good reason to think that his legal sense would evolve to some extent with the circumstances. He clearly understood law as being capable of embracing adaptation as well as innovation in pursuit of broad constitutional ends.

There is also room for significant doubt concerning McNamara's claim that Hamilton saw no role for the national government in providing for the material welfare of individuals. He glosses over important differences between Hamilton's views on political economy and those of Adam Smith. Hamilton challenged Smith's laissez-faire assumptions at their core, and in numerous writings he gave expansive interpretations of the general welfare and other key clauses in Article I, Section 8. The fact that Hamilton wanted the national government to spur, protect, and enhance a vibrant, diverse economy and reshape the habits of Americans through public policy hardly suggests he wanted individuals left strictly to their own devices. Lumping Hamilton and Smith together as classical liberals obscures far more than it enlightens in this regard. One wonders too if Hamilton's sense of liberality might take him further with the general welfare clause and the blessings of liberty than either Federici or McNamara want to admit. In such matters there is more than a little uncertainty about Hamilton's thought. The Supreme Court acted slowly and then with artful reticence under the reign of John Marshall in his early years as chief justice, so Hamilton had no opportunity to comment and mature his views concerning any kind of judicial activism. As Forrest McDonald observed, Hamilton did at times change some of his views as he gained experience and observed the unfolding political dynamics of the era. It is difficult at best to anticipate how his thinking might have evolved concerning judicial politics in subsequent generations, but it is not unreasonable to expect that it would evolve. What we do know about Hamilton's own jurisprudence is that it was energetic and expansive in its interpretation of the ends as well as the means of government. This undercuts the fundamentalist aspect of originalism touted by its modern proponents, including Federici and McNamara, and enables an ambitious and active public administration in broad and multifaceted service to the public.

On the Protection of Rights

Today we look with curiosity and some skepticism at Hamilton's opposition to appending a bill of rights to the body of the proposed Constitution. As Federici puts it, he is "commonly characterized as neglecting individual rights for the sake of political and social order."[36]
Curiosity is warranted, for the arguments he (and Madison) made on
this matter could not stand against the tide of opinion among their
Anti-Federalist colleagues, much less the general public, and are now
largely forgotten. At the time, some state constitutions included a prefixed bill of rights, and others did not, including that of Hamilton's
home state of New York. Nevertheless, many New York politicians as
well as members of the press insisted on one for the national constitution. Hamilton thus penned *Federalist* essay 84, the major part of which
dealt directly with the issue. His arguments there are logically compelling and historically accurate but not well suited to the temper of the
time. Accordingly, a compromise was struck to append a bill of rights
immediately after ratification. Ratification could not have succeeded
without the promise of meeting that condition.

Hamilton's arguments, however, do not indicate insensitivity to individual rights. To the contrary, they reveal deep devotion to them,
especially in light of his record as an attorney and/or advocate for
the rights of disparaged minorities—for example, ending slavery, extending rights to African and Native Americans, protecting the property rights of Tory loyalists, and, interestingly, protecting freedom of
the press. In his usual style, Hamilton dealt point by point with the arguments for a bill of rights. First, advocates in New York argued that although their state constitution included no prefixed bill of rights, the
body of that document contained "various provisions in favor of particular privileges and rights which, in substance, amount to the same
thing." Hamilton replied that the proposed national constitution did
as well, with provisions for criminal trial by jury, severe restrictions on
conviction for treason, no bills of attainder, "establishment of the writ
of habeas corpus, prohibition of ex post facto laws, and of TITLES OF
NOBILITY" that provided greater securities than were present in the
New York Constitution. To Hamilton, the prohibition on titles of nobility provided the most critical guarantee, the cornerstone of a fully
republican form of government. In toto, these protections would prevent arbitrary government and preserve liberty as well as or better than
any state constitution.[37]

The second argument by New Yorkers for a bill of rights claimed that since their constitution had grafted on the common law and statutes of Great Britain "in their full extent," other rights not expressed in the document would therein be secured. Hamilton quickly responded that the English law in both forms was made subject in the state constitution "to such alterations and provisions as the legislature shall from time to time make concerning the same," and therefore "at any moment liable to repeal by the ordinary legislative power, and of course have no constitutional sanction." Thus, these bodies of law can form "no part of a declaration of rights."[38]

Hamilton then added important historical context to the whole issue. Bills of rights emerged in the context of royal monarchy as "stipulations between kings and their subjects, abridgments of prerogative in favor of privilege, reservations of rights not surrendered to the prince." These are hardly relevant, he remarked, "to constitutions professedly founded upon the power of the people and executed by their immediate representatives and servants." The vestiges of royal legacy should not carry over. Instead, "the people surrender nothing; and as they retain everything they have no need of particular reservations." The proposed preamble to the national Constitution provides "a better recognition of popular rights than volumes of those aphorisms" that populate the bills of rights of state constitutions "and which would sound much better in a treatise of ethics than in a constitution of government."[39] As Federici indicates, Hamilton's approach here "illustrates the great distance between Hamilton's day and the present. The Constitution he described was 'merely intended to regulate the general political interests of the nation' not to regulate 'every species of personal and private concern,'"[40] as was the tendency of New York and other states under their constitutions. The vexing complications of federalism and the fourteenth amendment were yet to be realized.

To these points, Hamilton added two others. First, he suggested that bills of rights not only were unnecessary "but would even be dangerous. They would contain various exceptions to powers which are not granted; and, on this very account, would afford a colorable pretext to claim more than were granted. For why declare that things shall not be done which there is no power to do?" Why declare, for example, "that the liberty of the press shall not be restrained, when no power is given by which restrictions may be imposed?" Ultimately, Hamilton argued, the security of such rights "must altogether depend on public opinion, and on the general spirit of the people and of the government."[41]

He later successfully tested this point in a controversial New York seditious libel case, *People v. Croswell* (1804), where he argued on behalf of Croswell, an editor of a Federalist newspaper who allegedly "traduced and vilified President Thomas Jefferson."[42] Lower court judges relied on a precedent in English common law that required no proof of the truth or falsity of statements made in the paper, nor questioned the motives involved, but only the determination that damage had been done to the reputation of President Jefferson. Hamilton traced the key precedent to the English Star Chamber (fifteenth–seventeenth centuries), a court notorious for its abuse of both English subjects and general principles of law. This aroused heated public attention, putting the state supreme court judges under intense scrutiny. Hamilton then identified earlier precedents in the common law that clearly contradicted the obnoxious Star Chamber precedent, making truthfulness and intent of statements once again central to proof of libel. From these cases, and from general principles of law, he then fashioned fifteen propositions for a law of libel acceptable to a free society. The argument deadlocked the politicized state supreme court, letting the lower court decision stand but effectively averting a prison sentence for Croswell. Significantly, and to the point, the New York state legislature in the next session declared Hamilton's propositions the law of the state. As Forrest MacDonald notes, "In time [his position] was embraced throughout the American Republic and formed the legal foundation, firmer than the first Amendment, for the ideal of a free and responsible press."[43]

Hamilton concluded his argument against an appended bill of rights by offering the point "that the Constitution is itself, in every rational sense, and to every useful purpose, a bill of rights." "Is it," he inquired, "one object of a bill of rights to declare and specify the political privileges of the citizens in the structure and administration of the government?" "Is another object . . . to define certain immunities and modes of proceeding, which are relative to personal and private concerns?" Both were answered in the affirmative by the framers, in an "ample and precise manner," and "comprehending various precautions for the public security which are not to be found in any of the State constitutions."[44]

The arguments in *Federalist* essay 84 reflect Hamilton's deep concern for how individual rights could most effectively be enhanced and protected. The lasting influence of his propositions in the *Croswell* case provide evidence of their merits, despite their being overshadowed by the Bill of Rights. In hindsight it is easy to say that the Anti-Federalists had the stronger argument on this matter. They prevailed, and it is now impossible to imagine that the republic could fare well without bills of rights. But that should not detract from Hamilton's devotion to rights as the centerpiece of his designs and practices. As described earlier, Hamilton was ahead of his time in advocating for the rights of disparaged minorities. This was reflected in both his public policy recommendations and in his law practice. In the latter, he demonstrated unflinching support for property rights, due process of law, and freedom of the press. In the former, he advocated far more egalitarian measures than most of his colleagues could stand, and he set into law the enabling doctrines for enhancing the liberties of the people through an energetic national administration.

Hamilton's Enabling Doctrines

Hamilton, more than any other person, enunciated the legal rationale for energetic national administration. This did not mean he attended to the executive power exclusively. As has been shown, he sought to strengthen the entire administrative superstructure of American national government, with the executive branch as a leader among equals. The competent powers of each branch would extend to the subordinate administration as well, providing high tone throughout the government. Clinton Rossiter's analysis of Hamilton's legal thought comes to much the same conclusion. He identified four basic constitutional problems to which Hamilton directed most of his energies as constitutional theorist. These were: "(1) the division of authority between the nation and the states, (2) the nature and reach of the powers of Congress, (3) the nature and reach of the power of the President, and (4) the role of the courts as guardians of the fundamental law."[45] The legal doctrines that Hamilton applied to these four problems were calculated to strengthen dramatically the administrative capacity of the nation. They provide important legal and normative justifications for far-reaching administrative powers, and thus constitute enabling doctrines for American public administration.

As described in chapter 1, Hamilton clearly sought a greater portion of authority for the national government. His construction of the supremacy clause in *Federalist* essay 33 and in his Lucius Crassus papers provides the best public statements of his position.[46] The continued survival and prosperity of the nation depended on the supremacy of the national government and its laws. The establishment and maintenance of a stable, nationwide financial system, a free-flowing commerce among the states, a well-planned postal and customs system, a system of district courts to protect contracts and property development, and a much more effective common defense are but a few of the necessities the states themselves could not provide. The supremacy clause made a durable union possible. Hamilton argued that the principle of union became ascendant with independence in 1776. The states were at best artificial beings, and the Articles of Confederation amounted to an unfortunate "abridgement of original sovereignty."[47] The new Constitution was much better suited to the needs of the Union, though it still faced the prospects of encroachment by the states, as he predicted in *Federalist* essay 17.[48] Only by "much better administration" could the national government win the support and affection of the people necessary to maintain its supremacy over the states. The supremacy clause provided the national administration an opportunity to demonstrate what that meant.

Maintaining national supremacy by improving the national administration required liberal interpretations of specific constitutional clauses that addressed Congress, the president, and the courts. In Article I, Section 8, Hamilton applied liberal construction to the taxing and general welfare powers, commerce power, war powers, and the necessary and proper clauses in an effort to establish a broad legislative authority for Congress. In a variety of works, such as *Federalist* essays 22 and 30–35, his addresses at the Poughkeepsie Convention, the *Report on Public Credit*, the *Opinion on the Constitutionality of the Bank*, the *Report on Manufactures*, and his brief in *Hylton v. U.S.* (1795), Hamilton dealt with the taxing, general welfare, and commerce powers. *Federalist* essay 23 and his Pacificus essays addressed war powers, and his *Opinion on the Bank* made the definitive statements on the necessary and proper clause.[49]

Hamilton applied to each of these clauses his basic standard of providing means adequate to support the ends for which the national government may be responsible. For example, Congress should have broad powers of taxation because "the contingencies of society are not reducible to calculations; they cannot be fixed or bounded, even in imagination."[50] He was prepared to sanction almost any kind of tax, depending on the abilities and contingencies of society.[51] As Rossiter stated, he "took a large view of the power of Congress to tax because he took a large view of its power to spend."[52] In his *Report on Manufactures*, he argued that "the power to raise money is plenary and indefinite" and is applicable to a broad range of explicit and implicit concerns. Clauses on "necessary and proper" means and the "gen-

eral welfare" easily extended the national government's reach, especially over economic affairs.[53] Congress should, therefore, possess the
discretion "to pronounce, upon the objects, which concern the general welfare, and for which under that description, an appropriation
of money is requisite and proper." This meant discretion to promote
and regulate commerce, manufactures, agriculture, education, and
science and technology.

Hamilton's construction provides the rationale for a large national
budget in order to support a service- and regulatory-oriented bureaucracy. As secretary of the treasury, Hamilton oversaw the largest bureaucracy of his day, some five-hundred-plus treasury and customs
agents, the budding coast guard, and the mint, and he coordinated
and advised the activities of various governing boards. It was not difficult for him to envision the growth and maturation of many more
agencies required to develop the economic and military affairs of the
nation. His *Report on Manufactures* presented an inventory of natural
resources and economic potential along with a plan of national economic development. Though the particulars of that plan did not come
to fruition, it illustrates the broad sweep of national administrative
power he believed to be compatible with the Constitution.

Hamilton applied the same logic of contingency to the war powers
of the new government. Such powers "ought to exist without limitation, because it is impossible to foresee or define the extent and variety of national exigencies." In his mind, this justified the power "to
levy troops; to build and equip fleets; and to raise the revenues which
will be required for the formation and support of an army and navy in
the customary and ordinary modes practiced in other governments."[54]
Through the combination of broad congressional and executive powers, Hamilton provided the rationale for an extensive military and foreign affairs establishment.

In regard to executive powers, Hamilton again takes the same approach. The president should make "well digested plans" and lead
in ambitious policy formulation as well as execution. In terms of the
Constitution, he would "claim the exercise of implied powers [for
the executive] as well as the Legislative. In a word there is no public
function which does not include the exercise of implied as well as express authority," and this has been a matter of "uniform practice of the
Treasury and War Departments." He even cited examples of how the
former government under the much more limited Articles of Confederation still exercised implied powers through its executive boards.[55]

He also advocated active use of the veto for proposed laws that the president "deems contrary to the public interest." He believed the president had power to "direct the common strength" in times of war as commander in chief and to engage in hostilities when a state of war is established *in fact*, though without a formal declaration. It is hardly unusual for a nation to find itself at war before a legislative body can act. A congressional declaration of war can only apply when it wishes to commence a war, that is, *when the nation is at peace.* He believed the president had power "to proclaim [without approval from Congress] temporary suspensions of hostilities. Generals of armies have a right ex officio to make truces. Why not the Constitutional Commander in Chief!" Incident to such events, it is therefore also essential that the executive possess broad discretion concerning the expenditure of public funds.[56]

Hamilton expanded on the defense of broad executive power in his Pacificus essays, which he later deemed his best work on the subject. They addressed the specific issue of whether the president could proclaim neutrality. In the first essay, he established the executive "as the *organ* of intercourse between the Nation and foreign Nations— as the interpreter of the National Treaties in those cases in which the Judiciary is not competent." In doing so, he also voiced "the general doctrine of our constitution that the Executive Power of the Nation is vested in the President; subject only to the *exceptions* and *qualifications* which are expressed in the instrument." He contrasted the "different modes of expression" in the vesting clauses of Article I and Article II, arguing that Article II's vesting clause conferred general executive power on the executive branch, subject only to explicit restrictions.[57]

In the same essay, he buttressed this expansive grant of power with the obligation to "take care that the laws be faithfully executed" and with the power of "command and disposition of the public force." In the context of growing tensions with France, the lack of a declaration of war by Congress meant that the president must do what he can to prevent war and is thus empowered under the Take Care clause to proclaim neutrality. Beyond that, he asserted the president's role as the leading partner in treaty administration and, therefore, in foreign affairs generally. "Though treaties can only be made by the President and Senate, their activity may be continued or suspended by the President alone." The president, then, holds the executive power with only a few specific restrictions such as the participation of the Senate in treaties and appointments and the power of Congress to declare war and grant letters of marque and reprisal. Because these are restrictions, as opposed to grants, of a general power, "they are to be construed strictly—and ought to be extended no further than is essential to their execution."[58]

With respect to "command and disposition of the public force," Hamilton would grant the executive broad emergency powers. As stated earlier, he would give Congress broad taxing powers to support spending for unpredictable contingencies, and the same rationale applies to war powers for the executive. In times of emergency, its powers ought to be sufficient to provide for any contingency. If "the means to be employed must be proportioned to the extent of the mischief," then the government must be capable of resolving the worst calamities. He admitted an "aversion to every project that is calculated to disarm the government of a single weapon, which in any possible contingency might be usefully employed for the general defense and security."[59] He conceded that such power increases the risk of abuse but believed the risk was necessary. Such emergencies require the government's immediate response. Again, paradoxically, undue restrictions on such power tend only to weaken the law and the government it establishes. He explained in *Federalist* essay 25 that restrictions in law that *cannot be observed* in administration encourage a lax attitude toward law, and ultimately this "impairs that sacred reverence which ought to be maintained in the breast of rulers towards the constitution of a country."[60] In times of emergency, then, the president should have broad discretionary powers, and whenever possible, these should, for prudential reasons, be construed within the bounds of laws which are framed in general terms.[61]

The fourth constitutional problem Hamilton dealt with concerns the courts. The judicial power functioned as the "cement of union." The court's independent judgment upon the constitutionality of both federal and state laws provided a crucial bulwark against the encroachments of both Congress and the states. They would protect the rights of individuals, especially property and contract rights, while guaranteeing the supremacy of national law.[62] The courts should construe the powers of the national government liberally and protect its supremacy aggressively. Judicial review should also be used to protect the constitutional division of powers, which, for Hamilton, primarily meant protection of the executive's prerogatives and leadership against congressional usurpation. This did not mean that courts should construe congressional powers strictly. As already illustrated, he viewed the clauses of Article I, Section 8 as a bestowal of broad legislative authority.[63] The courts were to insure that they were used to support rather than stifle the energetic executive.

Though the Constitution includes no provision for judicial review, Hamilton deduced, expounded, and defended it as an integral part of a limited constitution. It is an inherent power flowing from the logic of the constitutional scheme. He defined a limited constitution as one that "specified exceptions to the legislative authority," and he saw judicial review as a primary means of preserving those exceptions from legislative encroachment. Chief Justice John Marshall would rely heavily on Hamilton's extant reasoning in his assertion of judicial review in *Marbury v. Madison* in 1803.[64]

In Hamilton's mind, the third branch constituted a vital power for national public administration. As Clinton Rossiter summarizes, "The courts . . . were to interpret the laws of Congress, support the exertions of the President, and police the boundaries of the federal system in such manner as to strengthen the Union upon which the *salvation* of America rested." Chief Justice Marshall would play a large role in asserting national power in language appropriated from Hamilton's work.[65] Moreover, late in his career, Hamilton reiterated his desire to "surround the constitution with new ramparts and to disconcert the schemes of its enemies" who were attempting through the Virginia and Kentucky resolutions of 1799 "to unite the state legislatures in a direct resistance to certain laws of the Union." New ramparts included the "extension of the Judiciary system" by subdividing each state into smaller federal districts, "assigning to each a Judge . . . and other Conservators and Justices of the Peace . . . to give efficacy to the laws the execution of which is obstructed by want of similar organs and by the indisposition of the local Magistrates in some states." Though this would raise immediate objections, "it would carry with it its own antidote, and when once established would bring a very powerful support to the Government."[66] The expansion of federal courts would precipitate many battles over judicial appointments and thereby bring judicial politics to the fore in the early nineteenth century. Hamilton seemed ready to play in that arena when he saw the need.

Preservation of Hamilton's Enabling Doctrines

With the ascendance of Jefferson and the Republicans to power in 1801, Hamilton despaired that his efforts at nation building would be reversed. Certainly much of what occurred in the new century dismayed him. However, even before his death, there were signs that not all was lost. The most significant was John Adams's appointment of John Marshall to the Supreme Court. As Ron Chernow observes, "During thirty-four years on the court, John Marshall, more than anyone else, perpetuated Hamilton's vision of both vibrant markets and affirmative government."[67] As chief justice, he converted much of Hamilton's jurisprudence into constitutional precedents, and it all began with the *Marbury* case.

In *Marbury v. Madison* (1803), Marshall asserted judicial review over acts of Congress. His decision drew heavily from Hamilton's arguments in *Federalist* essays 78–82. Because "the powers of the legislature are defined and limited" by a "superior paramount law," the court, as the ultimate judicial power, is obliged to review the constitutionality of legislative acts. Marshall established in fact what Hamilton had asserted in theory. It is also significant that, in the same case, Marshall called for deference to the broad administrative powers of the executive, arguing that the court's role was "to decide on the rights of individuals, not to inquire how the executive, or executive officers, perform duties in which they have discretion." The courts should exercise restraint in these matters, implicitly and explicitly "supporting the exertions of the President."[68]

The *Marbury* case arose because of the outgoing Adams administration's midnight appointments to the Federal courts. These were overtly partisan in nature, and the outraged Jefferson administration, through James Madison's office (secretary of state), refused to issue their commissions. Marbury and three other appointees sued for writ of Mandamus. The Marshall court unanimously denied the petition, holding that while the appointees deserved their commissions and that it was the main province of the courts to protect such individual rights, the Constitution did not give the Supreme Court power to issue such writs for lack of original jurisdiction in the matter. Marshall's implicit lecturing of President Jefferson about individual rights and the unanimous assertion of judicial review sparked heated reaction from Jeffersonian Republicans, which resulted in the repeal of the recent Judiciary Act of 1802 that had established the new courts. But the Jefferson administration failed to mount a serious challenge to the asserted power, so judicial review stood and became solidly institutionalized as part of the constitutional design. That paved the way, as Clinton Rossiter characterized it, for a "series of major Supreme Court decisions in the next two decades which established the basic principles of American constitutional law" and provided fertile ground for a robust national administration later on.[69]

The Marshall court began securing the national government's authority over the states and economic development in a manner that would have pleased Hamilton. President Jefferson appointed three Republican justices to the court during his terms, but to his frustration they fell under Marshall's sway and became ardent supporters of his nationalist jurisprudence. President Madison appointed Joseph Story to the court, and he actually rivaled Marshall in his zeal for Federalist jurisprudence. So the early decades of the nineteenth century witnessed a tour de force of Federalist judicial statesmanship via the Supreme Court, much to the consternation of the strict-constructionist party of Jefferson and their successor party of Jackson. Thus began a century-long era characterized by historian Stephen Skowronek as "the era of courts and parties."[70] The old Federalists entrenched their legacy through the auspices of the Marshall court, over which the ghost of Hamilton loomed very large.

In *U.S. v. Peters* (1809), Marshall denied the power of the states to annul judgments of national courts. In *Fletcher v. Peck* (1810), Marshall held Georgia's recision of Yazoo land grants in violation of the Constitution's contract clause. This was the first instance of the court invalidating a state law for being contrary to the Constitution, rather than to federal statute or treaty, and it broadened the category of devices that counted as contracts, in this case, land grants—a matter that Hamilton addressed in a 1796 draft opinion concerning Georgia lands. As Julius Goebel observes, "Marshall's analysis of the issues followed almost exactly Hamilton's reasoning, with the result that State legislatures would not be allowed to rescind them."[71]

The *Fletcher* case held tremendous ramifications for national economic policy as well as national supremacy. It spawned land investment booms during the nineteenth century and served as precedent for a line of cases, the most important being *Dartmouth College v. Woodward* (1819). There, the court expanded the application of the contract clause to corporate charters and joined Hamilton's earlier argument that, to adapt to the exigencies of the times, the courts should not be bound by framers' intent but based on broad textual interpretation. The case secured a new approach to property law that favored developmental interests over the traditional static conception of property and sparked an "explosion in the use of corporations for commercial purposes."[72] As Albert Beveridge puts it, "Instead of protecting established, passive wealth, [it] encouraged economic growth that altered the status quo."[73] Goebel, the editor of Hamilton's legal writings, concurred, stating that Marshall followed Hamilton's arguments closely in relating the contracts clause to national development.[74]

Marshall's support of Hamilton's economic policy and of plenary

powers for Congress is also borne out in his commerce clause interpretation. In *Gibbons v. Ogden* (1824), despite some equivocation, Marshall gave broad definition to the term "commerce" and expressed
sympathy for Daniel Webster's Hamiltonian argument as counsel for
Gibbons that Congress's power to regulate commerce among the states
was exclusive and therefore prohibited to the states. "This power, like
all others vested in Congress, is complete in itself, may be exercised
to its utmost extent, and acknowledges no limitations, other than are
prescribed in the Constitution." The power is plenary and vested "absolutely as it would be in a single government."[75]

The Marshall court buttressed further the national government's
authority through appellate jurisdiction controversies framed in *Martin
v. Hunter's Lessee* (1816) and *Cohens v. Virginia* (1821).[76] In the *Hunter's
Lessee* case, the Supreme Court, per Justice Story, ruled that the logic of
national supremacy and uniformity dictated that federal courts be able
to review and harmonize the decisions of state courts relative to the
application of the supreme national law. In the *Cohens* case, Marshall
relied directly on Hamilton's reasoning. "He made extended use of
Hamilton's argument [in *Federalist* essays 80 and 82] for the appellate
jurisdiction of the Court over the state courts in all the enumerated
cases of federal cognizance."[77] In doing so, he followed Hamilton's
lead in confining state sovereignty and according more sovereignty to
the national government exclusively. This line of cases rebutted the
argument that the national government did not possess sovereignty
but rather served as a mere agent of state governments.

Finally, Marshall helped establish Hamilton's principles of liberal
construction and implied powers in the nation's jurisprudence. In
McCulloch v. Maryland (1819), he closely paraphrased the heart of
Hamilton's argument. "Let the end be legitimate, let it be within the
scope of the constitution, and all means which are appropriate, which
are plainly adapted to that end, which are not prohibited, but consists with the letter and spirit of the constitution, are constitutional."[78]
Then, like Hamilton, he applied the reasoning to a variety of enumerated powers in support of the Bank of the United States specifically
and the incorporation power generally: "Although, among the enumerated powers of government, we do not find the word *bank*, or *incorporation*, we find the great powers to lay and collect taxes; to borrow money; to regulate commerce; to declare and conduct war; and
to raise and support armies and navies. It may, with great reason be
contended that a government, intrusted with such ample powers, on
the due execution of which the happiness and prosperity of the na-

tion so vitally depends, must also be intrusted with ample means for their execution."[79] Furthermore, he strengthened Hamilton's arguments addressing the necessary and proper clause by comparing the term to Article I, Section 10, which prohibits a state from laying "imposts, or duties on imports or exports, except what may be *absolutely* necessary for executing its inspection laws." For reasons unknown, Hamilton never alluded to this express distinction.[80]

The interpretations upheld in these cases were refined in later years; but, with the exception of the contract clause,[81] their essential nature has remained intact. A perusal of almost any constitutional history book will show how, at crucial times, these doctrines have been reasserted to support an expanding national administration.[82] Most of these histories attribute the enduring quality of these doctrines to the brilliant leadership of John Marshall, but as the analysis here indicates, Hamilton's arguments undergirded most of Marshall's opinions. Few constitutional histories acknowledge this fact. There are, however, some notable exceptions. For example, Edward S. Corwin states that the "modern theory of presidential power is the contribution primarily of Alexander Hamilton." Benjamin Wright says Hamilton "dominated the thinking of John Marshall," and Kelly, Harbison, and Belz point to Hamilton's tremendous influence in the *McCulloch* case.[83]

The significance of Hamilton's jurisprudence did not extend to Marshall alone. Other important figures in the legal and judicial community of the early nineteenth century helped preserve his enabling doctrines. Perry Miller indicates that a community of leading figures quickly arose to "a position of political and intellectual domination," founding its "massive philosophical formulation" on the "light and learning" shed by Alexander Hamilton.[84] Though others such as John Adams and James Wilson made important contributions to the development of American jurisprudence, Hamilton's formulation most inspired a small but highly influential legal community. Luminaries such as James Kent, Joseph Story, David Hoffman, John Marshall, Daniel Webster, Nathaniel Chipman, Joseph Hopkinson, William Pinckney, Nathan Dane, William Rawle, Lemuel Shaw, and Timothy Walker helped preserve his jurisprudence in the face of stiff opposition from the more numerous strict constructionists of the antebellum era. They were not only lawyers and judges but also leading politicians, administrators, and educators who borrowed heavily from Hamilton's work. One of the best indicators of this is found in the highly influential commentaries of Kent and Story.

James Kent and Joseph Story are commonly acknowledged as the preeminent jurists, legal scholars, and educators of the period.[85] Kent was, by his own admission, a devout student of as well as friend to Hamilton. He studied Hamilton in his own court and as an observer of him in many legislative sessions. He claimed Hamilton's arguments and oratory were the finest he had ever witnessed and dubbed him the great legal mind of the era. Story never knew Hamilton and was allied with the Jeffersonian Republicans in his early life, but as a Supreme Court Justice he "became the most Hamiltonian of judges." In private he acknowledged Hamilton as "one of the greatest men of the age" to whom, with John Adams, "we are mainly indebted for the Constitution of the United States."[86] These men made their influential commentaries "a repository of Hamiltonian principles of order and justice, and generations of lawyers who barely knew Hamilton's name were led subtly into the paths he had trod."[87]

Conclusion

Hamilton's jurisprudence has of course not survived in full form over the course of US history. This is the way of most legacies, and his was hotly contested from the beginning. Subsequent generations are shaped in part by them, but they also select, reject, and neglect aspects of that heritage as outcomes of their own thought and political machinations. Over time, legacies distort in myriad ways, to the point that while we may see their threads running through current affairs, the present fabric of society bears little resemblance to what came before. Hamilton's judicial review, for example, constitutes a prominent and continuous thread, a lasting legacy from the founding era, and yet he and his colleagues would likely be stunned to see how the practice played out in subsequent history.

The same can be said for his other enabling doctrines for energetic government. The liberal construction of law with implied powers to meet every exigency, the prominence he gave to the supremacy clause, his broad interpretation of executive and congressional powers, his case for a robust, professional military establishment, and his unflinching support of taxing and spending for the general welfare are threads appropriated especially in times of war and depression in American history. His doctrines were at times reviled and rejected, thrown into latency, and then rejuvenated as critical precedents in the next crisis, usually without attribution and with the gloss and permutations of subsequent eras. Their relevance today can hardly be denied and is in fact confirmed by the heated and persistent attacks of states' rightists and strict constructionists who want to gut the domestic side of the federal establishment. *Plus ça change, plus c'est la même chose.* The republic has endured mind-boggling change but has done so primarily through a politics grounded in arguments over constitutional propriety. In such debates, Hamilton remains the weightiest of figures.

4
Administrative Responsibility

> The ingredients which constitute safety in the republican sense
> are a due dependence on the people, and a due responsibility.
> —*Federalist* essay 70

> It is remarkable that the Constitution has everywhere used the
> language "Officers of the United States," as if to denote the
> relation between the officer and the sovereignty; as if to exclude
> the dangerous pretension that he is the mere creature of the
> Executive; accordingly, he is to take an oath "to support the
> Constitution," that is, an oath of fidelity to the Government; but
> no oath of any kind to the *President*.
> —Hamilton, *The Examination* (1802)

Administrative responsibility in a republic necessarily entails consideration of sources of authority, the relation of administrative officials to various principals, appropriate character for administrative officials, the ways in which they are held accountable and to whom, and the values they apply to public policy. Chapter 1 explained that Hamilton believed the people constituted the ultimate sovereign authority moderated through the constitution and moral obligations of natural law. Public officials possess plenary powers adequate to fulfilling the ends prescribed in that constitution, and they are both enabled and held accountable through a complex partition of powers. Chapter 2 illustrated how the three branches blend and delegate significant powers to the public administration primarily, though not exclusively, through the executive branch. Hamilton's designs included ample room for independent boards and quasi-governmental entities. Chapter 3 explained how Hamilton's constitutional jurisprudence established rule by law as the foundation for responsible governance and how the Constitution provided a platform from which to launch ambitious and far-reaching plans for the development of a complex political economy and supporting military defenses. This chapter illustrates (1) the type of character Hamilton deemed appropriate for responsible subordinate officials, (2) how he helped articulate a standard of public-spiritedness and professionalism quite different from the feudal standard that prevailed in European governments at the time, and (3) the type of public morality he deemed most appropriate for guiding the discretion of public officials in the formation and execution of the public policies he believed to be central to a commercial republic.

Hamilton's republican theory and constitutional jurisprudence normatively grounded his approach to administrative responsibility. The title quotations above clearly indicate that he believed public administrators are ultimately accountable to the people through the Constitution and to its root principle of rule by law. Thus, no simple hierarchical and instrumental relationship defines the nature and scope of their responsibilities. They must exercise discretion to maintain proper institutional relations among their many principals as well as with the general public and to formulate the policies and broad tasks of executive administration outlined in *Federalist* essay 72. Clearly implied in the quotations above is the possibility that bureaucrats may have to resist or even disobey the demands of superiors for the sake of protecting the public's interest in preserving the rule of law, as well as for preventing perversion of the public good for private gain. Administrative responsibility is therefore suffused with the tension between subordination and autonomy in service of the people. Hamilton believed that effectively maintaining this tension required certain qualities of character as well as proper incentives and external precautions against abuse of discretion.

Emphasis on Public Integrity

To Hamilton, public and institutional scrutiny secured through checks and balances would help limit the "spirit of favoritism in the presidency, and tend to prevent the appointment of unfit characters from state prejudice, from family connection, and from personal attachment, or from a view to popularity."[1] He argued this point relative to European regimes that suffered far greater abuses and inherent forms of corruption arising from feudal culture, where no distinction between private and public interests existed. Many older American founders inherited that feudal mindset and thus found it difficult to separate their private interests from their public duties. Hamilton had personally witnessed colleagues and friends readily conflate the two.[2] On several occasions he remarked with abhorrence the deleterious effects of such actions on the national character and the public good.

He expressed utter disgust with this behavior during the Revolutionary War as he discovered extensive profiteering in the arena of military procurement. He was so incensed that he confided to his close friend, John Laurens, "I whisper a word in your ear. I hate money making men."[3] One case in particular prompted his publishing three early letters as Publius, the figure who had overthrown Roman kingship and established the republican foundation of the government.[4] Samuel Chase, a Maryland congressman and future Supreme Court justice, provided insider information to associates about a congressional plan to supply the French fleet with flour. They cornered the local market to drive up the price to their benefit. Hamilton condemned the action as the worst kind of opportunism, taken by "a man appointed to be the guardian of the state." He is "forgetful of the solemn relation in which he stands" with the public and "descends to the dishonest artifices of a mercantile projector." He "sacrifices his conscience and his trust to pecuniary motives." As such, "there is no strain of abhorrence, nor punishment which may not be applied to him, with justice." Such persons "ought to feel the utmost rigor of public resentment, and be detested as a traitor of the worst and most dangerous kind."[5]

One can understand Hamilton's anger given his role as administrative aide-de-camp to General Washington, wherein he witnessed severe want of every necessity among allies and troops, but his irritation stemmed as much from their general effect on public office and public trust in a republic. Notably, he was concerned about the *public* character and reputation of these officials while expressing little concern about their private moral character. In the third letter of Publius, he remarked that he would let any defects of Chase's private character *pass untouched*, that it was "enough to consider you in a public capacity" as a member of Congress. "The station of a member of Congress, is the most illustrious and important of any I am able to conceive. He is to be regarded not only as a legislator, but as a founder of an empire. A man of virtue and ability, dignified with so precious a trust, would rejoice that fortune had given him birth at a time, and placed him in circumstances so favourable for promoting human happiness. He would esteem it not more the duty, than the privilege and ornament of his office, to do good to mankind; from his commanding eminence, he would look down with contempt upon every mean or interested pursuit."[6]

Hamilton understood full well the importance of public integrity at that early stage of the republic. As Chernow puts it, "Hamilton expected that someday the struggling confederation of states would be welded into a mighty nation, and he believed that every step now taken by politicians would reverberate by example far into the future."[7] While a politician's private life might exhibit serious moral failings, these should be tolerated so long as they did not compromise one's public responsibilities. McDonald notes one of Hamilton's favorite insights from Vattel, who argued that "private morality and private behavior were no reliable measure of performance in office. Men were in fact likely to behave more morally when acting in a public capacity than when acting privately." McDonald further observes that "the founding generation of Americans abounded with personally corrupt men who nonetheless, out of a sense of duty and love of country, served the nation well."[8] For Vattel and Hamilton, a vigilant populace, ever mindful of their elevated status in a republic, could be combined with an array of institutional checks and proper incentives for public officials to induce most of them to act honorably in public life.

Thinking thus, Hamilton crafted a new sense of public professionalism very different from that found in the British system, which at that time put public servants in a relation of fealty (absolute loyalty) and patronage to the sovereign King.[9] They became the King's property and his loyal instruments in a rivalry of power with Parliament and its control over the purse. Hamilton characterized that arrangement as one bottomed on corruption (mainly through sinecure and graft) and thus as normatively incompatible with US constitutional governance. In the American republic, the president presides over subordinates who share in *public* (not royal) power and in responsibility for things that advance the general welfare of a sovereign people. Thus, to be honorable, a public official's duties and sense of obligation are redirected to the public good, to one's reputation, which depends entirely on demonstrated good faith to the people through the governing process and on public achievement or results. This raised merit and honorable service above all other criteria for holding public office.

Federici identifies strong parallels in Hamilton's thought with Cicero's essay *On Duties*, a work Hamilton had taken to heart early in his education. Cicero emphasized honor and duty, which, though obligatory in all walks of life, are especially pertinent to life in a republic. "The good man will never, for the sake of a friend, act contrary to the republic, to a sworn oath, or to good faith."[10] Federici succinctly defines the two virtues: "Honor requires a greatness of spirit that lifts individuals above immediate self-interest to a place where virtue and benefit are joined. Cunning, deceit, and cruelty are contrary to what is honorable. Although the use of such means may sometimes seem beneficial, they will undermine the greatness of spirit on which honor and duty depend." It is the official's duty to pursue the public interest, even to the sacrifice of his or her immediate interests. Duty requires the qualities of disinterestedness, magnanimity, moderation in policy, and justice tempered by mercy, even toward "enemies in war, slaves, and foreigners"—all of which contributed to Hamilton's sense of liberality.[11]

As Federici indicates, few scholars "acknowledge the degree to which Hamilton's constitutional theory depends on quality of character." Many "overstate [his] and the American framers' emphasis on lower human motives." Both his words and actions "can be considered a reconstitution of older views that incorporate modern ideas," especially as found in writers such as David Hume, who provided a synthesis of self-interest and virtue through the hierarchy of passions.[12] Hamilton demonstrated his devotion to the abovementioned virtues throughout his life, with only occasional lapses in moments of despair. They culminated in an impressive show of public-spiritedness and desire for fame during his tenure as secretary of the treasury.

Fame and Public-Spirited Professionalism

Many of the founders jealously guarded against any threat or embarrassment to their public reputations. They avoided abuses of public office that might tarnish a reputation, and pursued policies that they believed would garner fame in the eyes of future generations. Hamilton's correspondence with colleagues is replete with expressions of concern for one another's reputations. Should someone directly impugn a reputation, the act demanded a quick and even panicked response, seeking immediate apology and retraction lest the matter precipitate an *affair of honor*—a polite reference to duels. Correspondence therefore manifested carefully written language with highly diplomatic expressions, protocols, and titles of respect, especially when conveying disagreement, lest someone take offense. When personal letters broached criticism, they artfully directed attention to issues and problems rather than to persons and treated the affected parties with great delicacy.[13]

The prospect of gaining esteem from one's colleagues and from future generations animated Hamilton's desire for public service. He adhered to Hume's theory of the hierarchy of passions from baser to nobler, with fame being the noblest because it approximated the love of virtue itself.[14] This connection of passions and interests provided him with a motivational set oriented in important ways to what we now call professionalism. Its attributes included a high level of maturity cultivated through rigorous training and tested through experience, a sincere respect for colleagues and the public, a grave sense of public responsibility, and a studied independence that preserved the capacity for sound judgment.[15] On these matters he led by example. He brought an unmatched level of expertise and experience in financial policy and organizational management to the new Treasury Department. He displayed a high level of public decorum and instructed his employees at length on its proper exercise in relation to the public they served—no haughtiness or imperious attitudes allowed. He carefully avoided even the appearance of conflict of interest with his public duties, refraining from all investments and market activity even remotely tied to Treasury policies, and then issued a rule barring any employees with official influence on Treasury policy from trading in government bonds and securities.[16] He suspended his legal practice and cut off all private sources of income to avoid any suspicion of conflict of interest, and he concentrated his energy solely upon his official duties, even though his salary at Treasury was so meager that he fell near to financial ruin during his years in office.[17]

Hamilton's independent judgment, cogent reasoning, and exhaustive research became indispensable to President Washington, especially as policy conflicts arose between rivals and their emerging political parties. He won so many of these battles because he conducted far more research and mounted more compelling policy justifications than any of his opponents. Jefferson considered him a "colossus against the Republic party." President Washington brought his own sound judgment and gravitas to bear with colleagues and the public, while Hamilton supplied the arguments and detailed information. Chernow characterizes their relationship as two figures playing against each other's weaknesses and complementing each other's strengths in a mutually beneficial relationship that was critical to the success of the new administration.[18] The relationship exemplified professionalism, which Hamilton likened to a bearing of *military confidence*. Thomas Flexner, drawing from his biographical research on Washington, finds that Hamilton "had consistently repelled manifestations of friendship on Washington's part, preferring instead 'to stand on a footing of military confidence than of private attachment.'"[19]

The analogy of military confidence is indicative of the proper working relationship in a constitutional republic among officials who must balance subordinate status with autonomy. Hamilton asserted that they should exercise "a firm and virtuous independence" of judgment because, ultimately, they are beholden to "the people *through* the government."[20] Their professional character ties them to an independence-conferring principle: rule by reason under law. Externally, the checks and balances of the Constitution impose oversight and accountability to that standard. All decisions must show evidence of at least some *rational basis* pursuant to law. Hamilton the lawyer well understood this, and he brought it to bear in all of his public plans and decisions with direct references to applicable laws. Internally, one's professional bearing hinged on fidelity to this principle in league with merit, and thus on the avoidance of rule by will, caprice, and abject loyalty. He therefore disdained appointments of "persons whose chief merit is their implicit devotion to their superior's will and to the support of a despicable and dangerous system of personal influence." Far be it, for example, that anyone permit "a glaring attempt to transform the servants of the people into the supple tools of Presidential ambition."[21]

Hamilton wanted "men of quality and weight who sought to win a name for themselves" as public officials in their own right.[22] The term "weight" applies in three ways. First, it relates to the sense of honor that grounds the conscience and defines moral limits beyond which the individual officer will not go. The official must maintain moral lucidity about such limits. Second, it connotes the weighty nature of their duties and, third, it applies to the stability and system these officials bring to the government as a whole. A perusal of Hamilton's many Treasury circulars (memos of instruction, standard procedures, and policy rules) to his far-flung subordinates reveal his awareness of their actual (if not official) impact on public policy in their own spheres and the probity and consistency required in their conduct— especially when making enforcement decisions that immediately affected public attitudes about the new government. These qualities contribute to public-spiritedness, a concept associated with patriotism that emerged in seventeenth- and eighteenth-century England as part of recurring efforts to balance public access and inclusion with the needs of security and order. Britains wrestled continuously with new liberties claimed in the wake of the Glorious Revolution of the late 1680s. Officially, the public was deemed to include only the various divisions (such as Court and Country parties) of the propertied elite, but public-spiritedness reflected the aspiration to rise above those divisions with policies aimed at achieving an overarching harmony of interests.[23] The attitude and virtues displayed by Hamilton and intended for his cadres of professional public servants seemed aimed at the same thing, though tailored to a constitutional republic staffed by people of merit rather than of wealth or birth. His tenure as secretary of the treasury provides ample evidence of this aim.

As mentioned earlier, the Treasury Department attracted Hamilton's interest because its reach extended into all affairs of the government and because its policies would impact the new nation immediately and with dramatic effect. Jacques Necker's three-volume *A Treatise on the Administration of the Finances of France* profoundly influenced him in this regard. Hamilton had read it soon after its publication in 1785. His Treasury reports and correspondence (especially his reports on public credit and manufactures) "are replete with quotes, paraphrases, and parallels to his work."[24] Of note here is Necker's description of "the qualities necessary for greatness in a minister of finance," a position hardly fit for the faint of heart and requiring an exceptional level of devotion to the public good. "There are men whose zeal ought not to be cooled: such are those who being conscious that they are qualified for great things, have a noble thirst for glory; who being impelled by the force of their genius, feel themselves too confined within the narrow limits of common occupations; and those, more especially, who being early struck with the idea of the public good, meditate on it, and make it the most important business of their lives. Proceed you, who after silencing self-love find your resemblance in this picture."[25] These words pair well with Hamilton's in *Federalist* essay 72, where he again spoke of the "love of fame, the ruling passion of the noblest minds, which would prompt a man to plan and undertake extensive and arduous enterprises for the public benefit."[26] It fueled his public-spiritedness and led him into work that friends warned would jeopardize his reputation. Ministers of finance suffered from intense suspicion and scrutiny over work that few understood, much less appreciated. It is also significant that Hamilton's *Federalist* essay 72 addressed fame in the midst of his review of the ingredients of executive energy—unity, duration, adequate support, and competent powers. In combination with institutional checks, they would help make power safer to wield. This reasoning applied in similar fashion to the subordinate echelons of the public service.

Duration and the Accoutrements of a Responsible Career in the Public Service

Hamilton argued that, as with senators, judges, and the president, subordinate public servants should enjoy long tenure to bring agency policies to fruition. They could invest their time and develop a sense of ownership in their duties. Without that, the temptation to abuse the office for private gain was enhanced rather than diminished. Moreover, longer duration seemed essential for ensuring some permanence and stability in administration. Frequent turnover would, in Hamilton's words, "occasion a disgraceful and ruinous mutability in the administration of the government," and thereby erode the public's confidence.[27] Lynton Caldwell concludes that he "clearly favored lengthy tenure of public office, consonant always with good performance and responsibility."[28] Hamilton explained his position in the Lucius Crassus essays (*The Examination*) in 1802. He wrote these essays mainly in defense of judges who were threatened with removal through repeal of the Judiciary Act of 1802, but in doing so, he remarked more generally upon the status of all officers under the Constitution: "Every office combines two ingredients of an interest in the possessor, and a trust for the public. Hence it is that the law allows the officer redress by a civil action for an injury in relation to his office, which presupposes property or interest. This interest may be defeasible at the pleasure of the government, or it may have a fixed duration, according to the constitution of the office. The idea of a vested interest holden even by permanent tenure, so far from being incompatible with the principle that the primary and essential end of every office is the public good, may be conducive to that very end by promoting a diligent, faithful, energetic, and independent execution of the office."[29]

He did not argue that permanent tenure is required under the Constitution, but he clearly believed it compatible and preferable. The specified term, permanent or otherwise, would be subject to law because the "office is holden not of the President, but of the *Nation*." To his way of thinking, long duration, like unity, should be a general principle subject only to specific exceptions. He did justify rotation in office where, as in the case of quasi-public agencies such as the Bank of the United States, "private opportunities and public responsibility were too closely interwoven to make the permanent tenure of directorships by the same individuals acceptable to the public or desirable to the government." In general, though, rotation of offices should be avoided. "I am convinced that no government, founded on this feeble principle, can operate well."[30]

As indicated in chapter 2, Hamilton made evident his concern for duration among high subordinates in *Federalist* essay 77, arguing that removal of high office-holders required the concurrence of the Senate. He never wavered in his belief that subordinate officers, even political appointees, should hold their offices beyond the tenure of the president who appointed them. Rather, as will be shown, he advised that they consider voluntary resignation if they came to fundamental disagreement over executive policy, and there is no record of him ever advising Washington to summarily dismiss such an official.

Furthermore, subordinates at all levels required long tenure because of the complicated nature of national governance. National policies require extensive coordination and complex administrative processes, as well as a wide variety of professional and technical competencies, even at the street level. As Caldwell notes, unlike many of his political opponents, Hamilton "did not believe the duties of office so simple that any person of ordinary ability could fulfill them."[31] His proposals for industry regulation and promotion, financial policy and management, a diplomatic corps, and professional naval and military organizations would require stable, expert-based government. The public administration would therefore entail a vast array of offices staffed by a career service, both military and civil. Caldwell argues that Hamilton's industrial policy alone foreshadowed the formation of a sophisticated career civil service.[32] Hamilton's advice concerning the "necessary accoutrements" for subordinate officers lends more evidence to this point.

Hamilton intended the accoutrements of office to include (1) sufficient pecuniary reward in order to live in style appropriate to one's station—a matter of professional dignity; (2) symbolic accessories and recognition, which stimulate a sense of honor and pride in public service; (3) a reasonable prospect of gradual promotion or advancement in responsibilities and rewards to recognize exertion, talent, and qualification; and (4) powers sufficient to excite officials about the prospect of making a real difference in office and thereby to distinguish themselves through their achievements.[33] He stood out among his peers as an advocate for adequate remuneration of career officials. "It is in itself just and proper, that all who are in the public service, should receive adequate rewards for their time, attention and trouble." He lamented Congress's tendency to skimp on rewards for office, so much so that in 1797 he felt compelled to write that "public office in this country has few attractions." Pay and benefits were "so inconsiderable as to amount to a sacrifice to any man who can employ his time with advantage in any liberal profession." These conditions weakened even the most virtuous individual's resolve and commitment to public service.[34] Good pay for public officials entailed small cost compared to that of the incompetency and irresponsibility fostered by low pay. "Experience will teach us that no government costs so much as a bad one." He wanted salaries tied to status. They should be high enough to allow public officials to live in a manner appropriate to their interests and station—where one's interests coincide with one's duties. A person must see that the many challenges of public office are worth accepting and that they will enjoy the social perks that come with such status.[35]

Adequate salaries also reduce the temptation to abuse of office over the course of a career. This was an important consideration, especially for street-level Treasury officials such as revenue collectors and customs inspectors. Hamilton argued that the "security of the revenue operations turns principally upon the officers of the lowest grade." It would, therefore, be wise policy to pay them enough to "prevent the temptation, from indigence, to abuse the trust." Interestingly, he also recommended exempting these officials from the strictures of the conflict of interest law that forbade "all officers of the United States concerned in the collection or disbursement of the revenues thereof from dealing in the funds or debts of the United States or of any state." He viewed that clause as unnecessary and inconvenient for those lower officials who had "no official influence upon Treasury policy." Allowing them to deal in public funds or debt instruments would "increase their personal interest in the exact collection of the revenue."[36]

Hamilton demonstrated his interest in securing important symbolic rewards for public officials through his rapt attention to military dress. In 1799, as Inspector General, he noticed that some military hats for new recruits were of poor quality, were the inappropriate style, and came without accessories such as buttons, loops, and bands. He objected strongly to this, saying, "Nothing is more necessary than to stimulate the vanity of soldiers. To this end a good dress is essential or the soldier is exposed to ridicule and humiliation." The hat "ought to be delivered with its furniture complete," for the men could not and should not be expected to procure the accessories for themselves.[37] Chernow notes that Hamilton attended to such matters at all levels of office, even for President Washington, with meticulous attention to design, etiquette, and protocol. He designed military housing for each rank, devised carefully orchestrated manuals for drill, and even conducted time and motion studies with vibrating pendulums for establishing the "ideal length and speed of the marching step"— an early foray into the methods of scientific management.[38] He addressed these improvements as much for the sake of bearing and decorum as for efficiency and effectiveness.

Finally, Hamilton deemed opportunities for promotion as essential. They helped especially to mitigate the effects of low pay and benefits at the lowest grades.[39] Furthermore, where "pecuniary compensations are moderate, special compensations to officers for special or extra service" are necessary, and the officers should be provided "indemnifications for extra expenses in peculiar situations."[40] Such provisions, Lynton Caldwell observes, indicate that Hamilton clearly intended a "public service open to all able men of moderate means." Without adequate compensation and opportunities for promotion, only "the few possessed of wealth and leisure" would hold higher positions, while "mediocrity [prevailed] at the bottom of the administrative structure."[41] Hamilton exemplified the able man of moderate means and humble origins, and his distinctly republican orientation to merit and office-holding belies the mistaken impression that he desired a government run by a wealthy class. Indeed, he intended his measures to serve as at least a modest bulwark against both state encroachment and the inevitably oligarchic tendencies of capitalism—a matter developed more fully below as an aspect of his public morality.[42]

Balancing Subordination and Autonomy in Practice

At the higher reaches of executive administration, Hamilton desired "a working unanimity among the members of the administrative family," as Caldwell characterizes it, in hopes of achieving unified positions on public policy and bolstering public confidence.[43] And yet these members must also possess a great degree of independence because they were expected to bring ambitious policy agendas into office. They should strive for harmony with their peers within the bounds of their convictions and sense of the public good. If senior executives came to view an administration's policies as broadly contrary to their view of the public good, then Hamilton advised resignation to avoid embarrassing the administration with internal squabbles and to pursue their opposition externally. Such persons are better fitted to serve the people outside the administration. "Let him not cling to the honor or emolument of an office . . . and content himself with defending the injured rights of the people by obscure and indirect means."[44]

In his Mettellus essays (1792), prompted by Jefferson's increasing differences with him over policy, Hamilton argued that a subordinate of the president should display a "firm and virtuous independence of character, guided by a just and necessary sense of decorum." He should "never sacrifice his conscience and his judgment to an office, . . . [he is no] dumb spectator of measures which he deems subversive to the rights or interests of his fellow citizens." He should "avoid a false complaisance" and always observe "the higher duty, which he owes to the community." However, if he disapproved of measures in another department, he "ought to manifest his disapprobation, and avow opposition, but out of an official line he ought not to interfere *as long as he thinks fit to continue a part of the administration.*" This was especially the case when the contested measure had successfully passed into law. Then a "contrary conduct is inconsistent with his relations as an officer of the government, and with a due respect as such for the decisions of the legislature, and of the head of the executive department."[45] So it was appropriate to speak out against policies one opposed, but to go further by trying to subvert an established policy through one's office crossed the line.

With respect to the relations of department heads to Congress, Hamilton generally held that they served as agents of the president and therefore were not formally subject to congressional supervision. However, as described in chapter 2, the Treasury Department necessarily exhibited ambiguity in this regard, and Hamilton often played both sides of the fence. The Treasury Act of 1789 required direct reporting by the comptroller of the treasury to the House, and Hamilton in his role sought direct access to its sessions. He was rebuffed, mainly for fear by Jeffersonian Republicans of his rhetorical powers. On the other hand, in 1794, he contested the House's superintendence of decisions he made pursuant to existing statutes and to verbal authorizations from President Washington. "The proper inquiry for the Legislature must be, whether the laws have been duly executed or not; if they have been duly executed, the question of sufficiency or deficiency of authority, from the President to his agent, must be to the Legislature, immaterial and irrelevant." To do otherwise would "interfere with the province of the Chief Magistrate."[46] This clearly supports robust executive power, but it does not equate with the unitary executive theory subsequently advanced by Andrew Jackson, who argued that Congress had no business directing or delegating powers by law to executive subordinates. Hamilton recognized that direct congressional delegation and limited forms of supervision even over street-level officials were at times necessary, such as when authorizing collectors of the customs to bring suit for nonpayment of taxes.

Within the realm of departmental administration, Hamilton articulated standards for relations between superiors and subordinates and for a range of discretionary powers. These are found mainly in his Treasury circulars and letters and are notable for their emphasis on harmony and cordiality.[47] They are polite, respectful, and direct, and they display an openness with regard to his reasoning on the subjects addressed. Instructions were accompanied by their rationale and a sincere invitation to return comment. When uncertain about the practical impact of his instructions, he admitted so and strongly encouraged subordinates' advice for improving and adapting them to local circumstances. Letters from many of his subordinates in the field indicate that they were very knowledgeable and articulate about applicable laws and not afraid to offer recommendations for making changes.[48]

Much of the Treasury operation was in its infancy and therefore more tentative than settled in its practices. Accordingly, Hamilton was hesitant to reproach when things went amiss. He communicated his impressions of improper or irregular action directly to the employees concerned and always left open the possibility of misunderstanding. He also repeatedly asked them for insight on how to improve street-level operations and reviewed all existing forms and procedures with them for the sake of simplification and ease in relations with the public. McDonald notes that, in this regard, Hamilton also tried to "prevent standardization from degenerating into the kind of bureaucratic stupidity in which mindless form-filling is substituted for substance [by granting] a measure of discretion to collectors in the larger ports" and improving the "two-way flow of information" in general.[49]

Hamilton required regular reports of collections and payment data, responded promptly and supportively when subordinates met complaints by merchants, and provided instructions on how to address thorny issues. His customs officials had to avoid in their enforcement actions timidity on the one hand and imperiousness on the other. For example, he counseled his revenue collectors to immediately file suit against any default on bonds relative to duties to be paid. Bonds were considered an indulgence (giving more time for payment of taxes due) and were not to be permitted to descend to undue procrastination. A tenor of consistent enforcement had to be set to maintain the order of finances, though not without limited forbearance.[50] He clearly expected good judgment rather than mindless complaisance from these low-level employees.

Nevertheless, a regular system of communications and instruction became essential given that most Treasury employees worked in locations far from the national capital. Many were accustomed to running things in their own fashion and at times felt hounded by Hamilton's close attention. He readily asserted his authority over noncompliant officials, sought more uniformity and consistency in street-level enforcement, and was adamant about bringing simplification and standardization in forms and reporting. He stated unequivocally his intent to establish well-reasoned "precedents, and to digest a general and uniform plan of custom house documents, which will conduce to order, facilitate business and give satisfaction."[51] In doing so, he set in motion a system that would provide regularity in the eyes of the public, as well as extensive and uniform customs data for his reports on public credit and manufactures.

In general, Hamilton seems to have treated subordinates with a high level of respect, in accordance with his view of them as public officials with their own standing and significant impact. Correspondingly, he expected a high level of maturity and a grave sense of responsibility. At times, he presumed too much regarding the motives of colleagues such as William Duer, his first assistant secretary. Duer secretly continued to speculate in debt instruments while in office, which precipitated an embarrassing scandal for the Treasury Department and eventually landed Duer in debtor's prison when his speculation failed. Hamilton refused to help him out of his troubles, and he eventually died in prison.[52]

In another instance, Hamilton clarified one aspect of the relation of authority and discretion among his subordinates in a Treasury circular in 1792. A situation arose in which some customs officers argued that they possessed independent discretion concerning the interpretation of law. They relied upon their oath of office as justification to "pursue [their] own opinion of the meaning of the law."[53] Hamilton responded by plying a distinction between superintending the execution of law and the actual execution of the duties of office. The power of superintending includes the power of "settling the construction of the laws relating to the revenue in all cases of doubt." The power to superintend necessarily implies "a right to judge and direct" and an "obligation to observe" the implementation of such directions. An officer cannot superintend the execution of law unless "he has a right to judge of its meaning." In this case, the secretary of the treasury was empowered by law "to superintend the collection of revenue," and customs officers should conform their conduct to his construction. Furthermore, "the responsibility for a wrong construction rests with the head of the department, when it proceeds from him." This maintains a clear line of accountability to the issuer. He also pressed more broadly the distinction between general superintendents and "those who are merely superintendents within particular spheres." The latter necessarily submit to the former.[54]

The general rule, then, was to follow the directions and interpretations of superintending officer(s). However, as with most general rules, Hamilton recognized reasonable limitations and exceptions to limit abuse of authority.[55] Subordinates should thoughtfully rather than blindly obey their superiors and seek clarification in doubtful cases. They should resist instructions that clearly violate law. In the same circular, Hamilton encouraged "freedom of observation on any instruction" or interpretation. "I shall constantly think myself indebted to any officer who shall give me an opportunity of revising my opinion, with the aid of his remarks, which may appear to him not consonant with law, with his own rights, or with the good of the service. To every communication of this sort I have always paid, and shall always pay careful attention. And as often as I can be convinced of an error, I shall with cheerfulness, acknowledge and retract it."[56] He seemed genuine in these remarks and to have gained the trust of the vast majority of his subordinates as a result. It would have been interesting to see his counsel to subordinates who encountered clearly inappropriate demands of a superior with an opposite attitude. Unfortunately, I have found no such account.

In the early going at Treasury, Hamilton oversaw execution in great detail, to the point where at times he micromanaged the affairs of those officers in whom he lacked sufficient confidence. As the operations developed, however, he steadily delegated more authority to subordinates, expanding their discretion in particular spheres. Later in his career, serving as inspector general of the army, he observed the general malaise in departmental management under James McHenry, noting its "want of proper organization of agents in the various branches of the public service, and of a correct and systematic delineation of their relative duties," which stemmed largely from McHenry's failure to properly delegate responsibilities. "It is essential to the success of the minister of a great department, that he subdivide the objects of his care, distribute them among competent assistants, and content himself with general but vigilant superintendence. This course is particularly necessary when an unforeseen emergency has suddenly accumulated a number of new objects to be provided for and executed."[57] Hamilton understood the basics of effective organizing and good management, and he viewed them as important elements of responsible administration. Effectiveness is a form of accountability in its own right and would, he believed, give the national government a chance to win hearts and minds away from state and local attachments. On the whole, the Federalist administration governed effectively, won a surprising degree of public trust and confidence in its operations, and left a roughly forty-year legacy of career administrators who quietly weathered the storms of partisan controversy.[58]

Responsible Governance and Public Morality

Public morality embraces the idea that it is important to distinguish in principle the norms for appropriate conduct and decision-making in governmental relationships from those that are appropriate to personal relationships. Hamilton took this distinction seriously and with it helped forge a new sense of public character and obligation appropriate to the constitutional republic he helped establish. The Constitution's principles and values should inform the roles public officials play, and its underlying premises, as Hamilton saw them, should inform public policy as well. His public morality thus drew attention to (1) the problematic condition of human nature, (2) a focus on power and interests, (3) the requisites and trade-offs of a commercial republic, (4) the weight of experience and evidence, (5) a strong juridical perspective, (6) a limited secularity, and (7) an overarching concern for public confidence and trust in government. Each is woven into the following analysis.

Lynton Caldwell observes that "Hamilton's conception of leadership was based on the premise that it is the business of politics to deal with things as they are and not as they ought to be."[59] This reflects the sober realism that underlay much of Hamilton's political thought and colored his republican vision. In a searching analysis of his writings, Federici concludes that Hamilton's realism was "a composite of Classical, Christian, and modern ideas" about human nature that "avoided the extremes of Hobbesian amoral realism and Rousseauistic romantic idealism." He was influenced as much by Aristotle, Plutarch, Tacitus, Cicero, and Augustine as by modern writers such as Hume and Steuart. Significantly, he did not subscribe to the abstract, modern liberal notions of a *state of nature* and *social contract*. Rather, he viewed foundings as historically situated and rooted in the permanent tension between good and evil.[60] This belief presumed a dualistic and paradoxical view of human nature, as illustrated in his *Defence of the Funding System* in 1795:

> The true politician on the contrary takes human nature (and human society its aggregate) as he finds it, a compound of good and ill qualities—endued with powers and actuated by passions and propensities which blend enjoyment with suffering and

make the causes of welfare the causes of misfortune. With this view of human nature he will not attempt to warp or distort it from its natural direction—he will not attempt to promote its happiness by means to which it is not suited, he will not reject the employment of the means which constitute its bliss because they necessarily involve alloy and danger; but he will seek to promote his action according to the bias of his nature, to lead him to the development of his energies according to the scope of his passions, and erecting the social organization on this basis, he will favour all those institutions and plans which tend to make men happy according to their natural bent, which multiply the sources of individual enjoyment and increase the national resource and strength—taking care to infuse in each case all the ingredients which can be devised as preventives or correctives of the evil which is the eternal concomitant of temporal blessing.[61]

Herein lay a key actuating premise of Hamilton's designs and policies for the new republic. No human good goes unblemished, so every institution and policy contains flaws against which officials must place "effectual precautions and preventives." Correspondingly, this made him critical of those who "content themselves with exposing and declaiming against all sides of things and with puzzling & embarrassing every practicable scheme of administration which is adopted."[62] The likelihood of flaw or abuse should not defeat a policy whose general effect is beneficial. "The truth is in human affairs, there is no good, pure and unmixed; every advantage has two sides, and wisdom consists in availing ourselves of the good, and guarding as much as possible against the bad."[63]

Furthermore, the very successes or achievements gained through effective policies may well contribute to their eventual decline or undoing—such as when having achieved conditions of prosperity, people begin to think the institutions or practices that brought them about are no longer necessary. Self-deception is a natural tendency of the human condition, and more often than not it is the product of hubris. Throughout his life, Hamilton alluded to this condition with a variety of maxims, such as "the natural consequence of success is temerity" and the idea that those who govern must guard against the effects of the condition in the course of public policy.[64] Governance is mired in continuing struggle with this condition, so maintaining stable institutions and policies presents constant challenges, even in a system designed to play competing interests against each other. He rejected the idea that such a system would automatically self-correct. Leadership at all levels of public service must play a critical and balancing role.

It follows that because human beings are incapable of perfection, politics should attend to the art of the possible. As discussed in chapter 1, this did not mean adherence to the status quo. That would trap a primitive nation forever in its dreadful circumstances. Rather, public officials should draw on the deep-seated inclinations common to their people and produce measures that develop and channel them for beneficial ends. Within the context of constitutionally limited government, Hamilton believed this meant improving the material conditions for ordered liberty through a political economy into which the diverse ambitions and interests of the populace can be channeled and then enhancing the procedural fairness of, and access to, the governing system. However, giving sway to basic inclinations does not guarantee success. Human beings are motivated by all kinds of things, and some are less well suited to durable interests than others. Distinguishing among these is a matter of political prudence.

Hamilton's prudence was grounded in reflection on experience both historical and personal, and it led him to eschew "political empyrics" who "travel out of human nature and introduce institutions and projects for which man is not fitted"[65] or who contrive systems that may be mathematically or geometrically elegant but bear little relation to the contingent world of politics. These were the products of "over-driven theory" that led him to observe "how widely different the business of government is from the speculation of it," and so too the "energy of the imagination dealing in general propositions from that of *execution in detail.*"[66]

As illustrated in the next chapters, Hamilton's attention to administrative detail and exhaustive research usually won the day against proponents of such theories. On that basis, he criticized some core doctrines of Physiocratic and laissez-faire theory for their abstract suppositions, especially that only agriculture produced surplus value and that the invisible hand of the market should supplant public leadership and intervention as a surrogate for the public good. Hamilton had learned from experience, as well as from Adam Smith and James Steuart, that real gains in value can be accomplished through commerce and manufacturing to even greater degrees than through agriculture. The refinement of agricultural staples into more diverse foodstuffs, for example, increased the outlets for trade and thereby increased value for all parties beyond that of mere subsistence. Entrepreneurialism guided into such activities becomes a source of value to both public and private life, and governments play a vital role in stimulating it. Hamilton clearly applied a public dimension to the way entrepreneurialism should develop and how it could be used for public benefit—a point reiterated more recently by Mark Moore in his work on public entrepreneurship.[67]

Furthermore, the generation of value and wealth ultimately rested in Hamilton's mind on the establishment and preservation of public trust. This is as central to financial credit and economic confidence as it is to confidence in government. Politics and economics were to his mind inextricably linked, the latter being a species of the former. The synthesis formed the new science of the era (political economy), and Hamilton was one of its ablest students. He quickly grasped the significant insight that if people believe something has or will have value, then even its anticipation can become of source of wealth if buttressed institutionally. As will be shown in the next chapter, Hamilton believed it the national government's role to both stimulate and restrain this wealth-creating dynamic to avoid wanton speculation and resulting boom-and-bust cycles that would destroy confidence. The system requires carefully adapted regulation and consistency from a source outside the markets themselves, and the national government is best suited to fulfill that role.[68]

The generation of wealth, however, also presents its own problems. Hamilton freely admitted that "great power, commerce and riches . . . may in like manner be denominated evils; for they lead to insolence, an inordinate ambition, a vicious luxury, licentiousness of morals, and all those vices which corrupt government, enslave the people and precipitate the ruin of a nation. But no wise statesman will reject the good from apprehension of the ill." This thinking led him to a troubling but prudent conclusion. At the New York Ratifying Convention he argued that vices are inevitable under any conditions but that some kinds of vice may be more useful than others to a commercial republic. "Experience has by no means justified us in the supposition that there is more virtue in one class of men than in another. Look through the rich and the poor of the community; the learned and the ignorant. Where does virtue predominate? The difference indeed consists, not in the quantity but kinds of vices, which are incident to the various classes; and here the advantage belongs to the wealthy. Their vices are probably more favorable to the prosperity of the state, than those of the indigent; and partake less of moral depravity."[69] Hamilton the realist would take advantage of the rich and their vices for public benefit. This did not mean, as some have argued,

that he favored the dominance of a wealthy elite, for he fully understood that wealth translates into power, and power of any kind must
be checked. In the Constitutional Convention, he stated unequivocally that the few and the many "ought to have power, that each may
defend itself against the other."[70] As Michael Chan indicates, he believed a number of conditions in society would help mitigate the tendency toward growing economic inequality. Hamilton remarked in
the same speech that abolition of primogeniture and entail (inheritance by eldest son only, women entailed) and "the present law of
inheritance making an equal division among children . . . will soon
melt down those great estates, which if they continued, might favor
the power of the few." He foresaw an end to the dominance of the
landed gentry in the thirteen states. House elections from larger districts would also help dilute their influence over the populace. Re-
districting would matter, and one of its core criteria should always
include balancing power among classes.[71] And finally, an adequately
paid public service open to all classes should serve as a check on the
influence of the rich in the halls of government and contribute to
the emergence of a middling class. He argued that "the character
and success of republican government appear absolutely to depend
on this policy."[72] However, as Chan also observes, Hamilton still "conceded that as America became richer, it would be more difficult for
poor men of merit to rise from obscurity and wield the reins of government." He made this point early in his career and seems never to
have abandoned it. Said Hamilton: "While property continues to be
pretty equally divided, and a considerable share of information pervades the community; the tendency of the people's suffrages, will be to
elevate merit even from obscurity. As riches increase and accumulate
in few hands; as luxury prevails in society; virtue will be in greater degree considered as only a graceful appendage of wealth, and the tendency of things will be to depart from the republican standard. This
is the real disposition of human nature: It is what neither the honorable member nor myself can correct. It is a common misfortune that
awaits our state constitution as well as all others."[73]

The ongoing challenge of a commercial republic is to stave off the
oligarchic tendencies of wealth for as long as possible and to find ways
to mitigate its effects as it ensues. And yet, Hamilton's realism convinced him of Aristotle's aphorism that regimes tend to die from an
excess of their own virtues. For a commercial republic the accumula-
tion of wealth would gradually take its toll. Like the rest of the found-

ing generation, Hamilton expressed serious doubts about how long the republican experiment could last, but that did not stop him or his colleagues from the venture. Their republican design, with its attention to limiting the play of power, held some hope for durability.

Preoccupation with Power

Hamilton's preoccupation with power shows most prominently in his *Federalist* essays, which of course were focused on the proposed *design* of the Constitution and how it avoids tyranny through the constraints of separation of powers and checks and balances. The *Federalist* is well known for its negative view of human nature, and Hamilton is often accused of holding the darkest view of it among the founders. However, as Forrest McDonald indicates, Hamilton followed David Hume in adopting the supposition of human venality as a matter of prudence, though not of fact. Hume stated that, "in contriving any system of government, and fixing the several checks and controls of the constitution, *every man* ought to be supposed a *knave*, and to have no other end in all his actions, but *private interest*. By this interest, we must govern him, and by means of it, make him, notwithstanding his insatiable avarice and ambition, cooperate to the public good."[74] Importantly, Hume added that this maxim is "true in politics though false in fact." Hamilton took that caveat seriously. One assumes the worst in human nature as a matter of prudence in designing a government. In matters of general governmental policy *after* establishing a government, he adopted a more balanced, empirical view of human nature. In defending his Treasury policies, for example, he argued that "the true politician takes human nature (and society its aggregate) as he finds it, a compound of good and ill tendencies, embued with powers and actuated by passions and propensities which blend enjoyment with suffering and make the causes of welfare the causes of misfortune."[75] Even in his *Federalist* essays, the picture of human nature is not as dark as some characterize it. In essay 76, he argued that the "supposition of universal venality . . . is little less an error than the supposition of universal rectitude" because the embrace of "delegated power implies that there is a portion of virtue and honor among mankind, which may be a reasonable foundation of confidence."

That said, the durability of the regime and its policies must still rely on a sober sense of human limitations. This became most evident in his approach to military and foreign policy. There, it had to do with maintaining a balance of power among nations to deter aggression on a grand scale and with focusing on cool calculation of mutual interests in forming alliances, determining maritime laws, and upholding the law of nations. Relations between countries require a different kind of thinking than do relations among colleagues or friends. For example, one must restrain the tendency to act toward other nations out of gratitude or to demonize them as evil enemies, because such sentiments are personalizing, and nations are not persons. Rather, they are entities through which the interests of their people are conveyed, and these are matters for bargaining and diplomacy, not gratitude or refined "metaphysical niceties about the justice or injustice" of a cause. The latter are seldom amenable to clear definition and calculation and thus make international relations unstable and less predictable. Stability, order, and predictability provide firmer ground for ensuring obligations of good faith and justice in that arena. Material interests "are definite and positive, their utility unquestionable [because] they relate to objects which, with probity and sincerity, generally admit of being brought within clear and intelligible rules."[76] Relations among nations are potentially so problematic that they must be cast in these modest, material terms and distanced from emotional displays that can embitter souls and embolden human aggression.

Finally, the thinking Hamilton employed in these matters flowed as well from his strong juridical perspective. The Constitution bases governance on the rule of law, and through its many legal provisions and economic powers subjects political and economic disputes to a form of republican proceduralism. The popular will is conditioned by an arrangement of institutions, processes, and mechanisms through which the responsibilities of public officials are carried out. In this fashion, administration by law provides a measure of solidity, and of results, by preferring material interests and rights to abstract causes. This is aided greatly by the confining of the ends of republican government to a lower order of moral goods and the leaving of the higher virtues and goods of individual and social improvement to other spheres. Hamilton's public administration under a *limited Constitution* is thus both juridical and secular in nature. The public morality of administration is thereby suffused with the language of representation, due process, equity, accountability, transparency, responsiveness, separation of church and state, contractual relations, and economic opportunity. These are the kinds of values that buttressed his sense of republican liberty, the primary end he meant the public administration to guarantee.

Conclusion

Hamilton offered a theory of administrative responsibility much broader in scope than the conventional theories in use today. While public administrators exercise significant degrees and types of discretion, they are typically treated as instruments of elected and appointed policy makers. They do not make policy; they just carry it out. The politics-administration dichotomy remains useful as a means of insulating civil servants from undue partisan influence—of that Hamilton would likely approve. But the broader tendency to treat their work as qualitatively different from politics, as strictly technical and instrumental, runs counter to his sense of them as constitutional officers in their own right who wield significant policy-determining power. He would likely see the extent and variety of decision-making procedures and legal mechanisms that comprise the administrative process today as an essential republican infrastructure—the political skeleton of the regime.

Moreover, it is quite apparent that Hamilton balanced his conception of "unity" in the executive with his extensive treatment of "duration in office." It is a mistake to treat one without the other. They combine to strengthen and energize presidential leadership, on the one hand, and, on the other, provide grounds for an extensive career public service possessed of an autonomy and sense of professionalism sufficient to resist being treated as servile instruments of unbounded ambition. As illustrated in the concluding chapter, we have not always wrestled effectively with the ethical tension Hamilton built into this relationship.

While Hamilton's theory embraced broad and ambitious roles for public administrators, his practice in terms of superior/subordinate relations remained somewhat simplistic, due in large part to the nascent stages of cabinet and departmental development in his day. It would have been interesting to see how his thinking evolved when the scale of departmental operations grew to many thousands of employees working in myriad agencies and programs and defending their turf in the dramas of bureaucratic politics. It appears that he would not have countenanced much of the bureaucratic guerilla government activity described today by Rosemary O'Leary, but such a conclusion must remain tentative. He wanted independent thinkers and doers among the ranks, and as O'Leary indicates, not all guerilla actions bear the same moral significance and status.[77] He might well approve of such actions if they resist or reverse decisions that degrade the integrity of an agency mission or violate individual rights. What can be said with confidence is that he articulated the primary standards for administrative responsibility under the Constitution that still require public administrators to wrestle with the tension between subordination and autonomy. In the end, that requires prudent judgment as much as checks and balances, so the character of the public service remains an abiding concern. This is especially important to consider in light of the current disaffection by a significant portion of the public with government in general and of siren calls for strongman leadership. This is a dangerous trend reemerging around the world, and one that our founders most feared and intended to resist. Hamilton's administrative republic, and the public morality he drew from its design, serves as a bulwark against such leaders.

His approach to public morality also deserves attention for other related reasons. First, his distinction between private and public character, wherein he advocated a measure of tolerance for private moral failings largely unconnected to public responsibilities, should be taken more seriously. The tendency today to expect politicians and public servants to be virtuous in all respects is simply unrealistic. It is also hurtful in the sense both of denying them some refuge in private life and of making public occupations so onerous and invasive as to deter many able persons from seeking public office. John Rohr and Patrick Dobel have made substantial contributions to this line of reasoning, but it appears that their points go unheeded.[78]

Second, Hamilton's realist approach to public policy deserves serious attention in administrative and regulatory practice, as well as in the academic fields of public administration and public policy. He is recognized in foreign policy circles as an early voice of the influential realist school, but the implications of his realism concerning public administration and policy in general remain unexplored. There is much to ponder, for example, about how his thinking may serve as a counterpoise to the dominant regulatory narrative that is informed mostly by applications of neoclassical economic thought and that has resulted in the withering of significant regulatory infrastructure and standards, especially in antitrust and financial policy arenas.

Finally, whether acknowledged or not, Hamilton's public-spiritedness informs the standards that prevail in American public service today. We no longer regard fame in any serious way, but reputation still matters. Moreover, public service motivation, as observed by James Perry and colleagues in myriad empirical studies, demonstrates that a significant number of public servants possess "other-regarding" values and a commitment to the public good.[79] The many ethics codes in effect within public agencies today also reinforce that sense with increasingly strict conflict-of-interest and related policies. However, the resolve of many public servants also appears to wax and wane with the moods of political society. These seem to follow what Arthur Schlesinger Jr. described as cycles of "private interest," when people neglect public things in favor of privatization and an "overriding quest for personal gratification," and cycles of "public purpose," when the excesses of the previous era demand reform and draw people back to concern for improving public life.[80] These cycles affect the morale and public-spiritedness of civil servants, so it is not uncommon during periods when private interest is ascendant to see an erosion of dedication among them, along with denigration of their public service as something less valuable than if they pursued truly productive work in business.

Nowhere has this phenomenon been more evident in recent decades than among regulators of the financial system during the run-up to the 2007–8 financial crisis. The prevailing idea at the time was an old one: let market competition clear the abuse and fraud in the system and thereby deny the raison d'être of regulatory work. Over time, the regulatory culture in the relevant agencies (Treasury, Federal Reserve, and SEC, primarily) eroded, with many employees seeking employment in the firms they were regulating, and neglecting enforcement of the laws governing financial practices.[81] This degradation of public-spiritedness amounted to a devastating loss of political and social capital. It should be thought of in those terms, as something that requires ongoing investment and preservation not only for individuals but also for the institutions they inhabit. The attitude of the public service matters. In the wake of the crash, the resulting loss of public trust in the financial system and of confidence in the economy and in government generally has been incalculable. As the next chapter will show, this is an arena of public administration and policy about which Hamilton had much to say, and much of it remains relevant to this day.

5
Public Finance and Political Economy

Building Confidence and Public Trust

> Money is, with propriety, considered as the vital principle of the
> body politic; as that which sustains its life and motion and enables
> it to perform its most essential functions. A complete power,
> therefore, to procure a regular and adequate supply of revenue,
> as far as the resources of the community will permit, may be
> regarded as an indispensable ingredient in every constitution.
> —Alexander Hamilton, *Federalist* essay 30

> A national debt if it is not excessive will be to us a national
> blessing; it will be a powerful cement to our union. It will also
> create a necessity for keeping up taxation to a degree which,
> without being oppressive, will be a spur to industry.
> —Letter to Robert Morris, 1781

> We can pay off [Hamilton's] debt in 15 years: but we can never
> get rid of his financial system.
> —Thomas Jefferson, 1802

Hamilton treated public finance and political economy as "natural
concomitants of [his] republican vision" and therefore as matters central to the work of public administration.[1] The European powers of the
day employed public finance to build royal treasuries and powerful
governmental prerogatives. As McDonald indicated, Hamilton repur-
posed it "to achieve political, economic, and social ends; and that
made all the difference in the world."[2] The new government should
pursue a constitutive republican agenda, promoting in Hamilton's
words a "general spirit of improvement" among the people. The national administrative infrastructure should stimulate "what amounted
to a social revolution" in the American way of life through a system of
credit and encouragements to industry of all types, and thereby "enlarge the scope of human freedom and enrich the opportunities for
human endeavor."[3] In his *Report on Manufactures*, Hamilton wrote that

"minds of the strongest and most active powers fall below mediocrity and labor without effect if confined to uncongenial pursuits. And it is thence to be inferred that the results of human exertion may be immensely increased by diversifying its objects." He thus conceived of an entrepreneurial society in its broadest sense, as a way of "cherish[ing] and stimulat[ing] the activity of the human mind" through development of a diverse array of vivifying public and private institutions.[4] Without such active administration and policy, liberty for average Americans would mean little as they scrabbled for bare subsistence.

This chapter describes Hamilton's efforts to establish the main organs of his financial system and the policy arguments he developed for achieving his constitutive vision of the American commercial republic. It begins with attention to historical context and details of emerging financial practice that help explain the significance of his contributions. He did not simply copy institutional designs and practices from Europe. He had to adapt them to the needs and concerns of Americans, and in the process, he became one of the leading minds of the day on the emerging science of political economy and public finance. His work would become revered long after his time by those who understood the significance of these subjects to an emerging new world.

Setting the Stage

Hamilton's new republic contrasted sharply with republics of old, which were steeped in ferocity and devotion to oppressively conforming notions of ultimate collective good. Ancient republics such as Sparta and Rome primarily espoused military virtues; they were city-states of soldiers that sought conquest and plunder to sustain themselves.[5] By contrast, the prospects for an industrious and relatively peaceful American republic became feasible through European innovations in political science (discussed in chapter 1), along with the development of modern trade, inventions of mass production, and liberalized financial practices that bolstered commerce, industry, and agriculture. Forrest McDonald, in *Novus Ordo Seclorum*, describes how this commercial revolution unfolded.[6]

Especially pertinent were institutional reforms adapted to domestic trading and financial practices from the law of international trade (*lex mercatoria*). The adaptations liberalized the use of interest on money, the negotiability of price, contracts for exchange, and the monetization of debt. Together, these transformed the political economy of Europe. Rates of interest on borrowed funds had always been fixed and relatively uniform within each country, and prices on goods had traditionally been governed by the standard of "just" or "intrinsic" value pegged roughly to the amount and quality of labor required to produce it.[7] These old standards kept market practices and prices very stable but also incapable of adjusting to rapid increases in production and exchange associated with the European Industrial Revolution. Adopting price negotiability between trading parties, and variable interest rates as used in international trade, accommodated these changes, though with increased potential for market instability. They also forced changes in contract law doctrines relating especially to restrictions against assignability to another party when a contract involved performance entirely in the future. Growing complexity in the volume and variety of trades required accommodation for assignable futures contracts in-country as well as internationally. This allowed proliferation in the variety and extent of commercial agreements in both established and emerging markets.

Debt monetization arose in response to the depletion of European government treasuries due to long and expensive wars. Extending credit had been heavily restricted in part because unified nation-states were only just emerging. In England, for example, the King had to borrow from a separate governing estate (the Commons, for example) for more revenue. Once the three estates, King, Lords, and Commons, were incorporated into a single state organ, it became possible to create more debt capacity through establishment of a central bank, for example, the Bank of England. Enlarging debt capacity included allowing not only for more debt but also for debt with no mandatory retirement period. The bank's new debt instruments thus paid perpetual interest. Moreover, its bills of exchange and bank notes could be made assignable to other parties and thereby circulated as forms of money. This made exchange of specie or bullion unnecessary, and banks could issue assignable (exchangeable) debt instruments far in excess of their actual holdings. This allowed rapid and immense market liquidity, though yet again more potential for market instability. Extraordinary financial booms and disastrous busts (such as the infamous South Sea Bubble of 1720) ensued and set off heated controversies over whether and how debt monetization should be used.

Sir Robert Walpole reformed and stabilized the English bank's practices first by making debt instruments redeemable after a stipulated period, then by establishing reserve requirements, and then by putting means in place to retire public debt. However, the damage done by previous financial bubbles provoked significant reaction against central banks and public debt in general. The controversy rippled to the American colonies, sowing deep distrust among large numbers of Americans about the mystifying practices of modern banking. Nevertheless, as McDonald observes, "no economic development in England's history would be so creative of the wealth of the nation" as this financial revolution.[8] This would apply to the United States as well, and eventually around the globe.

These changes, along with the Industrial Revolution, came more slowly to the United States, but strong social, economic, and legal ties to Europe, especially England, made them inevitable. The new constitution established on paper a national government capable of wielding the tools of modern public finance. Article I, Section 8 gave it "the power to borrow money on the credit of the United States," to "regulate commerce among the states," and to coin money and regulate its value. Hamilton played a central role in institutionalizing these powers with a central bank, a mint, and a sophisticated funding system. He had judged the American people already well suited in their dispositions to the commercial and industrial development that these new institutions would spur. He prepared himself for a leading role in these institutions by studying the great European ministers of public finance, many of whom, Thomas McCraw observed, were also foreign-born immigrants—a factor that enabled them to see things differently, more creatively, than the native-born, landed patricians who dominated the scene. These immigrants enjoyed a "wanderlust and readiness for bold action" oriented to urban rather than rural life, and thus they more quickly grasped the significance of a money economy. "They saw capital as rootless—movable, portable, migratory in the same sense that they themselves were" and how this "could serve the public good."[9]

Two European ministers, Emmerich de Vattel and Jacques Necker, weighed heavily in Hamilton's thought. Vattel's influence has already been described in terms of the "natural" ends of government and the public trust required to sustain republican governance.

Necker's study and practice of public finance led to more specific insights described by McDonald as involving the finance minister's responsibility for perceiving "the whole of a system and the relations of all its parts to one another and to the whole, knowing when to act and when to stop," and proceeding "slowly, step by step, so that they might not excite alarm."[10] The financial system must operate as infrastructure, with a quiet consistency and regularity that contributes to predictability and confidence, so much so that the system becomes taken for granted—like the air people breathe or the blood that quietly circulates as they live their lives—and all based on the morality of keeping commitments, on public trust.

Necker drew his insights from financial failures—boom-and-bust cycles fed by speculation and artifice with mystifying debt instruments. These were the enemies of public trust then and remain so to this day. When financiers mismanage these systems, whether through imprudence, incompetence, or clever mendacity, the effects can be devastating. Accordingly, Necker derived three moral principles for public finance that, if faithfully observed, would prevent calamity. Hamilton applied them "with exactitude—and often made enemies in the process." McDonald nicely summarized the principles: "First, said Necker, the [finance] minister must be attentive at all times to the interests of the people, especially the common people, and thus he must see to it that all laws concerning finance were made as simple as possible and that the main burden of new taxes should always fall upon 'objects of luxury and splendor' rather than upon necessities. Second, the financier must be guided by a strict and punctual adherence to promises, for there could be neither public credit nor justice otherwise. Third, Necker insisted on 'the infinite importance of making the state of the finances publicly known.'"[11] Simplicity, fidelity to promises, and transparency are difficult to achieve in money matters because so many financial transactions require elements of secrecy and complexity. And yet it is the role of the central financial organs of government to orchestrate the parameters of prudent financial practice and not to simply react to the innovations and dynamics of players in the system. Government must set the rules of the game, and the more simple and transparent these rules are, the easier it is to control their ill effects and observe good faith. In reaction to the most recent financial disaster (2007–9), the popular writer Michael Lewis concluded that the spirit of these principles requires "boring banking." "The ultimate goal should be to create institutions so dull and easy to understand that, when a young man who works for one of them walks into a publisher's office and offers to write up his experiences, the publisher looks at him blankly and asks, 'Why would anyone want to read that?'"[12] Hamilton would approve.

A Tenuous Start

The United States began its existence under the conditions of revolutionary war and severe depression. The governing arrangements under the Articles of Confederation made it impossible to effectively gather and manage the revenue required to conduct the war, much less stimulate the depressed economy. Its national government possessed no independent power of taxation or import duty and relied instead on requisitions from the states and on printing money. State requisitions were haphazard, unreliable, and entirely inadequate. The states continually reneged on their financial commitments, and printing money quickly turned disastrous.

National finances were at first handled by a commission, but they botched the job so badly that the Continental Congress decided to appoint a single head instead. Robert Morris, one of a mere handful of competent financiers in the country (and with whom Hamilton corresponded regularly), was selected for the post, but the Continental Congress so circumscribed his powers that he was forced to rely chiefly upon international borrowing and the issuance of IOUs domestically to accrue the most meagre resources. Forrest McDonald quipped sarcastically that "ordinary Americans and their duly elected representatives, it turned out, loved liberty so dearly that they were willing to pay for it with anybody's dollars but their own."[13] Morris operated under the eyes of highly suspicious state and continental officials who plagued him with accusations of impropriety at every turn. Founding-era officials in general treated public finance with intense distrust because of its complexity, because of the high stakes involved, and because of European experience with insider collusion, speculation, and corruption among financial officials. Morris resigned after an exasperating three years (1781–84) and with little hope that the new nation could survive without more sufficient measures for meeting its financial obligations. During most of the war, the new government had even failed to pay the interest on its growing debts, which meant that subsequent loans from foreign institutions came at very dear terms.[14]

The war cost the United States approximately $160 million in 1780 dollars, "more than the total budget of the national government over the *twenty years* from 1790 to 1810—years in which most federal spending went toward paying interest and principal on the war debt."[15] As loans became more expensive during the war, Congress resorted to printing money, issuing $241.5 million of it over five years. This sparked rapid inflation and the devaluation of the currency to about two cents on the dollar, thereby prompting the widely used exclamation, "Not worth a Continental!" Some states also printed money, as well as bills of credit, in excess of $200 million, all of which was quickly devalued for lack of good faith in meeting their obligations. Foreign loans from banks in Holland and France grew to around $11 million (including about $1.8 million in unpaid interest), which of course had to be paid back at face value plus yet higher interest.[16]

The new nation and its states had no real banking institutions until 1782 and were essentially bankrupt two years into the war. The Continental army resorted to issuing its own IOUs to farmers and merchants for food and equipment. As of 1792, the new government still ran budget deficits at around 38 percent of revenue, higher than at any other time in US history until 1992.[17] The scale of the debt boggled the minds of the founders and raised fears of financial ruin to the new republic. Shays's Rebellion (1786–87) against the foreclosure of central Massachusetts farmlands loomed very large for its broader implications and convinced many founders of the need to rework the Articles of Confederation into a more effective form.

Hamilton experienced the hardship of conducting war under these terrible financial conditions, and so during the slow winter months he schooled himself on the major works and periodicals of political economy and finance available at the time. He already possessed working knowledge of financial affairs through his counting house experience in the Caribbean. His subsequent immersion in works by James Steuart, Malachy Postlethwayt, Wyndham Beawes, Richard Price, Jean Baptiste Colbert, William Pitt the younger, Charles Montague, and Jacques Necker on both theoretical and practical aspects of commerce, trade, and finance significantly deepened his insight in two ways. First, as described above, he saw how to connect European reforms in trade and financial practices to the establishment of a more united and prosperous republic.[18]

Second, he learned the nuances and intricacies of managing money and banking for the sake of providing a stable source of public credit. He dove into these matters early on by helping design bank charters, first in New York, then for the national government, and also for Canada, using chiefly the Bank of England as his model, though with different principles and purposes in mind. Both Gordon and McDonald have noted that among the European empires, Britain was the first to figure out how to manage public debt through a central bank in a manner that created an immense and stable supply of circulating bank paper. It enabled the empire's ascendancy among its competitors chiefly because it could sustain a robust army and navy without impoverishing its citizens.[19]

Hamilton knew this would be even more essential for uniting a republic. The new constitution made it all possible by clearly establishing Congress's power to incur debt in Article I, Section 8, then by prohibiting the states from issuing their currencies in favor of a uniform national currency, and then by imposing uniform rules on bankruptcies. Its powers over commerce and taxation for the general welfare also constituted essential props for Hamilton's proposals, but he could do very little until Congress established the Treasury Department and delegated vital financial powers to its officers. Only then could he put some meat on the bones of the new government.

Hamilton told his friend Edward Carrington in 1792 "that most of the important measures of every Government are connected with the Treasury."[20] Through it, he could reach every arena of policy and every governmental institution and shape them in accordance with his national vision. He was eager to take the Treasury position provided that Congress structured it appropriately (e.g., headed by a single chief executive) and empowered it with sufficient independence from both presidential and congressional meddling. Madison, his indispensable ally and leader in Congress, succeeded in passing a workable design. The secretary would report to both Congress and the president, and subordinates received their own statutory powers to serve as not only key advisors but also independent checks on Treasury operations. As McDonald describes it, the new Treasury Act conferred upon the secretary of the treasury "a wide range of duties and a goodly measure of latitude in carrying them out. He was empowered to appoint his assistant, superintend the collection of the revenues, decide upon the forms of keeping accounts, prepare and report budgetary estimates. He was also to 'digest and prepare plans for the improvement and management of the revenue, and for the support of public credit.' He must make reports, 'and give information to either branch of the Legislature, in person or in writing (as he may be required), respecting all matters referred to him'—and then a most significant addition, 'or which shall pertain to his office.' Hamilton could scarcely have asked for more."[21] Upon his confirmation, he immediately took steps to develop a sophisticated financial and administrative framework. Given the depressed and chaotic economic conditions, this required establishing (1) reliable and affordable public credit, (2) a robust circulation of negotiable instruments to stimulate commerce, (3) a stable monetary system with uniform currency, (4) insular institutions (the Bank of the United States and the sinking fund) to manage public debt, (5) a reformed customs operation, (6) tax policy tailored to current circumstances but also capable of future expansion, and (7) protections and enhancements for the fledgling industries and trade operations that were needed to build a more diverse economy. Nothing would speak louder to the American people than dramatic actions that brought immediate and promising changes into their lives, and Hamilton wanted the new national government at the center of it. It must win their confidence early or lose the advantage to the states. Accordingly, with herculean effort he prepared a series of reports with accompanying legislative proposals over the first two years of the Washington administration (1789–91) to establish the institutions and policies needed to accomplish those ends.[22]

A System for Public Credit

> In nothing are appearances of greater moment than whatever regards credit. Opinion is the soul of it; and this is affected by appearances as well as realities.
>
> —Alexander Hamilton

Hamilton submitted his first report, *Relative to a Provision for the Support of Public Credit*, on January 9, 1790. The body of it ran some twenty thousand words, appendixes doubled its length, and it addressed every facet and nuance of the existing problem. Moreover, it laid forth both the necessity and the moral basis for the system. Hamilton pressed the case that all nations encounter the necessity for borrowing, especially in times of national emergency, and that the dire financial conditions of the country made it all the more imperative to manage the existing debt for public benefit. The country must be able to "borrow on *good terms*" and therefore "the credit of [the] nation should be well established." Otherwise, it will suffer the "constant necessity of *borrowing* and *buying dear*" with the result that its condition must continually spiral downward toward its dissolution.[23]

The argument seemed sensible, but it faced stiff opposition from those who feared that the tax burden for repaying the debt would fall disproportionately on average citizens and unduly benefit speculators and the rich. This led some to advocate full or perhaps partial repudiation of war debt to make it more affordable. Others opposed debt in general as an immoral condition—a public curse, unfairly binding future generations and stifling economic development and individual freedom. This group advocated rapid repayment through higher taxes, budget austerity, and the sale of public lands. Such arguments remain popular to this day, but Hamilton responded that none of these positions helped remedy the broader economic malaise, and further, they would hamstring the new government in meeting the ends entrusted to it. He proposed a radically different approach, which after six months of fierce wrangling in Congress became the law of the land. His approach treated the national debt as a national blessing.[24]

Hamilton construed public debt as a matter of "public faith." A government that violates good faith risks loss of public trust. Because the public debt was owed primarily to creditors who supported the war effort, reneging on that debt meant betraying their efforts as well as losing their investment. The debt tied the fortunes of many to the future of the country. The "observance of good faith is the basis of public credit," and it serves not only the "strongest inducement of political expediency" but also "rests on the immutable principles of moral obligation." Anyone, Hamilton believed, who sees the "intimate connection between public virtue and public happiness" will be repulsed by "a violation of these principles." The obligation is all the more solemn given that the debt was incurred as "the price of liberty," and its continued violation excited regret and resentment. A government that "may decline a provision for its debts, though able to make it, overthrows all public morality."[25]

Hamilton then suggested that the efforts made by both the state governments and the national government over the preceding years to "retrieve the national credit, by doing justice to the creditors of the nation," had raised hopes that both the national reputation and individual fortunes could be restored. It made no sense to dash these rising expectations, and they could easily be tied to the interests of the people as one nation. "To justify and preserve their confidence; to promote the increasing respectability of the American name; to answer the calls of justice; to restore landed property to its due value; to furnish new resources both to agriculture and commerce; to cement more closely the union of the states; to add to their security against foreign attacks; to establish public order on the basis of an upright and liberal policy. These are the great and invaluable ends to be secured, by a proper and adequate provision, at the present period, for the support of public credit."[26] He then cut to the most crucial insight of his report. Beyond the obvious advantages to nation and creditors of restoring value to existing debts lay a "less obvious, though not less true" consequence that a "properly funded national debt . . . answers most of the purposes of money." It is, in fact, "a *substitute* for money." Monetizing debt became the "new power in the mechanism of national affairs." It would answer the pressing needs of a new nation dreadfully short on cash. Hamilton's entire plan for restoring public credit relied on it. Existing debt instruments, if restored to their par value and backed by the full faith and credit of the United States, could be made assignable to other parties in commercial trading and thereby circulated as a form of interest-bearing money. Bullion need hardly circulate at all, and a national bank could hold it in reserve and issue tradable debt instruments far above its actual value. Chernow observed that even before establishing the Bank of the United States, Hamilton jumpstarted the circulation of paper instead of specie by "deciding that customs revenues could be paid with notes from the Bank of New York and Bank of North America, an innovation that began to steer the country away from use of coins and toward an efficient system of paper money."[27]

Furthermore, the war debts could be more effectively managed through the retirement of old securities in trade for a new and uniform body of federal securities. Holding these consistently at par value would also eliminate them as a source of speculation, which at the time was rampant, fueled by anticipation about how the new government would treat devalued debt instruments and currencies. So, a stably funded debt provided the solution to the want of money capital for both the new government and the national economy while suppressing wild speculation. The challenges lay in how to go about it.

Establishing reliable and affordable public credit first required assessing the extent and nature of the existing debt and then bringing some order to it. This was no easy task since it had been issued through a variety of instruments (bonds, IOUs, promissory notes, and various unbacked currencies) by both the state governments and the federal government, and they had been issued to thousands of individuals as well as to institutions. Hamilton tapped various institutional sources for data to arrive at serviceable estimates. The most unreliable sources were the states, whose estimates about how much they actually owed changed dramatically depending on whether they believed the new national government would recompense or obligate them for the cost of the war effort. The erratic nature of the auditing process during and after the war made it difficult to sort out their varying claims. Nevertheless, Hamilton managed to roughly assess state debt at $25 million (several states had already paid down some portion of their debt), national debt plus interest obligations at about $40 million, the amount needed to liquidate old Continental currency at another $2 million, and foreign debt at around $12 million. The new national government could not possibly pay the interest (most of it at 6 percent) on that bulk of remaining debt. As McDonald indicates, paying the interest on foreign debt alone would leave nothing for government operating expenditures, so Hamilton would have to figure out how to refinance the body of debt and seek delay in paying off part of the foreign debt until the revenue picture improved. The adoption of the new Constitution helped gain some forbearance among European creditors, but only for a short while, which made it imperative to act quickly.[28]

The greatest portion of income for the new government would come from a new revenue tariff imposed by Congress in 1789. Some would also come from excise taxes on domestically produced goods (mostly spirits at the time), but the matter hinged on settling whether the states or the national government should impose them. Given the depressed state of affairs, the new government dared not impose direct taxes, and Hamilton preferred in the short run to leave those to the states. Import duties and excise taxes were much easier to collect as well as to police against evasion if both were administered at the national level. However, assigning the excise tax exclusively to the national government left the state governments without any effective means of paying off their debts. The national government would have to assume them, and that is exactly what Hamilton proposed because they could then be monetized and reissued.[29] Thomas McCraw summarizes Hamilton's basic strategy. First, he needed the authority to refinance the entire foreign loan debt at a lower rate than currently obligated, from 6 percent to 4 percent. For the most part this was noncontroversial, and given the new government and Hamilton's appointment to the Treasury, the foreign banks were disposed to granting the more favorable interest rate. Second, he needed the authority to "issue new federal bonds to replace the total principal of all old securities, again at their entire face (or par) value." More importantly, the "new bonds would carry no dates of maturity. Nor could their holders receive from the Treasury more than a specified dollar amount each year." In effect this turned them into life annuities, which kept them circulating as money for a long period, thereby stimulating economic growth and "insulat[ing] the Treasury against excessive demands, should it run short of funds." Bondholders would be guaranteed a steady rate of return despite variation in interest rates in the market. Third, as with the foreign debt, Hamilton proposed issuing the new bonds at 4 percent rather than at the current 6 percent rate, though with different ways of subscribing to accommodate subscribers' varying interests.[30] This would substantially reduce the new government's annual interest obligations, which represented its most immediate budget liability. Complaints arose about the lower yield, but these were mitigated because Hamilton's overall plan promised a vastly more secure outcome for everyone, especially the bondholders.

Hamilton enhanced the stability of this arrangement by "set[ing] aside part of its substantial receipts from import duties" to make interest payments, thus avoiding the need for congressional appropriations and the "bitter annual controversies" that would spark. In matters of public finance, congressional politics over these appropriations posed too many uncertainties that would threaten the viability of the funding system—a truism that later informed the establishment of the Federal Reserve. Then, as a way of gaining the confidence of investors, he "specif[ied] that interest on the debt would be paid in gold and silver." This allayed nervousness among the general public about all the *paper* involved and enticed more people to invest.[31]

Fourth, Hamilton needed the authority to assume state debts, and on this matter he faced the stiffest opposition, including from his ally James Madison. The issues with this debt assumption centered on factors that ran to the heart of state and regional politics as well as to vitriol against speculators, whom many believed would profit most from Hamilton's plan. Speculators posed a serious problem for Hamilton because they had already been active after the war in buying up old debt from individuals at rock-bottom prices. They took advantage of the desperate straits many of these people faced. Few believed their securities would ever be worth anything, so even a trifling offer seemed compelling. Moreover, many of these speculators came from northern, commercially oriented states and preyed upon people from middle and southern states. The outrage played into fears that the northern states would gain a huge financial advantage through Hamilton's plan and threaten the balance of power among the states.

Accordingly, demands arose for discriminating between first and subsequent holders of war debt, requiring that original holders receive the first and greatest consideration. Though this seemed fair in one sense, it was patently unfair in another. Hamilton persuasively argued that to discriminate against the face value of a security would undermine confidence in the security-issuing and trading process in general. As importantly, it would pose an administrative nightmare to carry out, and with little guarantee that the most deserving holders (prior or subsequent) would get a just reward. In fact, by definition, discrimination meant that no one would get a truly just (par value) reward. The nuances and complications of thousands of transactions with the old securities simply defied sorting and verifying. Hamilton won the debate but at the cost of abiding resentment and suspicion by those who felt injured in the process.

The opposition to assumption and to the funding plan as a whole continued unabated, and to Hamilton's surprise, Madison joined in. Debate of the plan in Congress endured for about six months, mixing state and regional interests with both the pecuniary and the publicly interested motives of individual members. Many members of Congress held securities that were affected by the plan, but that hardly guaranteed their support since some would benefit more without it, especially those who traded securities internationally. Ironically, a deal to accept the plan centered on Virginia's state interests and on a land investment deal by Madison and a few of his Virginia allies. They had speculated on lands along the Potomac River in hopes of establishing a manufacturing and commercial city. As McDonald describes it, Madison and his group sought to tie their deal in logrolling fashion to the fortunes of Hamilton's plan in Congress. "The tactic . . . as it gradually emerged, was to seek out the most vulnerable part of Hamilton's proposals, block the passage of that part, and hold the line there until they could negotiate a bargain favorable to their region and to themselves."[32] Assumption was clearly the most vulnerable part of the plan, and their tactic put Congress to wrangling for the better part of four months before, of all people, Thomas Jefferson engineered a final compromise.

At that early point (June 1790), Jefferson saw Hamilton's plan as being critical for the nation's survival and for maintaining good relations with France over the issue of US debt. With war looming in Europe, he wanted the matter settled as quickly as possible. He likely did not yet see all the implications of Hamilton's design, especially those having to do with maintaining debt long term, but the exigencies at the time drove him to support it. The deal involved Madison's land along the Potomac but for a different purpose: locating a permanent place for the nation's capital, which had been temporarily located on Wall Street in New York City. With some wheeling and dealing in league with Robert Morris (an esteemed member of the Senate) from Pennsylvania, Jefferson achieved a compromise proposal to move the capital to Philadelphia for ten years (fifteen years was initially proposed), and thence to the parcel of land on the Potomac. Over what is now considered one of the most famous dinners in the nation's history, Jefferson met with Madison and Hamilton to orchestrate the deal.

Hamilton desperately needed it. Madison and Jefferson set him to winning enough votes from his northern colleagues and to making sure that Virginia got a favorable accounting of its sums due upon assumption—enough to fully settle its state accounts.[33] The deal, with some complicating compromises struck over interest rates on the new debt, was finally completed in early August. Hamilton then commenced establishing an administrative system for collecting old debt instruments from thousands of people and institutions. He placed loan commissioners in every state "to open books, receive and liquidate old certificates, issue new certificates, record transfers of ownership, pay interest due, and generally to perform related duties under the direction of the Secretary of the Treasury."[34]

Public Credit and the Sinking Fund

Hamilton proposed a sinking fund, patterned loosely on England's, as a final element in his report. Enhancing public credit necessarily included provisions for debt retirement. He thought it a "fundamental maxim that the creation of debt should always be accompanied with the means of extinguishment."[35] The proposal gained wide appeal, especially among those wanting the debt quickly eliminated. However, as already noted, Hamilton did not seek immediate extinguishment. Monetized debt must serve the purpose of money for many years to come. He intended only that provision be made for its eventual retirement after meeting the more important steps of making the government solvent and the economy more robust, and then only at the discretion of the board of the sinking fund, with very modest amounts to actually apply.[36]

Reducing the debt was not the most important priority in public finance. In fact, a too aggressive board would scare investors. The board could discharge debt, "either by purchases of stock in the market or by payments on the amount yearly redeemable on the principal of the new stock, until the whole debt was discharged." The money appropriated to this fund came initially from a $2 million foreign loan to endow it and subsequently from surplus post office revenues in an amount not to exceed one million dollars. The postal service never exceeded more than a few tens of thousands in surplus revenue annually. Hamilton also planned "that the commissioners be authorized to borrow sums not to exceed $12 million for the purpose either of converting the foreign debt to a lower rate of interest, or of purchasing domestic debt in the market when it was selling below par." This performed a stabilizing function, not a debt retirement function. As an additional check, the transactions of the sinking fund would be conducted "through the medium of a national bank" yet to be proposed.[37]

The administrative machinery of the fund was capable of retiring debt fairly quickly if given adequate and permanent sources of revenue, but this posed other problems that Hamilton wanted to avoid. As Swanson and Trout indicate, Hamilton recognized the sinking fund's vulnerability to looting by Congress if the fund held substantial sums, and it could also "delude politicians into believing that the debt problem was being solved . . . and then too easily spend more and ignore the need to tax accordingly." His concern still pertains with today's woeful penchant among politicians to *borrow and spend* rather than *tax and spend*. Hamilton chose instead to rely on the beneficial effects of compounding interest on government funds that would accrue due to his plan's limited redemption policy. If Congress chose, it could apply compounded funds through earmarking to the debt without need of annual appropriations. This "hidden sinking fund," as Swanson and Trout call it, prevented the looting and deluding problem and built more debt reduction capacity into the system than almost no one but Hamilton realized.[38] Early on, though, he was more interested in the sinking fund for its political and psychological value than for its ability to pay off the debt. The *appearance* of debt reduction at that time was far more valuable than *actual* debt reduction.

Donald Swanson described how Hamilton designed and managed the sinking fund to maintain this favorable appearance. First, he put the "highest officers in the government" in charge of the management of the sinking fund. These included the vice president, the chief justice, the Speaker of the House, the attorney general, and the secretary of the treasury. Ominously, Jefferson successfully lobbied for a position on it as Secretary of Foreign Affairs, replacing the Speaker of the House. Their impressive reputations, combined with the form and operation of the program, "gave the appearance that the debt was being paid and that all the ingredients of a well-constructed fiscal system had been furnished." Second, Hamilton exploited the "full psychological and political value out of what little debt redemption the sinking fund accomplished." He had newspapers publish every instance of debt reduction, giving the appearance of active and substantial debt retirement. Third, he occasionally proposed revisions to enhance the fund's debt reduction capabilities. In a later report suggesting measures for refining the design of the funding system, he proposed a more "systematic sinking fund" with supplementary and permanent sources of income. Though increased, these sources were intendedly insignificant in relation to the actual size of the debt, which had grown due to costly efforts to quell the Whiskey Rebellion and conduct the Indian Wars. In general it appeared that the debt was being reduced.[39]

Jefferson's experience on the board led him to believe that Hamilton had no intention of ever reducing the debt, and Hamilton felt no need to dispute the point despite his longer-run intentions to the contrary. Jefferson, like so many of his colleagues, failed to see the subtleties of Hamilton's design. Rather, he was convinced Hamilton was trying to create a perpetual debt like England's and to confuse and control Congress while transforming the government into a monarchy.[40] However, with his retirement from Treasury in 1795, Hamilton submitted of his own accord a serious plan for redemption of the debt in less than thirty years. By that time, both the government's and the economy's prospects had dramatically improved. He proposed a variety of new taxes and substantially strengthened the sinking fund. However, he built some flexibility into the plan to avoid having the fund operate at full capacity during periods of deficit spending caused by war or other emergencies. It should not operate at cross-purposes with the full functioning of debt spending when it was most needed, especially when operating for countercyclical effect. He wanted to maintain the fund's capacity for "adapting to different budgetary conditions."[41]

The machinery of Hamilton's sinking fund remained in place until 1834, when it successfully completed redemption of the public debt. The sinking fund would reappear at times during the nineteenth century as wars and depressions brought on more debt but was managed more rigidly than Hamilton would advise. It was not used in the twentieth century, but aspects of his debt management practice have been employed many times in the operations of countercyclical fiscal policy and for conducting open market operations (i.e., quantitative easing) comparable to those performed by central banks today.[42]

The Bank of the United States

The economic ideas that sprang from Hamilton's fertile, industrious mind have informed financial practice and monetary policy in this country for more than two centuries.
—Federal Reserve Bank of Minneapolis, 2007

Once passed, Hamilton's measures on public credit changed the investing mood at home and abroad and raised the new nation's economic prospects. As McDonald describes, "The public, instilled with illusions and expectations, changed its opinion about the value of all those pieces of paper." In just a few months, the market value of the paper tripled to about $45 million.[43] It remained, however, to create an institutional framework through which the restored public credit could be stabilized. A national bank figured most prominently in that design.

Hamilton viewed the bank as a public necessity for a modern commercial republic, though it should not be managed directly by government in its daily operations. It should bridge public purposes with private interests through a quasi-public form of governance and, in his words, provide a "foundation for a circulation coextensive with the United States, embracing the whole of their revenues, and affecting every individual, into whose hands the paper may come. . . . Public utility is more truly the object of public banks, than private profit. . . . Such a Bank is not a mere matter of private property, but a political machine of the greatest importance to the State."[44] Here, as McNamara notes, Hamilton differed from Adam Smith, who insisted that banks serve merely private interests. "Hamilton's bank would provide an important source of capital for the development of the country."[45] This was public entrepreneurship on a grand scale. The bank formed an integral part of his broader system of finance, going hand in hand with his plan to diversify and energize the economy. It also revealed Hamilton's conviction that financial markets are uniquely different from other markets. Financial institutions, both public and private, serve public purposes and incur public responsibilities because they form the financial spine for the entire commercial system.

Hamilton submitted his *Report on a National Bank* in December 1790. He opened by stating "that a National Bank is an institution of primary importance to the prosperous administration of the finances, and would be of the greatest utility in the operations connected with the support of the public credit."[46] He organized the report into three parts: (1) a quick review of the principal advantages offered by a national bank; (2) a thorough review and response to each disadvantage claimed by critics of the proposal; and (3) a fairly detailed description of its organization and governance. The report as a whole presented a primer on state-of-the-art banking at the time, with much of it still applicable today. Few if any in Congress could match his insight and expertise on the subject, and most had fallen under the thrall of his masterful reporting and extensive preparation.

He did not expect strong resistance to the proposal despite the intense dislike of banks in some quarters. The subject of a national bank had long been discussed in both American and European newspapers, as well as in journals and popular treatises. The need for more banks (there were only three at the time), especially a national bank, had become increasingly evident as the war effort and economy foundered. Then too the sudden positive turn in public confidence about his earlier measures added great momentum to the proposal. McDonald noted how the US economy made a prosperous turn just after passage of Hamilton's measures for restoring public credit, though it likely had as much to do with "continued crop failures and political turbulence in Europe, but Americans, as would ever be their wont, tended to attribute it to the doings of the administration."[47] Hamilton enjoyed a bit of luck in league with his efforts.

It also probably served Hamilton and his sympathizers that Adam Smith was favorably disposed to banks as engines of commerce, though as already mentioned, the two held different positions on the role of a central bank. Smith's treatise, *The Wealth of Nations*, was already quite popular in the United States among both Republicans and Federalists but for different reasons. Hamilton had read the massive work not long after it was published and knew he could use it to support some of his measures while carefully arguing against other ideas that he thought too abstract and problematic. He saved a direct and thorough critique of Smith's free market ideas for his *Report on Manufactures* (addressed below). In the bank report, he took great care in answering every significant objection.

Advantages of a National Bank

Hamilton reviewed three principal advantages of a national bank. First, it augments "the active and productive capital of a country" by turning *dead Stock* (gold and silver when used only for exchange or alienation of property) into *live Stock* by making it "the basis of a paper circulation." He used simple examples to illustrate how depositing one's gold or silver in a bank makes it available to the public and turns it into an investment yielding interest for the depositor. "His money thus deposited or invested, is a fund, upon which himself and others can borrow to a much larger amount," thus circulating notes indefinitely that "pass current as cash." A party to transactions with these notes is "often content with a similar credit, because he is satisfied, that he can, whenever he pleases, either convert it into cash or pass it to some other hand, as an equivalent to it . . . without the intervention of a single piece of coin." A proper ratio of bank reserves to the amounts loaned will ensure confidence among the investors "on the most rational grounds." In this fashion, banks contribute "to enlarge the mass of industrious and commercial enterprise" and thereby "become nurseries of national wealth."[48]

Second, a national bank provides a great convenience to government "in obtaining pecuniary aids, especially in sudden emergencies." Its capital, amassed and "placed under one direction," is "magnified by the credit attached to it" and "can at once be put into motion, in aid of the Government." The bank's directors can "afford that aid, independent of regard to the public safety and welfare," in the normal exercise of their careful and prudent management. This goes again to a point that the bank should be privately managed. Governmental management would expose the bank to potential politicization and related temptations to abuse its sound practices.[49]

Third, a national bank in two ways facilitates the payment of taxes and supplies other wants that require exchange. It is a particular benefit to those who pay duties and may need short-term loans "to answer with punctuality the public calls upon them." Next, and more generally, is the benefit of "increasing of the quantity of circulating medium and the quickening [velocity] of circulation," by making national bank notes conveniently available to businesses separated by distance who wish to transact without need or risk of transporting specie or coin between private banks. "The greater plenty of money . . . adds to the ease with which every industrious member of the community may acquire that portion of it, of which he stands in need; enables him the better to pay his taxes, as well as to supply his other wants."[50] A subtler point underlay Hamilton's thinking here because the fear of *paper money* was palpable given the recent experience with Continental dollars. Bank notes serving as an alternative form of currency were more desirable in the short run because they could be redeemed in specie if anyone got fearful of their loss in value.[51]

While these advantages of a national bank would help people in general, Hamilton was especially keen that they attract "the immediate interest of the moneyed men" because their transactions reached amounts significant enough for an initial spur to the economy, and as importantly, it would attract them as subscribers to the initial principal of the bank. Their investment in the bank would amount to an investment in the country. Hamilton proposed a starting capital of $10 million, a staggering sum relative to the capital of the other banks and "far more than the amount of all the gold and silver in the country."[52]

He knew the amount must be large to meet the demand of a suddenly stimulated national economy. He proposed that the government subscribe $2 million (paid through a loan from the bank itself) and that private subscribers put up the rest at 6 percent interest—a real attraction in a country with few competing investment alternatives. The sum fully subscribed within two hours of the bank's opening. The careful and subtle design, as McDonald characterizes it, was "almost poetic in its beauty and symmetry. Hamilton had found banking's equivalent of the philosopher's stone, whereby base elements are turned into gold."[53]

Disadvantages Overcome by Bank's Governance and Operation

It was Hamilton's style to clearly state objections or claims of disadvantage by critics and then answer them in order. He would often admit the merits of such criticism, giving opponents their due, but then show how his proposals would diminish or obviate the claimed negative effects. That is how he addressed the six main objections to the bank. Critics claimed the bank would "increase usury, tend to prevent other kinds of lending, furnish temptations to overtrading [or speculation], afford aid to ignorant adventurers, give to bankrupt or fraudulent traders a fictitious credit, and tend to banish gold and silver from the country."[54]

In response, he showed first that usury (unreasonable interest) arises in conditions of an insufficient money supply and that the new bank's large capital reserves would provide more than ample supply, thus obviating the concern. Second, though the national bank would by law have no national rival, nothing would prevent establishing banks in the states, thus affording alternative sources of lending. And while banks will generally favor short-term commercial loans, the general increase of capital by the new bank will eventually supply "a copious stream" of capital sufficient for longer-term loans and mortgages. Third, though the potential for rampant speculation always looms as a possibility, it is greatly diminished by the presence of a stable banking system that prudently manages its loans and interest rates and is backed by governmental oversight and stipulations on types of loans and reserve ratios. Thus, the bank as designed would stymie more than encourage speculation. Hamilton treated the fourth and fifth objections about ignorant adventurers and fraudulent traders together and emphasized that all the precautions proposed for the national bank would induce careful diligence by its directors in the vetting of its clients, such that the chances of issuing unwise loans were greatly mitigated. Moreover, the possibility of a few bad loans would be vastly compensated by the myriad good loans afforded to so many deserving parties.

The final objection took more effort to answer. The fear of a drain of gold and silver away from the country "rests upon their being an engine of paper credit, which by furnishing a substitute for the metals, is supposed to promote their exportation." A partial answer to this is "that the intrinsic wealth of a nation is to be measured, not by the abundance of the precious metals [the United States had very little at the time], . . . but by the quantity of the productions of its labor and industry." This presented a dynamic or *active* conception of wealth still relatively new in the minds of that generation, though receptivity to it was bolstered considerably by Adam Smith. Nevertheless, conceded Hamilton, the matter of gold and silver held or lost "can hardly ever be a matter of indifference." The metals were held in high regard as the most stable standard of value, and thus could not be ignored. Then, through a long explanation of the relations of banking and commerce, he concluded that "well constituted banks favor the increase of precious metals" rather than their decrease. "They augment in different ways, the active capital of the country." Prudent banking "generates employment; which animates and expands labor and industry," which leads to more production "furnishing more materials for exportation, conduces to a favorable balance of trade, and consequently to the introduction and increase of gold and silver." In short, he construed public credit and prudent national banking as a spur to economic diversification through new industries that could turn the balance of trade and the stock of specie in our favor.[55] Hence the importance at that time of establishing the conditions of sound governance and policy in the national bank.

Hamilton contrived every aspect of the bank's design and governance to instill confidence in its operation. It should be chartered for twenty years, making its existence contingent upon congressional renewal; its directors would be rotated with limited terms to prevent financial cabals; states could still charter their own banks in competition with it; it should be "prohibited from issuing notes and incurring other obligations in excess of its capitalization"; foreign stockholders would hold no voting rights' and the secretary of the treasury would routinely inspect its accounts and require statements of its condition.

Moreover, Congress would regularly demand reports of its condition pursuant to their fueling the bank with tax revenues to service the massive interest payments on the national debt.[56]

The Bank bill passed resoundingly, and the institution functioned effectively over the life of its charter. It provided the funds necessary for a variety of governmental exigencies, including the Indian Wars, the Whiskey Rebellion, and Jefferson's Louisiana Purchase.[57] It stimulated investment in all kinds of enterprise and became an essential aid to the Treasury in regulating the interbank settlements in the growing state bank system, thus anticipating a function of the Federal Reserve banks in twentieth- and twenty-first-century America. It became the first quasi-central bank in America, and most subsequent central banking institutions and regulations (including those in Canada) were adapted from its plan. And yet, "the excellent record of the Bank of the United States and the friends it won did it insufficient good politically."[58] The bank's charter required renewal in 1811, but the effort failed due to an odd combination of political and economic dynamics.

As Jefferson hoped, the Republican Party had by that time come to represent all number and kinds of factions, among them old Anti-Federalist agrarians and planters, as well as some old Federalists and wealthy businessmen. The agrarians opposed the bank as a stimulus to, and symbol of, the commercialism of the northern states. The business lobby disliked the bank's regulatory influence on state banks, viewing its controls as an unnecessary check upon commerce. And both groups formally opposed it, once again, on grounds of constitutionality.[59] More moderate and conservative spokesmen for the bank knew its value both to government and to the private sector. Albert Gallatin, Jefferson's able secretary of the treasury, strongly supported it, with Jefferson tolerating it largely at his urging. In the end, however, the rechartering effort failed in Congress, which precipitated unregulated growth of state banks to fill the lending gap without any central regulative machinery enabling the Treasury Department to affect the activity.

The War of 1812 created dire need for Federal government borrowing and reawakened interest in centralized fiscal policy and national banking. Ironically, James Madison as president came to realize its necessity and convenience. A newer wing of Republicans with Hamiltonian predilections joined with Madison to charter a Second Bank of the United States in 1816. Among this group numbered such luminaries as Henry Clay, young John C. Calhoun, John Quincy Adams, Mathew Carey, Friedrich List, William H. Crawford, John Forsyth,

John Taylor, S. D. Ingham, William Lowndes, and William Rush. Rush became secretary of the treasury in the late 1820s and publicly alluded to Hamilton's "comprehensive genius" and farsightedness to support active national government policies. The second bank functioned adequately at times, but as Bray Hammond concludes, the great "difficulty was one of having not merely to replace a necessary institution, . . . but of undoing the unnecessary mischief that arose from its abandonment,"—a problem that became common in the cycles of US politics and reform.[60]

The Mint

The establishment of a mint (early 1792) was mostly uncontroversial, though its administration staggered for many years thereafter. Possibly because Jefferson had earlier made coinage a pet project, Washington gave its management to his State Department, but it languished there for lack of attention. Jefferson's diplomatic duties crowded his time, especially since he arrived late to the position. Leonard D. White notes that the mint's development was hampered not only by poor management but also by a general lack of knowledge in the new nation about starting one and by a lack of technical expertise and adequate machinery for metallurgy and coinage. As years progressed, it became a source of frustration to the bank especially because of scarce copper coinage. Its failings led to attempts at privatization, but the efforts were stymied until its operations eventually improved with Hamilton's advice and intervention.[61]

Hamilton had prepared the report on the mint, taking insight from a prior report by Jefferson. Both approved of the final report. Hamilton, in his usual manner, conducted an exhaustive survey of European practices to refine his recommendations. He recommended a bimetallic standard but valued gold more highly than silver, as the latter was readily available from the West Indies trade. Either metal alone presented disadvantages as a sole standard because that might "abridge the quantity of circulating medium."[62] Further, though Hamilton would have preferred a new name for the base currency, he settled on the dollar because it was by far the most common in circulation, due in part to the Continental Congress adopting it as its currency.[63]

Everyone understood the need of a common currency. At the time there were as many as fifty different currencies floating around the nation, causing yet more confusion in the process of evaluating debt, conducting market transactions, and assessing taxes. Chernow indicates as well that "so many gold and silver coins were adulterated with base metals that many merchants hesitated to do business for fear of being shortchanged." McDonald noted that coins were traditionally used for larger international transactions, but Hamilton desired minting them in small denominations such as dimes and copper cents to be used in the general population for encouraging lower prices: "As he pointed out, the lowest price for any commodity would often sell for half a cent if such a coin were available." Significantly, this met another of his "overall social objectives: he wanted to get everyone accustomed to handling money. In a nation in which most people rarely used money as a material object, the effects of that change could be profound."[64]

Revenue and Taxation

Upon Hamilton's initial assessment of the new government's debt burden, he quickly surmised the need to improve its sources of revenue. The chief source had come, and would continue to come, for almost a century from import duties or revenue tariffs, the type that is kept low enough to not dissuade production and importation yet in the aggregate provides a sizeable flow of revenue. Chernow indicates that, at the time, "three quarters of the revenues gathered by the Treasury Department came from commerce with Great Britain." That meant keeping good trade relations with the British when anti-British sentiment ran strong among Americans in the wake of the Revolutionary War. The fact that Britain's protectionist policies kept Americans from trading directly with West Indian and other colonies just exacerbated the angst. Furthermore, Jefferson, ever the Francophile, controlled much of the foreign policy apparatus, so Hamilton had to work through separate lines of communication with British interests—a matter that gravely intensified Jefferson's distrust. "The overlapping concerns of Treasury and State were to foster no end of mischief between the two men."[65]

The turbulence inherent to international relations convinced Hamilton that other sources of revenue would be necessary to stabilize the financial condition of the nation. As White discovered, the hopes of significant revenues from nontax sources, such as excess postal revenue and sale of western lands, never materialized. Over the first ten years of its existence, the new national government took in more than $50 million from import duties, just over $3.6 million in excise taxes on domestic goods, and just under $400 thousand from nontax sources.[66] The excise tax became Hamilton's only significant alternative. Fortunately, his earlier measures on public credit had helped turn the economy around, and conditions of international trade worked strongly in the country's favor. As a result, the Treasury accrued an operating surplus, which helped meet the interest on the debt without extravagant appropriations from Congress. Though fortunate in that sense, it also worked to Hamilton's disadvantage in proposing to broaden the tax base. Americans, still smarting from English tax policy, exhibited an almost pathological hatred of taxes, so Hamilton would fight an uphill battle on the matter throughout his career.[67]

He proposed new and increased excise taxes in his second report on public credit (December 1790), arguing that despite being disliked, they were eminently preferable "to taxes on houses and land." Besides, the latter could be construed as *direct taxes* that could only be levied "in proportion to the Census" yet to be taken, plus they are of a type better reserved for more general needs of communities and the exigencies of public safety, such as war. He wanted excises laid on all distilled spirits, graduated by proof and volume of sales, and on tea and wines. He proposed enforcing them through the existing Treasury force of inspectors and collectors, but to keep them from becoming too imperious and aggressive, he denied them the power of summary jurisdiction in favor of trial by jury for alleged violations. In addition, he limited the powers of search to "those places, which the Dealers themselves shall designate."[68] Within those bounds, he pressed his agents to inspect frequently and thoroughly, which of course ignited a great deal of public resentment and protest, culminating in the Whiskey Rebellion among small distillers in western Pennsylvania. He put the rebellion down in part to clearly establish the federal government's power over taxation in general—a much-needed action but also one that forever tarred him as an advocate of despotic central government.

At various times in his career, Hamilton advocated for a more diverse system of taxation, articulating the principle of progressivity and even mentioning the possibility of income taxes at some distant point in the future. During his career in office, however, he spent most of his effort defending the excise tax. There, he helped set an important Supreme Court precedent in *Hylton v. U.S.* (1796), the first case in which the court exercised judicial review, though in this case to uphold an act of Congress rather than to declare it unconstitutional. Acting as counsel for the government, he spoke eloquently despite being severely ill and convinced the court that taxes on carriages were not direct taxes but clearly of the nature of an excise. He thus helped establish a broader definition of excise taxes, and a much narrower definition of direct taxes, than many people wanted at the time.[69] Beyond that, his most significant opportunity for expressing a fuller position on the national government's power of taxation came in his *Report on Manufactures*.

Diversifying the Economy

> There is at present juncture a certain fermentation of mind, a certain activity of speculation and enterprise which if properly directed may be made subservient to useful purposes; but which if left entirely to itself, may be attended with pernicious effects.
> —Alexander Hamilton

Harold Syrett and Jacob Cooke, the editors of Hamilton's papers, aptly characterize the *Report on Manufactures* as "an integral part of Hamiltonian finance." In it he defends the bank and the funding system established pursuant to his earlier reports and "reiterate[s] his view of the public debt as an acquisition of artificial capital available for the promotion of manufactures." They note as well that "an equally close relation exists between the Report and his attitude toward foreign policy,"[70] which is the subject of the next chapter. His desire for diversifying the American economy through manufactures and trade bridges finance and foreign affairs to round out his strategy of administration for a vibrant republic.

Hamilton worked on the document periodically through the year 1791, submitting it that December. He wrote five drafts, integrating significant content in the first draft from a report by Tench Coxe, his assistant secretary of the treasury and a respected writer on the subject, and adding insights and new data from myriad sources with each draft. The final version presents an elaborate argument favoring public encouragement of manufactures as a way of diversifying the means of employment and contributing to the general welfare. It is an impressive work of applied macroeconomic analysis, focusing on the synergies gained through blending the "aggregate prosperity of manufactures and the aggregate prosperity of agriculture."[71] Peter McNamara characterizes it as "in many respects . . . a theoretical document" because it addressed head on the political-economic ideas and arguments of the day to which many Americans seemed fervently attached.[72] As already discussed in chapter 1, the most prominent of these ideas issued from Physiocratic, free trade, and small republic advocates in support of an agrarian republic—very much the status quo, especially among the mid-Atlantic and southern states. Hamilton proffered a vision based upon a trajectory of dispositions in the American people that could bring about a more diverse, opulent, and united commercial republic. This required the "incitement and patronage of government" to ignite a *spirit of improvement* toward that end. The country's entrepreneurial disposition needed both spur and rein.

Mired as the young republic was in agrarian conditions and mindset, Hamilton's report swam against the current and was largely ignored in Congress. Its prescience would never be fully appreciated in the United States, though some of its ideas and measures sporadically bubbled into public policy throughout the last half of the nineteenth century and much of the twentieth. Its relevance as a body of political-economic theory remains salient for its thorough analysis and critique of Smith's free market theory and for explaining much about how the American economy actually developed. As an example of the latter, McCraw cites as "most prescient" of all Hamilton's prediction that skilled immigrants "would probably flock from Europe to the United States to pursue their own trades or professions, if they were once made sensible of the advantages they would enjoy." He notes that many copies of the report were distributed in England, receiving particular attention by skilled craftsmen, many of whom emigrated to the United States and formed a hub of new manufacturing and machining expertise that would transform cotton and other raw materials production.[73] Ironically, the report received more attention in Europe than in the United States throughout the next century because of efforts by American System advocates such as Mathew and Henry Carey, Henry Clay, and Friedrich List. Their agenda fully embraced Hamiltonianism, and List spread its program to the European continent.[74]

The report's many sections and vast details need no recapitulation here. Much of it supported a broad argument for establishing national industrial policy, a matter sadly ignored by most politicians throughout US history. The work's real significance lay in its policy arguments for governmental intervention to spur national economic development in diverse directions. Hamilton's arguments contribute cogent support to one side of the never-ending debate over American economic policy and, in the process, help provide justification for an aggressive system of promotive and regulatory administration. His main subject of manufactures entailed two lines of argument: (1) that it added to the *regularity* of production in general, thus supplying opportunities to fill agricultural downtime with paid work (a combination that would work well throughout subsequent US history); and (2) that it would lend much added value to the domestic economy through the refinement of agricultural and other goods and to the stock of new and diverse occupations for the American people. These things could not come about in a timely fashion without significant intervention by the national government.

Hamilton believed that the integration of agriculture and manufactures would eventually help knit the country's clashing regional (north/south) interests together in a complex system of interdependent markets. Much of his analysis borrowed insights from Smith's work in *The Wealth of Nations* in support of a diversified economy. He departed, however, from Smith's belief that such development would occur naturally if the economy were left to itself. Government must play a critical role in stimulating and sustaining a diverse political economy, lest other nations continue to deprive the agrarian republic of opportunities in international trade. Without at least some temporary protection, they would trade at a severe disadvantage, creating both gluts and shortages in languishing home markets.

He easily demonstrated how the current practices of other nations made international trade anything but free. The United States had been "precluded from foreign commerce," to the extent that we could not even secure principal staples without serious obstructions. We needed much from Europe, while Europe needed much less from us. This want of reciprocity worked to our disadvantage, and Europe was not about to relinquish its advantageous situation for our benefit.[75] With this in mind, Hamilton justified the use of tariffs, bounties, premiums, and related aids designed to induce reciprocity abroad, develop home markets, and encourage domestic manufactures. He was not an isolationist but advocated protectionist measures as a means of getting infant industries to a more mature state so they could compete on a more even playing field. He argued that truly free market conditions were at best hypothetical in that era and that the more prudent course required adopting measures to make the United States competitive. *Free* markets are not necessarily *competitive* markets.

Debunking Laissez-Faire Economics

Hamilton offered five cogent reasons for rejecting the fundamental assumption of "invisible hand" theory, that is, that human beings are rational calculators of their own interests and that leaving them alone to do so would result in an automatically correcting economy.[76] First, he argued that people are more strongly influenced by "habit and the spirit of imitation" than laissez-faire doctrine can admit. "Experience teaches that men are often so much governed by what they are accustomed to see and practice, that the simplist and most obvious improvements, in the most ordinary occupations, are adopted with hesitation." The "spontaneous transition to new pursuits" will come, if at all, only with great difficulty and often "be more tardy than might consist with the interest either of individuals or of the society." The "incitement and patronage of government" is therefore required "to produce desirable changes."[77] People are generally creatures of habit, more socially than economically oriented, and so must be prodded and enticed into new entrepreneurial pursuits.

Second, related to man's social nature is his fear of failure in new and untried enterprises. These pose tremendous uncertainties and risks that deter people from serious investment of time and effort. Their fears require mitigation through governmental support and protection. In short, governments must selectively subsidize risks and limit liabilities that deter investment. Ample evidence exists to show that both were used routinely in the founding era and have been ever since.[78]

Third, government must help overcome "intrinsic difficulties incident to first essays towards a competition with those who have previously attained to perfection in the business to be attempted." Getting into the market is in great part a matter of gaining the trust and confidence of potential buyers of products and overcoming the price, scale, and technological impediments imposed by dominant firms. The government must offer "a degree of countenance and support . . . as may be capable of overcoming the obstacles, inseparable from first experiments." It must, therefore, reduce barriers to market entry to gain the "confidence of sagacious capitalists both citizens and foreigners" and employ "judicious regulations for the inspection of manufactured commodities" in order to boost consumer confidence at home and abroad.[79] The states had already employed inspection laws of their own, and Hamilton pressed their aggressive use nationally.[80] He treated market regulation as a necessity wherein "the avarice of individuals threw trade in channels inimical to public interest, when desirable enterprises might otherwise not be undertaken for want of sufficient private capital, or when unexpected causes thwarted a prosperous flow of commerce." He factored such problems, especially the avarice of speculators, into his financial and economic designs.

McDonald observes that his "contemplation of the extent of their avarice convinced him that speculators, far from being stable props for a national system of finance, were greedy enough to erect their own fortunes upon the ruins of public credit. Immediate private interest was simply too unreliable."[81] Hamilton was well aware that free markets could break down or conduce to monopoly through unrestrained avarice.

Fourth, the "greatest obstacle of all to the successful prosecution of a new branch of industry consists . . . in the bounties, premiums and other aids which are granted, in a variety of cases, by the nation in which the establishments to be imitated are previously introduced." He cited commonly known examples of bounties, indemnifications, and exemptions offered to enterprises in other nations that "enable their own workmen to undersell and supplant all competitors in the countries to which those commodities are sent." Unaided *private interests* cannot on their own "surmount all [these] adventitious barriers."[82] Hamilton treated these incentives as among the "most efficacious means of encouraging manufactures," simpler in their market effects than duties and more easily administered. Bounties and premiums were controversial and rejected by Congress at the time, challenged in part as being unconstitutional. To this, Hamilton gave a spirited reply, again invoking broad construction of Article I, Section 8 powers in advance of "common defense" and the "general welfare," terms "doubtless intended to signify more than was expressed or imported in those which preceded; otherwise numerous exigencies incident to the affairs of a nation would have been left without a provision." He saw "no room for a doubt that whatever concerns the general interest of *learning*, of a*griculture*, of *manufactures*, and of *commerce* are within the sphere of national Councils *as far as an application of money*."[83] He anticipated common use of such incentives later, especially tax exemptions, to attract and guide various kinds of market development locally as well as nationally.

Finally, Hamilton dealt with the argument that protecting domestic firms from foreign competition would increase domestic prices and conduce to monopoly practices at home. To this he replied that evidence to the contrary already existed in the United States and that "the internal competition which takes place, soon does away everything like monopoly, and by degrees reduces the price of the article to the *minimum* of a reasonable profit on the capital employed." Moreover, as manufactories grow and refine their processes, the improvements exert downward pressure on prices as marginal costs likewise go down, thus taking advantage of economies of scale. Concluding, he noted the complementary effect that the decreasing prices "enable the farmer to procure with a smaller quantity of his labor the manufactured produce of which he stands in need, and consequently increases the value of his income and property."[84] All of this is made possible at first through the stimulus of "artificial, circulating capital" introduced through the system of public credit, and thence to real gains in production and income. Artificial capital begets real capital.[85]

These arguments remain valid as criticisms of classical and neoclassical economic doctrines and are supported in the findings of institutional, critical, and behavioral economists today. Hamilton of course emphasized the prevalence of these factors in a nation dominated by agrarian life, bereft of the means for refining its agricultural products to a competitive scale and in an efficient manner. His critique focused on the need to protect and enhance infant industries, but his extant remarks clearly indicate that nations would take steps necessary even for mature industries to secure their niche, perhaps even dominance, internationally if their products and services are deemed vital to national interests. The practice among other nations confirmed the point. However, he also strongly cautioned against extended use of tariffs for protective rather than revenue purposes, arguing that a less-restrained competition must still play an important role in robust markets. The stimulative and regulative functions of government should work to improve competition in general, not retard it. He again pressed the point that markets left to themselves hardly guarantee competitive markets over the long run.

Conclusion

From the years 1789 to 1795, when Hamilton left the Treasury, he engineered one of the most remarkable reversals of national fortune in the history of any regime. He pressed his advantage early to establish the core administrative organs of the new republic and put them to work on policies designed to cultivate a new entrepreneurial outlook and corresponding habits in average Americans. Within those years, the economy turned completely around, public confidence rose to an all-time high, and as McCraw notes, a cadre of entrepreneurs coalesced and commenced chartering 311 limited liability corporations, making the 1790s the most prosperous decade in the nation's early history.[86] Hamilton had set the new republic on a sound commercial path in large part by first setting its government upon a sound administrative footing. In the remaining years of his public career, he turned his attention to matters of military and foreign affairs, for these were necessary complements to ensuring the country's security as well as its prosperity.

6
Military and Foreign Affairs for the Republic

> Those who have had opportunities of conversing with foreigners respecting sovereigns in Europe, have discovered in them an anxiety for the preservation of our democratic government, probably for no other reason, but to keep us weak. Unless your government is respectable, foreigners will invade your rights; and to maintain tranquility, it must be respectable—even to observe neutrality, you must have a strong government.
>
> —Hamilton, Speech to the Constitutional Convention

Hamilton treated military and foreign affairs as integral aspects of a nation's public administration. Though both remained nascent and weak in the United States during his life, he provided the rationale and prepared plans for their expansion as events would dictate over subsequent generations. He argued that no nation could ignore the development of military and foreign affairs institutions for long without incurring grievous harm from foreign intrigue, if not outright invasion. Many of his colleagues disagreed, thinking the new republic's circumstances allowed it to forgo especially a standing military force and to provide only a fledgling foreign affairs department. Later in their lives, the force of events made some leading opponents (Madison and Jefferson among them) see the wisdom in his designs. The challenge Hamilton faced lay in convincing people that a strong, well-managed military force and a discerning foreign policy establishment could be safely restrained and reconciled to republican principles and yet maintain the might and readiness necessary to deter and repel all forms of foreign aggression. He convinced very few at the time, but aspects of his theory and argument remain relevant to the current day.

Toward a Republican Military

Karl-Friedrich Walling depicts Hamilton above all else as a military officer because that is how many of his contemporaries referred to him, first as Colonel Hamilton and then as General Hamilton. Much of

Hamilton's life revolved around war or the threat of war, and the successful launching of his political career came from his distinction first as a highly spirited and disciplined artillery officer and then as a brilliant aide-de-camp to General Washington. As Walling notes, even as a youngster in the West Indies, Hamilton wrote of wishing for war, viewing it "as an honorable way for an adolescent orphan with no money to rise quickly in the world."[1] While secretary of the treasury, he attended to the organization and management of the Department of War, and through his management of the Customs Service and a fledgling Coast Guard, he oversaw the protection of harbors from French privateering as the French Revolution ensued. He also equipped militias and helped Washington lead in the successful effort to quell the Whiskey Rebellion in western Pennsylvania in 1794.[2] When war loomed with France in the late 1790s, he returned to the military as a major general, second-in-command to General Washington, serving also as inspector general of the Provisional army until 1800. He laid extensive plans and lobbied hard for the establishment of the navy, for the outfitting of a small standing army, and for professional military academies in which to train military leaders and subordinate officers in matters ranging from broad military policy to the technology of warfare.

Walling observes that one can easily mistake Hamilton's preoccupation with military affairs as the sign of an ardent militarist with pretensions to turning a republic into an imperial monarchy through military necessity.[3] His enemies certainly accused him of such designs, but both his writings and his actions reveal a very different intent. In his *Continentalist* essays he observed that "political societies in close neighborhood must either be strongly united under one government, or there will infallibly exist emulations and quarrels. . . . A schism once introduced, competitions of boundary and rivalships of commerce will easily afford pretexts for war." In *Federalist* essays 6–8, he illustrated how a loose confederation would eventually demand that each sovereign state establish its own standing army to stave off the depredations of the other members, in much the same manner as occurred throughout the history of Europe as well as of ancient Greece. Commerce in the confederative setting could not enjoy any kind of pacifying tendency but rather would simply "change the objects of war" and multiply the sources of internal enmity.[4] He described the typical path of such confederacies in *Federalist* essay 8: "Frequent war and constant apprehension, which require a state of constant preparation, will infallibly produce [standing armies]. The weaker States, or confederacies, would first have recourse to them to put themselves upon an equality with their more potent neighbors. They would endeavor to supply the inferiority of population and resources by a more regular and effective system of defense, by disciplined troops, and by fortifications. They would, at the same time, be necessitated to strengthen the executive arm of government, in doing which their constitutions would acquire a progressive direction towards monarchy. It is of the nature of war to increase the executive at the expense of the legislative authority."[5]

Hamilton then noted that in history it was not unusual for smaller republics with well-organized and disciplined armies to "triumph over large states, or states with greater natural strength, which have been destitute of these advantages." The larger states would in turn build their own military forces and engage "the same engines of despotism which have been the scourge of the old world." Hamilton sought to break this horrid tendency by engaging "the industrious habits of the people of the present day, absorbed in the pursuits of gain and devoted to the improvements of agriculture and commerce" among united states, rather than build a nation of warriors—"the true condition of the people of those [ancient] republics."[6]

Hamilton's reasoning led to a conclusion that many of his generation were not yet ready to accept, namely, that a united commercial republic demanded "disciplined armies, distinct from the body of citizens."[7] He wanted to isolate the military as much as possible from domestic affairs, take away control from the states, and professionalize it as an arm of national foreign affairs. Only rarely should it ever exercise its powers domestically, and then only to quell insurrection. The Whiskey Rebellion presented such a challenge early on with no standing army yet in place, and the whole incident reinforced in Hamilton's mind the necessity of establishing one as soon as possible.

The rebellion stemmed from Congress's adoption in 1791 of an excise tax that fell principally on distillers of spirits. It was the only internal tax levied by the national government at the time, and it enraged southern and western farmers, who often converted their crops into alcohol to make a profit. The excise taxes imposed by England before the revolution still fired resentment and anger, and the new nationally imposed excise stirred anxieties that the new government was already emulating British despotism. The Scotch-Irish farmers and distillers of western Pennsylvania were the most militant in their opposition, and they subjected the federal tax collectors in their districts to beatings, tarring and featherings, the burning of their homes, and other tactics of humiliation and scorn. This was bad enough in Hamilton's eyes, but the scales tipped dramatically when state officials and their members of Congress abetted their efforts rather than trying to restrain them. Such encouragement led to the formation of a more organized rebellion, and when called to put this down, local militias turned to favor the insurgents instead. The rebellion grew to roughly six thousand activists and, in the eyes of Washington's administration, presented a serious threat to federal authority in its infancy, and thus to the new constitutional order as a whole. Hamilton was especially piqued by the situation and recommended as strong a response as could be mounted by activating neighboring state militias to make a decisive show of force, and if necessary, to use that force to quell it outright.[8]

President Washington wisely took his time in deciding what to do, letting events unfold in hopes of finding a less drastic solution and then constituting a three-man commission to try to negotiate with enraged citizens. Hamilton informed the commission that he would accommodate "any reasonable alterations" to the excise that would help dispel anger and "make the tax more palatable."[9] The efforts failed, and Washington resolved to make a show of force. Due to other distractions, General Knox, the head of the Department of War, was away and unable to prosecute the effort, so it fell to Hamilton, working with Major General Henry Lee, to lead the operation. He poured his energy into organizing and outfitting the multistate militia and then joined Washington and Lee in the field to conduct the operation. They had amassed a force exceeding twelve thousand troops, but logistical challenges exacerbated by disorganized militias greatly slowed their advance. Their eventual arrival on the scene, however, quickly dissipated the insurgency. Though Hamilton wanted stern measures applied to the leaders of the rebellion, his greatest hope came to pass—that making a decisive show of force would deter the need to inflict harm. Ultimately, both Washington and Hamilton conducted affairs in the field in such a measured and careful way that very few citizens were actually prosecuted, and those convicted were granted clemency in the aftermath. Chernow notes that "public opinion applauded the way Washington balanced firmness and clemency in suppressing" the rebellion and that "he and Hamilton had brought new prestige to the government and shown how a democratic society could handle popular disorder without resort to despotic methods."[10]

On the international scene, Hamilton believed the military should function in a similar fashion, though the immediate circumstances warranted a more cautious approach. The nation should build toward a strong force that commands respect not only for its might and readiness but also for its restraint, good judgment, and proportionality in response to hostility—elements that characterize just use of military force to this day. Walling concluded that his "fundamental political objectives were to enable the American Republic to avoid war when possible; to wage it effectively when necessary; and to preserve both political and civil liberty in time of war." Hamilton broke new ground in thinking about how a republic could combine great military power while preserving liberty.[11] He especially wanted to avoid war in the early years of the republic because it lacked the funding and effective means for conducting war and because so little will existed for establishing a standing army. These conditions, however, did little to inhibit popular passions for war.

The commencement of the French Revolution in 1789–90 sparked a heated ideological battle over the issue of whether the United States should back the new French republic out of republican sympathy and friendship for its cause while it declared war and revolution against the rest of Europe. The ideological fervor revealed the same "furious and dark passions" that Hamilton had witnessed with the Tory confiscation acts, but on a grander scale, and this raised anew his fear that the young nation would destroy itself in a bout of republican zeal. In his *Phocion* letters, penned against Tory discrimination and denial of their rights, he stated that "nothing is more common than for a free people, in times of heat and violence, to gratify momentary passions, by letting into government, principles and precedents, which afterwards prove fatal to themselves."[12] In the Tory cases such precedents entailed the angry denial of their due process rights, confiscation of their property, and even banishment. In the zeal for the French Revolution, it entailed breaking important treaty and commercial agreements with Britain (which then constituted the bulk of US foreign trade) in favor of loyalty to the new French republic and the prospect of joining it in an ideologically driven war against monarchy. Both situations revealed a "pernicious spirit of bigotry in politics, as well as in religions," which is inimical to the "spirit of toleration" required to sustain a commercial republic. With respect to religion, he observed, "It was a long time before the kingdoms of Europe were convinced of the folly of persecution, with respect to those, who were schismatics from the established church. The cry was, these men will be equally the disturbers of the hierarchy and of the state. While some kingdoms were impoverishing and depopulating themselves, by their severities to the non-conformists, their wiser neighbors were reaping the fruits of their folly, and augmenting their own numbers, industry, and wealth, by receiving with open arms the persecuted fugitives. Time and experience have taught a different lesson; and there is not an enlightened nation, which does not now acknowledge the force of this truth, that whatever speculative notions of religion may be entertained, men will not on that account, be enemies to a government that affords them protection and security."[13] With respect to politics, a strong, national republic could appeal not only to the need for protection and security but also to the prospect of liberty for persecuted émigrés as well and thereby win their loyalty and perhaps even their affection. That depended, however, on the ability and willingness of the national government to resist the *republican* brand of bigotry. As Walling notes, Hamilton's chief concern was that, "by degrees, the rhetoric of virtuous republicanism would issue in the reality of a vicious despotism." Leaders would be needed to restrain and calm its dark passions, and a professional military and foreign affairs establishment would play an important role in the effort.

A Steady and Permanent Military Administration Being Necessary to a Free Republic

Early in his military career, Hamilton became convinced that a standing army and navy were essential not only to the survival of the new republic but also to its prosperity and moderate temper. He witnessed firsthand the disastrous effects of state-controlled administration of the Revolutionary War and how that system relied so heavily upon patriotic voluntarism, and with it the severe and disparate sacrifice of those least able to afford it. The results were perverse and dispiriting. He briefly recounted the resulting condition of the Revolutionary army to his friend James Duane in September 1780: "It is now a mob, rather than an army, without cloathing, without pay, without provision, without morals, without discipline. We begin to hate the country for its neglect of us; the country begins to hate us for our oppressions of them. Congress have long been jealous of us; we have now lost all confidence in them, and give the worst construction to all they do. Held together by the slenderest ties we are ripening for a dissolution."[14] He found reliance upon the states "precarious, because the states will never be sufficiently impressed with our necessities. Each will make its own ease a primary object, the supply of the army a secondary one." Moreover, the multifarious channels of supply abetted hidden and irregular transactions and multiplied "the opportunities of embezzling public money." The problem was so pervasive that it convinced Hamilton of the need to take arms production and supply entirely out of private hands, essentially nationalizing the industry.[15] As significantly, he observed that the system of state militias relied too much on a popular spirit that lacked durability and sufficient attentiveness to a disciplined or "rigid responsibility" as well as "diligence, care or economy." This turned the administration of the war into a highly mutable affair, resulting in more expense and far less effectiveness than if it were run through a stable and uniform national system.[16]

The fix for these problems, Hamilton advised, included a stable, national financial system to fund the war effort, appointment of "great officers of state" who could bring energy and system to it, and the initiation of a series of administrative reforms that would convert the ragtag military into a professional and public-spirited corps. Congress should immediately abandon the state-based military supply system in favor of a nationalized system, adopt a military draft with three-year terms in place of state bounties, which rewarded only short-term enlistment, and give officers half pay for life (as opposed to just seven years) as a means of "binding them to the service by substantial ties" and keeping them available in the event of future conflicts.[17] All of this must be abetted with extensive training and discipline instilled by experienced officers. During the war, Hamilton had recruited foreign officers such as the Baron von Steuben and the Marquis de Lafayette to lead and train a regular army, which carried on much of the effective fighting. Their professional experience and leadership instilled a more durable courage in their troops than could ever be obtained through the haphazard leadership of irregular and inexperienced officers over a militia. As Walling notes, Hamilton distinguished between two types of courage—the *natural* versus the "*artificial*, which is the effect of discipline and habit."

> Hamilton implied that the "artificial" courage of professional soldiers would normally be superior to that of ordinary citizens in the militia. The professionals had the advantage of experience, or habituation to the confusion and danger of war. Professional soldiers acquire confidence in the use of arms and in working together in large groups through repetition of essentially mindless tasks. Though free-spirited members of the militia would normally balk at such tedium, professional officers would compel their troops to practice such tasks until they were second nature and the men had acquired artificial courage. . . . [They would] borrow their courage from their officers. . . . The natural cour-

age of free citizens was a product of enthusiasm, which waxed and waned, according to the fortunes of war; but the confidence of professionals, who acted bravely in combat because they had performed the same tasks a thousand times before in drill, was much more reliable.[18]

Though Hamilton clearly favored the artificial to the natural form of courage, he also saw how a republic could draw upon both to "develop a unique martial character, a mix between the natural but unreliable courage of the [republican] militia and the more reliable but artificial courage of a European army." This he thought could result in a military that acts "as a repository of American patriotism" marked by public-spiritedness and devotion to republican liberty, all under the auspices of permanent administrative institutions that could maintain the professional army as a smaller and relatively insular corps. A larger navy would obviate the need for an expansive army and thereby reduce any threat to domestic usurpation.[19] The modern American military evinces this character, and it extends as well to the successor of the state militias, the National Guard. At the time, however, none of this was obvious, and it fell to Hamilton to argue that the circumstances of the new republic demanded such a military establishment as an integral part of national administration.

In the *Federalist* essays 23–29, Hamilton argued that an appraisal of the country's circumstances, as well as its commercial bearing, would illustrate the necessity of maintaining army and naval forces even in times of peace. The European empires controlled the seas and the lands bordering the United States. They held dominion over many new settlements, as well as posts and routes from which they could harass the United States at will. The British restricted American access to West Indies trade, especially to the region held by the French. If US citizens wanted freer trade, their national government must expand and improve its military strength to improve its negotiating position. It needed a navy to police and protect lanes of commerce at sea and on its rivers; it needed active dockyards, arsenals, coastal and inland fortifications, and garrisons sufficient to house a rapidly expanded army when war loomed.[20] The mere presence of these military institutions and resources would deter foreign meddling and aggression.

In addition, the new nation might have to act offensively to expand and secure it borders. The territories to the west and south were deemed vital to US interests by most early statesmen, and Hamilton suggested that invading them in stages may be necessary for security and advantageous for commerce. "There are, and will be, particular posts, the possession of which will include the command of large districts of territory, and [will] facilitate future invasions of the remainder."[21] Finally, the danger of internal rebellion also loomed and had already led Pennsylvania and Massachusetts to establish standing forces of their own. Hamilton emphasized "how little the rights of a feeble government are likely to be respected, even by its own constituents."[22]

These arguments faced strong opposition, so Hamilton did not press them very hard. Instead he assured the continued existence of state militias, emphasizing the security they offered against an encroaching national army and the necessary support they provided while the nation lacked a sufficient standing force. He also played down the need for a large standing army if a smaller professional corps were established that could readily expand forces as events required. He expected, however, that the press of future crises would lead to the results he desired.

Halting Steps toward Military Establishment

Hamilton's theory of a republican military and his arguments for permanent military institutions languished until the twentieth century. Until then, the Anti-Federalist belief that standing armies presented the most serious threat to the life of a republic persisted. Armies were the engines of budding despots and led inevitably to either subversion or outright overthrow of republican institutions. The nation, the Anti-Federalists contended, must rely on the ability of the states to mobilize their citizen militias when hostilities seemed imminent or when the national government became too overbearing. Anti-Federalist Republicans were not about to let the new national government build a rival military establishment. Thus, the first Congress failed even to authorize inspections of the state militias by the new Department of War, much less allow it to order their affairs. State jealousies about the matter ran too strong for even President Washington to make any headway, so the new department languished in a sea of ill will.

Its administration suffered further for three related reasons: first, because of poor leadership and management by Henry Knox and then by James McHenry (both military men with little administrative acumen); second for lack of key subordinate administrative officials such as quartermasters and paymasters; and third for lack of adequate troops, which during the early administrations varied in number from two thousand to five thousand and were poorly trained and equipped. This led to some embarrassing defeats with Indian campaigns of the early 1790s, which prompted investigations that resulted in giving yet more responsibilities to Treasury and Hamilton's oversight. His prompting and instruction of Knox and McHenry got little in the way of positive results, and Congress gave him no help with resources.[23]

The first Congress had decommissioned naval ships provided for the Revolutionary War effort, and the only new ships commissioned were revenue cutters, which operated under Treasury supervision. As White observes, not until 1794, when the United States found itself in hostilities with Algerian corsairs (English allies) for their predation on commercial shipping, did Congress relent to building six new warships, and even that must cease if peace were achieved before completion.[24] Congress tasked Hamilton with managing their construction through the Treasury Department. In the end, only three of the six ships got built because hostilities ceased earlier than expected. Caught on the problem of sunk costs, Congress compromised in preserving the three already nearly built. The navy was not formally established as a separate institution until 1794, and that only after heated political battle. The construction of ships commenced rapidly thereafter (expanding to thirty-three) under more competent management and organization until Jefferson became president in 1801 and he halted all such efforts.[25]

Resistance to a permanent military establishment stemmed as well from the growing belief among Jeffersonian Republicans that Hamilton plotted to engineer the government into a monarchy. If Washington was a budding monarch (as many of them believed), then Hamilton was his prime minister. The resistance grew so intense and became so personal that it eventually persuaded Hamilton to leave the secretary of the treasury position in 1795 and return to his law practice. At Washington's pleading, he remained available for advice carried on extensively through correspondence, but he did not return formally to public service until 1798 when called to serve with Washington in command of the military under President John Adams. By that time, relations with the French had soured, and a naval war of sorts (often described as a "quasi-war") ensued. Adams needed to mobilize a military but had little with which to work. Thus, he called upon Washington to lead the effort, and the former president agreed, contingent upon Adams appointing Hamilton as second-in-command. Once accomplished, Washington essentially handed over the operation to his deputy.

Hamilton used the tense situation with France to try to convince Congress to create a well-rounded military establishment. Working through Oliver Wolcott, Timothy Pickering, and other administration officials, he proposed that Congress empower the president to raise ten thousand troops immediately and then prepare a corps of professional officers to eventually train fifty thousand more troops. He knew this was unlikely but hoped at least to establish "a competent number of persons qualified to act as instructors to additional troops, which events may successively require to be raised."[26] To this he added plans for the development of military academies, the building of more ships and frigates for the navy, the development of arms manufactories, and the appropriation of secret operations funds.[27] As Broadus Mitchell indicates, though circumstances remained favorable to such development for only a short time, Hamilton, "practically alone, devised the principal features of the [military] establishment. He laid the foundations for the national defense system" and planned "for expansion and amendment, so that outlines need not require change."[28] In the process, he offered instructions to Knox and McHenry on the proper management and organization of the fledgling military.

Managerial Instruction in the War Department

Chernow characterizes Hamilton's knowledge of military affairs as "encyclopedic" and claims that he "laid down the broad outlines of the entire military apparatus" in the short period of his military appointment under Adams and Washington. White likewise concludes that Hamilton "went far in managing the War Department" during his tenure at Treasury and later as inspector general.[29] In the latter position, he laid out his plans for a military academy and provided War Department leaders with a wealth of managerial advice.

Hamilton held a military academy as "an object I have extremely at heart," and he sought advice from military-minded experts abroad for its design.[30] He seemed as much interested in the technical aspects of military education, such as training engineers and artillery experts and improving cavalry systems and naval science, as he was in training for leadership and management of military organization and deployment. Chernow notes his yen for learning from the highly developed military practices of European nations, and his disappointment in the American attitude of "self-sufficiency and a contempt of the science and experience of others," a trait that Chernow links with Hamilton's "dismay over the Jeffersonian faith that Americans had much to teach the world but little to learn from it."[31] He set his sights on a fortress complex at West Point and supplied McHenry with plans for five schools to teach military fundamentals, engineering and artillery, cavalry, infantry, and navy. He offered detailed lists of necessary administrative positions and professors in the various sciences as they applied to military operations and action, as well as of the subjects to be addressed in each school. He especially emphasized the importance of maintaining a sufficient number of sergeants to rapidly train an army of fifty thousand men and offered a detailed plan of organization for the military specialties at headquarters and in the field.[32]

A review of Hamilton's correspondence with Secretary McHenry during the period from 1797 to 1799 reveals the extent to which Hamilton schooled him on virtually every aspect of departmental management, including matters of communications, purchasing and procurement, contracting, organizational structure, rulemaking and legal draftsmanship, data collection, and personnel policy. Regarding communications, he advised developing a reporting system between the War Department and the commander in chief to routinely provide information on such things as "the state of public supplies and the measures in execution to procure others" and detailed arrangements for the collection and storage of information pertinent "towards plans of general defence."[33]

Regarding procurement, Hamilton urged McHenry to centralize the function under one head and then to divide it from needs assessment and oversight functions, which were to be performed by the quartermaster general. In this arrangement, Hamilton distinguished between "civil and military functions." He deemed procurement a civil function and needs assessment and oversight as military functions and declared that they were thus far "discordantly mixed." Apparently, the quartermaster general had been involved in the business of procuring and purveying supplies in addition to assessing supply needs and insuring that they were met—a combination that invited too much secrecy and abuse and frustrated the efficiency gained by separating the functions.[34]

Hamilton illustrated the ethical trade-offs as well as practical implications for McHenry on contracting versus direct purchasing by "agents of the government." Purchases by government agents "are liable to much mismanagement and abuse." It is, therefore, often less economical than contracting but is still preferable in regard to the "quality of supplies, satisfaction of the troops, and the certainty of supply." Contracting, on the other hand, is more economical, but because "the calculations of contractors have reference primarily to their own profit, they are apt to endeavor to impose on the troops articles of inferior quality." The troops will get into the habit of expressing dissatisfaction about this, "even where there is no adequate cause." Military operations should not rely so heavily "on combinations of individual avarice." The government would be forced into much additional expense "to obviate the mischief and disappointments of those failures." Accordingly, Hamilton proposed that McHenry combine both modes in a manner more advantageous to the government. He suggested letting contracts for the laying in of magazines while providing transportation and issuance of supplies "by *military agents,* who must likewise be authorized & enabled to provide for the deficiencies of the contractors and for whatever may not be comprehended in the contracts." This scheme would "admit the competition of private interests to furnish supplies at the cheapest rate" while diminishing the potential for abuse by "public agents."[35]

Regarding organizational structure, Hamilton urged McHenry to consider systematic propriety and span of control in the arrangement of regiments, battalions, companies, platoons, sections, and demi-sections. System, uniformity, and order should be imposed wherever possible so long as important military ends were not frustrated in the arrangement. The "proportion of officers to men ought not to be greater than is adequate to the due management and command of them." Hamilton suggested appropriate ratios in light of a variety of factors. In general, he suggested a higher proportion of men to officers than had before been practiced. This made the operation more economical, but as importantly, it made the officers' positions more respectable, thereby enticing more and better applicants and stimulating "that justifiable pride which is a necessary ingredient in the military spirit." He fixed the upper limit on span of control by tactical considerations such as maneuverability in the field.[36]

Hamilton's counsel to McHenry on personnel matters addressed appointments, officer grades, quartering, pay, and benefits. For example, he advised that appointments be made with less emphasis on political beliefs and more on military competence, "especially in reference to lower grades. . . . Military situations, on young minds particularly, are of all others best calculated to inspire zeal for the service." Due regard should be paid to "appointing friends of the government" to the higher offices, though not without regard to general competence. Furthermore, he advised McHenry "to adopt as a primary rule the relative representative population of the several States" in the recruitment and selection of commissioned officers, though "this principle must frequently yield to the most proper solution of character among those willing as well as qualified to serve." This coincided with Washington's general policy on personnel appointments to all government positions in the new administration, a matter watched carefully by state leaders. Regarding officer grades, they should not be unduly multiplied and confused with half-grade distinctions such as lieutenant colonel. Too many grades would erode the respect and distinction needed to make each rank desirable. Titles of rank that have a history of respect and honored usage should be preferred over new titles or titles that have become obsolete.[37]

Hamilton's advice on quartering troops and provision for their rations reflected his desire to keep military operations separated from the domestic life of the country. This stemmed in part from the intrusive ways in which British troops had been quartered in the residences of private citizens in colonial times, but it also related to his desire to avoid undue mixing of martial life with the citizenry. Thus, the quartering of troops should take place away from the nation's "great cities." "The collection of troops there may lead to disorders and expose more than elsewhere the morals and principles of the soldiery." The War Department should provide all rations as well, rather than furnishing monetary allotments as a substitute. Monetary allotments too often facilitate "marauding and desertion" and dispose the soldiery "to lay out too much of their money in ardent spirits . . . which besides occasioning them to be ill fed will lead to habits of intemperance."[38]

In addition to advice on general rates of military pay and benefits, Hamilton instructed McHenry on extra allowances for expenses incurred while traveling on military business and for other "peculiar duties." He advised adoption of a system of fixed rates rather than leaving it unstructured and dependent upon each officer's report of extra expenses. Fixed rates were less liable to abuse, though also "not easy to regulate so as to unite economy with justice." A special appeal procedure could be instituted to handle extraordinary cases. Pay policy should be tailored to the types of incentives inherent in a given position. For example, the head of the procurement department should have an especially "ample pecuniary compensation [because] military honor can form no part of reward." Such considerations assumed of course the cooperation and assent of Congress, the lack of which drove Hamilton to despair about the nation ever achieving sound military management.[39]

Finally, Hamilton's instructions on rulemaking and legal draftsmanship in the War Department revealed the centrality of rules and standard operating procedures to military organization and policy and their connection to the rule of law as the primary means of reconciling military power with the liberty and consent of the governed. Rulemaking went hand in hand with the efforts to systematize and make accountable the entire military organization. Hamilton wrote many of these rules himself and coached McHenry on such elementary points as making rules nonretroactive in their effect. "The [retroactive] application of a new rule may produce hardship and injustice, when the service may have been performed in the expectation that practice on former occasions would prevail."[40]

In drafting laws for consideration by Congress, Hamilton suggested that McHenry first propose bills that provide for fundamental arrangements of military forces. The subsequent bills for "augmentation need only define the number to be raised and the duration of service, and the mode of raising." This would eliminate the necessity of Congress reviewing administrative arrangements with every new bill and would therefore lend stability to the existing force structure. It was vital to determine the level of administrative detail appropriate for congressional bills. For example, in 1799, Hamilton sent McHenry a draft of a bill for establishing a medical hospital system for the military (and for veterans). In the cover letter he called McHenry's attention to the structure of the bill. It should deal with "nothing but an organization with a general outline of duty." Detailed and more flexible regulations would follow in the executive departments, where they could be "varied as experience advises."[41] Here again Hamilton demonstrated his administrative orientation to law. Regulations structure discretion but are easily changed to suit new circumstances. Statutes should usually be framed in general language for broad yet limiting purposes, with the details left to administrative agencies.

Like the rest of the government, the suffusion of law throughout the military system would subject it, first, to a degree of uniformity and accountability that could never be achieved in a system of separate state militias and, second, to the general superintendence by civilian authorities poised to restrain military ambition. In the end, as Walling notes, Hamilton shared with Anti-Federalists an aversion to military imperialism but believed their confederation to be fundamentally flawed as the means to preventing it. The better path lay through national union, led by an energetic government promoting the blessings of liberty at home and strength abroad. In that context, a professional military, publicly spirited in nature and bound to the Constitution, should operate as an arm of foreign affairs rather than of internal suppression or imperial overreach.[42]

Hamilton's Foreign Policy

> The foundation of this doctrine [of alliances], is the utility of clear and certain rules for determining the reciprocal duties of nations—that as little as possible may be left to opinion and to subterfuge of a refining or unfaithful casuistry.
> —Hamilton, Pacificus no. 2

The French Revolution commenced in 1789 and continued for ten years in tumult, anarchy, and war. Its chaos made conditions ripe for a dictator, and Napoleon's coup establishing him as first consul of the government made it a reality in 1799. The course of that revolution exerted defining influence on US politics and its foreign policy in the founding era. As Gilbert Lycan recounts, in its beginning, the American people expressed enthusiastic support for French commoners throwing off the yoke of oppression under the ancien régime and following the spirit of the American Revolution in establishing their own regime of liberty.[43] The good feelings stemmed in part from the alliance of 1778, which secured France's cooperation and support with the new United States against the English, but it also stemmed from pride in a newfound fraternity of republicanism that aroused strong ideological fervor. That fervor led many Americans to advocate alliance with France in its war against monarchy in general and to rationalize and excuse heinous acts committed by French republicans in successive reigns of terror over their own people.

Though favorably disposed toward the revolution at first, Hamilton backed away as French good sense gave way to "horrid and disgusting scenes" born of intemperate zeal.[44] The intense and violent actions of the revolutionaries, combined with the popularity of French philosophes who to his mind espoused radical and utopian ideas that encouraged "an unexampled dissolution of all the social and moral ties," soon convinced him that the revolutionary experiment would fail. By 1794, in his Americanus essays, he predicted that "after wading through seas of blood, in a furious and sanguinary civil war, France may find herself at length the slave of some victorious Scylla or Marius or Caesar."[45] In the meantime, France's instigation of war against the rest of Europe presented important opportunities for the United States if it could avoid being drawn into hostilities, including the chance to annex vital western and southern borderlands and to cultivate more favorable trade relations abroad. These became Hamilton's chief foreign policy goals.

The fault lines of discord among Americans about the progress of the revolution in France followed rather consistently the divide between Federalists and Jeffersonian Republicans, with Hamilton leading Federalist opinion in numerous essays against the folly of supporting the French in war and in favor of proclaiming strict neutrality instead. Jefferson and his party (which soon came to include Madison) believed that the United States was obligated through the defensive treaties signed in 1778 to come to France's aid against what they viewed as aggressor nations, especially England and Austria. Bitterness toward the English remained fresh in the hearts of many Americans, including Jefferson, who had always felt slighted by their diplomats.[46] He sympathized with the French people, having witnessed conditions there as foreign minister at the onset of the revolution, and had acquired a far more tolerant view of bloodshed as a sad but unavoidable result of revolutionary progress. However, he and a group of his leading colleagues did not want the United States to join the war with France—the United States had no real capacity to help in that regard. Even the French governments, royal and then republican, did not demand that, but they did expect other means of support from their republican brothers. Jefferson's group thus hewed to the idea of maintaining a stance of qualified neutrality, with strong rhetoric defending the French cause and accusing the British especially of heinous treaty violations and abuses to both France and the United States.

Intended or not, this opened the door to many other Republicans who, in Hamilton's words, sought to "provoke and bring on war by indirect means without declaring it or even avowing the intention." The fact that the British continued to discriminate against and even obstruct American trade with anyone but themselves through a combination of navigation acts and wartime impoundment orders further inflamed the situation. So too did informal British alliances with Algerian corsairs to raid American ships operating in their trade routes, and as well with various northern Indian tribes who plagued settlers and towns on the northwestern borderlands. These soured relations provoked several retaliatory bills by Madison and other congressional

Republicans who, as Hamilton again characterized it, wanted to reduce British commercial ties and "perpetuate animosity between the
two countries without involving War."[47]

Although these proposals never passed, they inflamed the Republicans who desired war. The subtle differences in approach between
the two Republican factions became lost in the fray of subsequent
events, which seemed to impel the United States toward war, though
with Congress continually rejecting any substantial preparations for
it. As Lycan put it, "Partisan considerations seemed to have unseated
reason, at least for the time. The Republicans wanted commercial war
with Britain, and some would even appropriate British property, but
they rejected all measures for national defense."[48] Moreover, they ignored the glaring fact raised continually by Hamilton that the United
States conducted about three-quarters of its trade with Britain. They
also ignored the fact that the French committed depredations and
sponsored privateering on American territory and shipping when it
thought it advantageous, even as its ministers courted American favor.
He predicted rightly that all the European powers would continue to
act this way to advance their own interests so long as the United States
remained weak and vulnerable. Their control of US borderlands presented a dire threat that led both Hamilton and Jefferson to quietly
consider plans of invasion if negotiation failed.[49]

Hamilton found both Republican positions untenable, arguing
that "wars oftener proceed from angry and perverse passions than
from cool calculations of interest" and that either Republican strategy
stirred the former to the sacrifice of the latter.[50] Madison and Jefferson wanted to believe that speaking strongly against Britain in favor
of France would induce British leaders into favorable compromises
for fear of losing significant trade with the United States. This seemed
plausible, but events surrounding the arrival of the French republican
envoy and firebrand, Edmond (or Citizen) Genêt, in 1793 soon scut-
tled their hopes and swung momentum among many political leaders
toward Hamilton's position of strict neutrality. In his view, the United
States should try to enforce neutrality with all parties and negotiate
patiently with each nation bilaterally while building its own military
power to deter future depredations on its borders and shipping. President Washington articulated this approach with a now famous line,
"If we desire to secure peace, it must be known that we are at all times
ready for war."[51] These words captured the essence of Hamilton's philosophy of military and foreign affairs. Through his correspondence,
back-channel diplomatic efforts, and prolific public essays, he helped

keep the United States out of the European war. And throughout that written work, he advocated the propriety of a realist foreign policy that has ever since contributed to the continuing debate over the proper course of American diplomacy and engagement in war.[52]

Realist Foreign Policy

Hamilton intended that foreign policy buffer the nascent American political economy from foreign competition and military aggression. The ability to do this depended in large part on the creation of a diplomatic corps backed by strong military capacity. As Mitchell indicates, he proposed the establishment of the diplomatic corps and consular service as early as 1783, and in notes to his military pay book (1777), he expressed concern for acquiring detailed knowledge of the strengths, interests, views, and resources of foreign nations, thus anticipating the need for a variety of intelligence-gathering functions to inform diplomacy as well as military preparedness.[53] Through this array of institutions, he wanted to project both the perception and the reality of a powerful nation.

The exercise of power in foreign affairs, Hamilton maintained, should be guided by "sober and palpable" assessments of national interest and should studiously avoid impassioned appeals to ideology or any other cause that might lead people to sacrifice that interest. In his Pacificus essays, Hamilton argued that inherently tenuous relations between nations can be stabilized only through calculations of "*mutual* interest and *reciprocal* advantage." It is a "general principle that the predominant motive of good offices from one nation to another is the interest or advantage of the nation which performs them," and this constituted the basic standard against which the actions of foreign affairs administration must be evaluated.[54] However, he did not advocate a policy "absolutely selfish" in this regard. Rather, he advocated pursuit of national interests "as far as justice and good faith permit." More often than not, "the interests of the nation, when well understood, will be found to coincide with their moral duties."[55] Conversely, "violent and unjust measures commonly defeat their own purpose."

The coincidence of interest with moral duty is made easier by adopting low but clear expectations and reciprocal forms of justice and good faith. Foreign affairs is no place for "metaphysical niceties about the justice or injustice of the cause." Overly refined and impassioned views frustrate each nation's ability to determine a fair, if yet imperfect, outcome. Mutual interests and reciprocal advantages focus on material objects and concerns that are amenable to negotiation and settlement through treaties and other types of agreement. Here again, Hamilton strongly preferred a process orientation marked by agreements with clear triggers for response or action. He illustrated the point in an argument over whether an existing treaty with France was *defensive* and how obligations to come to one another's aid in that case should be determined.[56]

In Pacificus no. 2, Hamilton recited the opening passages of the treaty, which clearly characterized the entire document as defensive in nature. Invoking the rules of conventional legal construction, he stated that "it is sufficient that it be once declared [up front], to be understood in every part of the Treaty, unless coupled with express negative words excluding the implication." He thus rejected the tendency of Republicans to pick clauses out of the document for offensive purposes without reference to the document's explicit defensive premise. That settled, one must then determine whether France was engaged in an *offensive war* or a *defensive war.*[57]

Citing conventions of the law of nations, he asserted, "No position is better established than that the Power which *first declares* or *actually begins* a War, whatever may have been the causes leading to it, is that which makes an *offensive war*. Nor is there any doubt that France first declared and began the War against Austria, Prussia, Savoy, Holland, England and Spain. Tis the commencement of the War itself that decides the question of being on the offensive or defensive." This greatly simplifies the task of determining whether one's legal or "positive treaty" obligations are triggered in otherwise extremely complicated conditions. Venturing into the quagmire of prior causes is "too vague, too liable to dispute, too much matter of opinion to be a proper criterion of National Conduct." For the sake of argument, Hamilton then illustrated how France was "not blameless in the circumstances which preceded and led to the war with those powers; that if she received, she also gave cause of offense, and that the justice of the War on her side is, in those cases, not a little problematical."[58]

His next point directly challenged general and ideological calls to arms, such as France's Decree of November 1792, which granted "*fraternity* and *assistance* to every People who *wish* to recover their liberty and charge the Executive Power to send the necessary orders to *the Generals* to give assistance to such people, and to *defend those citizens who may have been or who may be vexed for the cause of liberty.*" He reasoned that it may be "justifiable and meritorious to afford assistance to the one which has been oppressed & is *in the act of liberating itself*; but it is not warrantable for a Nation *beforehand* to hold out a general invitation to insurrection and revolution." This would permit a country to do "what France herself had complained of—an interference by one nation in the internal Government of another." Decrees of this sort "disturb the tranquility of nations, excite fermentation and revolt everywhere."[59] These passages illustrate Hamilton's penchant for clear, stable, and self-restraining criteria by which to conduct international relations. They are much more amenable to moderating intense emotional reactions (whether born of injustice or fanaticism), which exacerbate rather than calm tensions among the affected nations.

In this regard, diplomats should display an amiable and patient manner in negotiations, always seeking to achieve a mutual understanding of situations and interests. As Lycan observes, Hamilton wanted to heal breaches rather than win points or prevail in "a contest of words." Many of his political opponents wanted to defend the righteousness of their cause and to ridicule and blame the actions of their perceived enemies (usually England) as justification for construing treaty provisions in France's favor. To Hamilton, defending the rightness or wrongness of parties in such disputes was misplaced. "The *rule in construing treaties* should be to suppose both parties right, for want of a common judge."[60] This conveys respect to each side as a precondition for constructive dialogue and negotiation toward settlement of grievances. It brings them to the table with their dignity intact.

Hamilton then dealt with claims of obligation to France out of gratitude for their invaluable aid during the Revolutionary War. Such claims, he argued, entail a mistaken sense of reciprocity and are misplaced in foreign affairs. Here, once again, he distinguished between the obligations of personal versus public morality.

> Instances of conferring benefits, from kind and benevolent dispositions [e.g., gratitude] without any other interest on the part of the person who confers the benefit than the pleasure of doing a good action, occur every day among individuals. But among nations they perhaps never occur.
>
> Indeed the rule of morality is in this respect not exactly the same between Nations as between individuals. The duty of making its own welfare the guide of its actions is much stronger upon the former than upon the latter; in proportion to the greater magnitude and importance of national compared with individual happiness, to the greater permanency of the effects of national than of individual conduct.[61]

The relation of public officials to their people begets an obligation to see to their interests first, and thus does not enjoy the right of sacrificing national interests out of gratitude. Public officials should operate by a different principle of action: "Rulers are only *trustees* for the happiness and interest of their nation, and cannot, consistently with their trust, follow the suggestions of kindness or humanity towards others, to the prejudice of their constituent."[62] This standard is not absolute: it is still bound by considerations of justice and good faith, but in general, sentiments such as gratitude frustrate the ability to anticipate material and reciprocal benefits or costs, or to delimit appropriate actions and responses. Thus, "refinements of this kind are to be indulged with caution in the affairs of nations, [in favor of more palpable interests that are subjectable to] clear and intelligible rules."[63]

Hamilton illustrated the inappropriateness of acting with gratitude toward France by showing that its motives for aiding the United States during its revolution were self-interested. Neither France nor Spain lent support out of some altruistic interest in our independence or liberty. France joined American forces because it was advantageous in redressing the balance of power with England and Spain. Each country vied for control of US borderlands and wanted to make England's war with its colonies extremely expensive, thereby weakening her war making and commercial capacities over the long run. An English empire divided from within worked to their distinct advantage.[64]

Basing foreign policy on the play of interests does not completely rule out considerations of friendship, esteem, or good will. Friendships can be useful as well as enjoyable, and "esteem and good will [with France] ought to be cherished and cultivated, but they are very distinct from a spirit of romantic gratitude calling for sacrifices of our substantial interests; preferences inconsistent with sound policy; or complaisance incompatible with our safety." Esteem and good will can do much to facilitate agreements to mutual benefit, but the weak status of the United States led Hamilton to the judgment that at least in the short run it should avoid any long-term commitments and hesitate to ally itself too closely with any nation, lest it "make its own interest subservient to that of another."[65] That prospect posed an existential threat to the young nation's honor and reputation.

Subservience of a nation's core interests to another nation constituted debasement of its character and dignity as an independent country. In his third essay of *The Warning*, he drew from the example of France's domination of the weak and vacillating states of Holland and Italy (1797). "The honor of a nation is its life. Deliberately to abandon it is to commit an act of political suicide. The Nation which can prefer disgrace to danger is prepared for a master and deserves one." There is a point, among nations and people, at which forbearance no longer demonstrates good and patient character but rather indicates humiliation and disgrace. Such mental debasement is the "most pernicious of conquests which a state can experience" because it dulls one's "sensibility to insult and injury." It destroys "pride of character which prefers any peril or sacrifice to a final submission to oppression."[66] The French were not offering genuine friendship to the United States. They simply wanted to manipulate the United States for their own ends, heedless of US interests.

Hamilton believed that adherence to national interest as a guide to foreign policy logically compelled the United States to recognize and respect the legitimate interests of other nations. The judgments and conduct of other nations, which are calculated from their interests, should not be interfered with except as they affect US interests. He cited Vattel in support of this principle. No nation is justified in "taking cognizance of the administration of the sovereign of another country, to set himself up as a judge of his conduct or to oblige him to alter it."[67] Strict observance of this principle avoids the temptation to self-righteousness and checks the tendency toward ideological evangelism. He observed this tendency in the excesses of the French Revolution. France's revolutionary zeal for republican liberty eroded its respect for nonrepublican nations and led to declarations for their overthrow. Hamilton dreaded this kind of moralism. No nation enjoyed a monopoly of virtue, and there was no single governing form or principle appropriate for all. He deemed France's tendency so dangerous that he spared no effort at distinguishing the US republic from that of the French.[68]

Regard for national interests provided Hamilton with a solid and modest basis upon which to conduct foreign relations. Such regard confines a nation's moral reach to what is administratively feasible, making diplomatic responsibilities less complicated on all sides and enhancing the prospect of more accountable and predictable relations. Nations with widely varying political forms and cultures can more easily cultivate a common ground for international agreements. Commitments, in the form of debts, treaties, and trade agreements can more easily be honored in good faith or renegotiated as the play of interests evolves or breaks down.

The greatest threats to these arrangements arose from two different sources. The first is an egregious imbalance of power among the

affected nations. The weak condition of the new United States made it
so vulnerable to predation by European powers that few of the founders felt confident about its long-term prospects. Hamilton, more than
most of his colleagues, saw grounds for hope if it could stay out of war
and play the competing powers against each other while the United
States built its own commercial and military power. Then it too could
achieve prominence and contribute to a more stable balance of power
in the western hemisphere and perhaps around the world. In the short
run, he favored allying more closely with Britain as a bulwark against
the continental powers and because the extensive trade between the
two countries posed more severe consequences to both parties in the
event relations broke down.

The Jeffersonian Republicans believed that Hamilton in fact wanted
to bring the United States back under the English Crown, and they
published numerous essays and made countless speeches to that effect. The vitriol galvanized their party in support of France by demon-
izing a common foe. For Hamilton, the "excessive partiality for one
foreign nation & excessive dislike of another" revealed a dangerous
form of moralism and constituted the second major threat to effective diplomacy. In written drafts of George Washington's Farewell Address, Hamilton characterized this imbalanced and excessive partiality
as "one of the most baneful foes of republican government. [It] leads
to see danger only on one side and serves to veil & second to resist
the arts of influence on the other."[69]

He witnessed this one-sided, distorting moralism in full play with
the impassioned and ideological devotion so many Americans displayed
toward France's revolutionary cause. The Edmond Genêt affair illustrated the dangers.

Genêt, appointed in 1793 as French minister to the United States,
arrived with great fanfare at the port of Charleston, South Carolina,
not at a port closer to the new capital, Philadelphia. He carried with
him a large number of letters of marque, which could be used to
convert private American vessels into privateers on behalf of France.
These would take British prizes and share the wealth between the
United States and France, thus sealing their mutual pecuniary interests. He also came with the clandestine purpose of organizing agents
to attack British and Spanish holdings in the US borderlands. Overtly,
he planned to rouse republican sentiments to a fever pitch to convince US leaders to increase support of all kinds to the French war
effort and even drag the United States directly into hostilities—all in
direct violation of the neutrality proclamation. As his six-week jour-

ney to Philadelphia commenced, he embarked on a campaign that, as Chernow describes it, made him look "more like a political candidate than a foreign diplomat." He attended banquets, gave spirited speeches about republican brotherhood, and "spawned 'Republican' and 'Democratic' societies whose members greeted one another as 'citizens.'"[70]

Genêt stirred popular frenzy and euphoria wherever he traveled, and upon arriving in Philadelphia, he began making audacious claims to the US administration (and to Jefferson especially) that France had every right to use American ports and other facilities for military purposes and "that he rejected the notion of American neutrality." Most alarming, "he said that he planned to go above Washington's head and appeal directly to the American people, asking their assistance to rig French privateers in American ports."[71] This set off a firestorm of controversy, with Republican and Federalist presses pouring out vitriolic articles and embroiling the Washington administration in the hottest of internal squabbles, as well as arguments with British diplomats. All who spoke for neutrality, or just tried to calm things down, were reviled as traitors and monarchists.

Washington needed badly to dismiss Genêt and send him back to France, but the intense internal dissension and the risk of insulting France made him hold back. The prospect of being drawn into war, despite so much effort to avoid it, seemed imminent. Jefferson too faced a dilemma because while he ardently supported the French, he was obliged as a member of the administration to support Washington's neutrality proclamation. He tried to restrain Genêt's antics but to no avail. As Harper describes it, Jefferson, as secretary of state, had to explain the subtleties of US obligations under the neutrality proclamation in a letter to Genêt, but "Genet dismissed Jefferson's arguments as old-fashioned legalisms and beneath the dignity of republican diplomacy." Increasingly he viewed Jefferson as "endowed with good qualities, but weak enough to sign what he does not believe and to defend officially threats which he condemns in his conversations and anonymous writings."[72]

Genêt's reaction to Jefferson's advice is telling for its naïveté and dismissiveness toward important legal distinctions and diplomatic practices. Jefferson performed his duty with the required subtlety and aplomb, and it is quite common to have to make official statements that one personally disagrees with. For Genêt, the cause of republican fraternity should sweep all that aside. His wider antics with the American public displayed the same recklessness toward its governing institutions and processes in general. He thought whipping up the passion for republican liberty would suffice to meet his ends—impelling his American brothers into a war for the cause.

Genêt's fortunes, however, took an ironic turn. The same passions he stirred in the United States were also aflame in France and lead to a Jacobin coup (led by Maximilien Robespierre) against the Girondist faction to which Genêt belonged. He became persona non grata in his home country and faced the guillotine should he return. As Chernow indicates, Hamilton "urged Washington to allow him to remain in the United States, lest Republicans accuse Washington of having sent the brash Frenchman to his death." He was granted asylum, became an American citizen, and "married Cornelia Clinton, the daughter of Hamilton's nemesis, Governor George Clinton."[73]

Foreign intrigue and passion for the republican cause waxed and waned for many years thereafter. It hit an especially high point shortly after Hamilton resigned in 1795, and in a moment of weakness, the invective lured him onto the street to confront directly some of its most vociferous agents, only to be stoned and challenged with duels for the effort.[74] He struggled with this kind of fervor throughout much of his career, fearing its reckless tendencies and incitement to mob rule and despairing at times about whether the new government could survive its onslaughts. He appealed constantly in the press for calmer measures, provided insightful analyses of powers and interests at stake, and argued as persuasively as anyone could for what he saw as the better policy. In light of the country's vulnerable situation, his counsel amounted to this: "Permanent alliance, intimate connection with any part of the foreign world is to be avoided. Confine relations to palpable interests and reciprocal benefits, let engagements be fulfilled—with circumspection indeed but with perfect good faith. Here let us stop."[75]

Conclusion

Biographers often note that Hamilton possessed the ability to survey the American scene as an outsider. Most of his prominent colleagues could not do this well because their perspectives were rooted in long lineages of state origin and identity. Hamilton expressed affection for his adopted state of New York, but his loyalties clearly belonged to the nation as a whole and to its prospects rather than to its colonial and state-centered legacy. This improved his ability to think purely in terms of national rather than state interests. He could write reports on national policy and administration calculated purely for national benefit and design them for impact on foreign audiences as well as domestic ones. Certainly, his mammoth reports on public credit, the bank, the mint, and manufactures were calculated to influence European leaders and financial institutions as much as his colleagues at home. Harper's interpretation of Hamilton's *Report on Manufactures* as "a lever to push British policy in a more liberal direction, and to counter Jefferson's confrontational strategy," makes a lot of sense. "It would bring pressure to bear on Britain gradually and indirectly, without unleashing the kind of devastating trade war that would follow from the Madison-Jefferson approach."[76] It would also project to the wider trading world the direction of development and the prospects for future trade with the United States. Even if the United States only stumbled in this direction, as it did, its trajectory seemed more evident to outsiders like Hamilton than to its homegrown citizens. Hamilton's vision of America's future as an urban society with an integrated political economy and immersion in international commerce fit that trajectory.

In a sense, then, Hamilton displayed a unique brand of nationalism for his time. As Federici indicates, the term is now loaded with very different, negative connotations, so one must take care to distinguish Hamilton's version from other strains. His realism informed his nationalism, so his attitude included a strong element of national introspection or self-criticism. Federici thus characterizes him ironically as "one of the first anti-nationalists, because he recognized that nations are not the ultimate measure of goodness or justice. He often found fault in his own nation while recognizing the virtue in other nations. He was aware that nations, like individuals, must be judged by transnational standards that embody the wisdom of historical experience." This contrasts with what Hamilton saw in the Jacobinism of the French Revolution, which amounted to "an ideological movement engendered by a national hubris that is prone to meddling in the affairs of nations it considers less enlightened." The "jingoism, racism, and nativism" associated with nationalism in subsequent centuries bears strong resemblance to the Jacobin strain and therefore should not be linked to Hamilton except by his revulsion to it.[77]

Federici finds a much better characterization of Hamilton's modest nationalism as cosmopolitan patriotism. Borrowing from John Lukacs, he explains that patriotism respects, even reveres, the traditional institutions of a political society and "is restrained by transnational standards like natural law and conceptions of transcendence." Thus, as

Lukacs describes, "patriotism is defensive, nationalism is aggressive. Patriotism is the love of a particular land, with particular social and political traditions; nationalism is the love of something less tangible, of the myth of a *people,* justifying many things, a political and ideological substitute for religion."[78]

A further distinction, made by John Schaar, differentiates the "natural patriotism" described by Lukacs from "covenantal patriotism," which applies with even greater force to the United States. For Schaar, patriotism in general embraces a sense of indebtedness to where one is raised—to its social, religious, and political legacies. The United States exists in profound paradox because its origins lie both in consent and conquest, and as such, the ties of its people to its lands are more tenuous. As Schaar characterizes it (quoting Robert Frost), "The land was ours before we were the land's." Only Native Americans can fully claim the latter. Instead, the largely immigrant nation finds its patriotic indebtedness in its covenantal charter—in the values and principles embodied in its Constitution. In that sense, the founders were quintessential patriots, with Hamilton the most cosmopolitan among them because he so thoroughly embraced the idea of a *more perfect union* and because of his deep desire to adequately defend it.[79] Close and thorough reading of his extensive writings and speeches reveals his deep attachment to a defensive rather than imperialistic military and foreign policy. His example and his advice on these matters deserve our continued regard in our current era of American exceptionalism and seemingly permanent war, as a guide to sober introspection, at least for those who try to govern wisely.[80]

Conclusion
The Hamiltonian Legacy

Legacy. What is a legacy?
It's planting seeds in a garden you never get to see.
I wrote some notes at the beginning of a song someone will sing
for me.
America, you great unfinished symphony, you sent for me.
You let me make a difference.
A place where even orphan immigrants can leave their fingerprints
and rise up.
    —Lin-Manuel Miranda playing Hamilton, in *Hamilton*, act 2

Surveying the landscape at this end of history, the American republic bears the distinct imprint of Hamilton's vision. It is a vibrant and
opulent commercial republic, devoted to liberty and entrepreneurial
in spirit. It projects the most powerful military force in the world, and
American foreign policy dominates the international scene. National
government supremacy is firmly established, much to the consternation of ardent states' rightists and libertarians. Presidents energetically
exercise powers and reach unimagined in earlier times. An amazing
variety of professions and technical occupations staff myriad institutions across all sectors, reflecting strong meritocratic norms. An array
of financial institutions constitute the financial spine of the economy
at all levels and even across the world. Money and debt operate syner-
gistically, supplying lifeblood to the system, with most other nations
pegging their currencies to the almighty dollar.

In all of this, the public administration figures prominently, as Hamilton intended. He offered a compelling theory of constitutional government that fused responsibility with power for the sake of achieving "liberal and enlarged plans for the public good." His opponents
dwelled on intense suspicion of power, preferring strict limits on both
means and ends in hopes of preserving an agrarian and state-centered
status quo. But the plan adopted at the Constitutional Convention
offered much broader language—much of it due to ambiguities and
conflicts the framers themselves could not resolve—and an ingenious

design that Hamilton found capable of energetic administration. By the standards of his day, his vision and model were progressive and constitutive in nature. He built and managed institutions, proposed policies, and planned for a future he saw as eminently reachable given the dispositions of the American people. He is thus not only a leading founder of the American republic but also the preeminent founder of its public administration.

Hamilton's theory and practice present us with a complex and nuanced view of the role of American public administration because it flows from a complex constitutional superstructure. If the analysis conducted in the preceding chapters offers a central insight, it is that his words and actions must always be couched in the context and integrity of that superstructure. The analysis shows that he and his colleagues took a very pragmatic approach to the blending of powers that flowed from it. He was neither formulaic nor doctrinaire in his thinking, and he well understood that the abstract categories of legislative, executive, and judicial power were not entirely clear, much less absolute. The framers wrestled with these distinctions knowing full well their indeterminacy, especially in relation to other existing conceptions of governing power (such as the federative power) they found in European regimes. Hamilton stood out for his brilliant grasp of these subtleties and for seeing that in the mix of powers there existed an opportunity to bolster the executive branch to make the overall administration of the government more effective.

High-toned government required that significant powers be granted to it as a whole, with much of its delegative and appointive powers concentrated in both the legislative and the executive branches. Hamilton's application of liberal construction to enumerated Article I powers, and his close interaction with members of both houses, clearly indicates that he intended for Congress to play a serious role in the overarching administration of the government. Furthermore, his actions as secretary of the treasury showed that he readily included the courts in even the minutiae of street-level administration.[1] And despite his general preference for a tidy hierarchical form of departmental organization, he displayed remarkable readiness to employ boards, commissions, and interbranch collaborations that mixed and integrated all three powers for entrepreneurial and other special purposes. In his view, the Constitution was permissive regarding both organizational form and interbranch participation.

Hamilton is of course best known as the great advocate for a powerful executive. That is what people remember most about his theory of government. But the broader aspects and nuances of his theory and practice are too often neglected in favor of a narrowed and more doctrinal view that divorces his thoughts on executive power from its context. Most pertinent in this regard is his conception of unity in the executive. It has been much used and abused in US history, resulting in unfortunate effects on both the presidency and the public administration. As one might expect, the most telling distortions arose through presidential claims of expansive, even total power over the national public administration. Most prominent with such claims were Presidents Andrew Jackson, Theodore Roosevelt, and Franklin Delano Roosevelt—each very popular as well as controversial leaders who did much to shape the eras in which they lived.

The Abuse of Unity in the Executive

Andrew Jackson is well known for marrying Hamilton's unity in the executive with Jefferson's Republican virtue, born of simplicity, in such a way that he could claim a democratic mandate from the people to make the national government more truly representative and responsive. His primary mechanism for doing so lay in his reform doctrine of rotation in office, in which he claimed the exclusive right as president to remove long-standing administrative officials at any level and replace them with common folk—especially friends and followers who were personally loyal to him. The *Decision of 1789* loomed large in his thinking, and he used the removal power to equate all of federal administration with the executive branch, as well as to claim that Congress could only channel its oversight and delegation through his office. This constituted an early version of *overhead democracy* and *unitary executive theory*, which treats the public administration as the exclusive preserve of the executive and his party.

In the early years of Jackson's presidency, Congress railed against such claims, at one point even passing a resolution condemning his firing of successive secretaries of the treasury before finding one who would obey his command to remove funds deposited by law in the second Bank of the United States. However, as Lawrence Lessig and Cass Sunstein observe, Jackson's argument eventually prevailed against the objections of such luminaries as Henry Clay, John C. Calhoun, and Daniel Webster, as well as against the Supreme Court in *Kendall v. U.S.*, where the justices unanimously rejected his thesis. Congress would later (1837) expunge its prior resolution condemning Jackson, which for Lessig and Sunstein "indicates at the least that by then, the nation's

conception of the Presidency had begun its mammoth transformation." Significantly, they note that among the many who objected to
this transformation was James Kent, an influential Hamiltonian judge
and legal commentator, who remarked, "I begin to have a strong suspicion that Hamilton was right [that the removal required the concurrence of the Senate]."[2] Kent's reservations, shared by most Whigs,
were drowned in a tide of spirited democratization that found the
simple, instrumentalizing logic of Jackson's argument compelling.
How could an unelected Treasury official at any level be held accountable if he holds a power independent of the elected president, the direct representative of the people? Brian Cook observed that Henry
Clay spotted the quite predictable flaw in *General* Jackson's argument—
that it was "altogether a military idea, wholly incompatible with free
government. There exists no such responsibility to the President. All
are responsible to the law, and to the law only, or not responsible at
all." This thread of Hamilton's sense of responsibility, bolstered by
duration in office, then fell into latency, replaced with what Cook describes as "a harsher instrumental conception of administration and
an even greater estrangement of public administration from its constitutional roots."[3]

Theodore Roosevelt came to the presidency in 1901 as a patronage
reformer bent on cultivating public opinion in favor of an expanding administrative state, centralized under the executive branch and
staffed by an expert civil service. Parties and patronage hiring dominated the latter half of the nineteenth century, which, as Peri Arnold
indicates, turned the public service into "a satellite of congressional
interests and party requirements" that produced fragmented, quasi-
independent administrative organs as manifestations of congressional
fiefdoms and party machines. The fusion of parties with administration gave elected officials new powers over governmental largesse, including jobs and contracts, along with veterans' pensions and land
grabs. They introduced a system of feudal-styled corruption similar
to that exercised by the British Crown in earlier generations but fitted to a distributive party state.[4]

Roosevelt attacked the corruption and waste inherent to this system, and in its place, he touted a *stewardship* role for the presidency
that, like Jackson, overtly attempted a synthesis of Hamilton's strong
executive with popular rule. He asserted inherent presidential powers,
greater in his mind than ever before seen in either republics or constitutional monarchies, and especially in foreign affairs. He claimed
what amounted to a roving commission to do whatever he thought

necessary, short of explicit constitutional prohibition, as a steward of the people.[5] Absent from this approach is the founding generation's sense of *limited government* through *enumerated powers*. Scholars of the Progressive Era aptly characterize him as "ushering in the rhetorical presidency," whereby the president, through tactics of popular rhetoric, serves as a direct conduit to, and informer of, popular will. He becomes the "steward of the public welfare," which Theodore Roosevelt interpreted as a matter of meeting public wants and needs as he saw them.

In that context, the national public administration should take on a nonpartisan character, reinstate duration and merit in office through a civil service system, and serve as the "instrument of executive-centered government."[6] Cook concludes that Roosevelt and his Progressive Party "clearly anticipated the full-blown administrative state, and even the welfare state that came fully into being during the New Deal."[7] Their program focused not only on cleaning up the spoils system but growing and adapting the federal administration, especially in response to the powers and abuses of the burgeoning corporate industrial system. Hamilton's manufacturing agenda had come fully into being, though without his prescribed regulatory framework. Roosevelt set about establishing that framework and, along with it, proposed new public institutions such as a national health service and a social insurance program to deal with industry's deleterious effects.

Roosevelt's presidential political rival, Woodrow Wilson, also embraced the Progressive Reform agenda, and as both a scholar of political science and president, he built on Roosevelt's stewardship theory in a more systematic way, especially pertaining to the role of public administration under the executive. As Cook observes, Wilson viewed administration as the chief part of governing but also as distinct from politics because, in his mind, it addressed different questions and processes. In general, administration deals mostly with policy management but also plays a vital role in policy development through its immersion at street level in the dynamics of social life. As the "State's experiencing organ," it would "test the laws already on the books" and gather the knowledge required to inform the development of new laws. It would thus operate at the edges of law, serving in "adaptive, guiding, and discretionary" roles. The administrative process is therefore "organic" in nature, and for Wilson this required the integration of all governing powers in order to efficiently fulfill governing functions. He prescribed the critical bridging role among the branches for the executive, uniting them in practice through presidential and party leadership over public opinion. He sought to collapse the separation of powers by way of administrative theory and executive leadership.[8] From the standpoint of Hamiltonian theory, this is getting the cart before the horse and acquiesces to Pope's notorious aphorism: "For forms of government let fools contest, that which is best administered is best." Roosevelt's stewardship model, with Wilson's refinements, set the groundwork for Franklin Delano Roosevelt's (hereafter, FDR's) managerial presidency and has heavily influenced presidential assertions of power over public administration ever since.

Like Andrew Jackson and Theodore Roosevelt before him, FDR sought to blend Jeffersonian ideals with Hamilton's strong executive, but clothed in the modernized garb of liberal economic rights and democratizing leadership. As Cook describes it, "FDR sought to use the presidency, and the public administration, to give shape, substance, and guidance to the inevitable democratic tide."[9] That tide had swelled during the nineteenth and early twentieth centuries, achieved democratizing successes in the Populist and Progressive eras, and then in the near total breakdown of the political economy in the 1930s found new expression and hope through FDR's New Deal—his own, much-expanded version of Hamilton's "liberal and enlarged plans for the public good." The severe want inflicted on millions of Americans through ever-deepening boom-and-bust cycles over roughly fifty years had prepared the way for FDR's fundamental rethinking of economic rights as a charter for safety net protections and an individual's *positive liberty* to earn a living.[10]

Positive liberty stood in contrast to the *negative liberty* conceived as freedom from governmental restraints to pursue one's life as one saw fit, primarily through the use of one's own property. The latter conception had dominated American thought since the founding era, but the country's political economy developed in a feverish, haphazard, and weakly regulated fashion, creating vast disparities in wealth, with political and economic powers steadily concentrating in new patrician elites and their large corporate trusts. Their abuses helped stimulate populist and progressive movements that demanded governmental intervention on behalf of a rapidly growing, disaffected, and dispossessed population. FDR attacked these elites as the enemies (economic royalists) of policies that could enhance the positive liberties of average people. As Cook indicates, he converted the old individualistic version of humanitarian liberalism into a programmatic version that he defined as liberal and to which he contrasted the conservative or laissez-faire liberalism that he blamed for causing repeated economic collapses. That distinction "has continued and increased in intensity," defining the basic divide between the Democratic and Republican Parties.[11]

FDR then treated the public administration as the vital engine for stable, programmatic implementation of government services and protections. It should buffer these programs from partisan strife under the leadership of a managerial presidency. As Cook describes it, "FDR sought to make the president the center of national electoral politics *and* the engine for the programmatic liberal transformation of American government and politics outside the parties. Public administration, so vital to the creation and sustenance of that liberal program, would replace party as the institutional home for programmatic liberalism because it could be more easily and permanently attached to the president."[12] His plan thus required exclusive control over the public administration under the president and a gathering of the resources and staff needed in the White House to effectively manage all the new and old departments tasked with rebuilding the national economy. That plan was laid out in an elaborate report prepared by the President's Committee on Administrative Management, now commonly referred to as the Brownlow report. John Rohr's analysis of the report underscores its intent "to make the executive branch of the federal government supreme over Congress and the courts." Its underlying premise drew essentially from Andrew Jackson's assertion that true democratic accountability to Congress demanded that all administrative agencies and personnel report directly to the president and be subject to both his appointment and his removal. He should have a *free hand* in all such matters. As Rohr indicated, this far surpassed even Hamilton's "exuberant defense of executive power" in the first Pacificus essay. "Nowhere . . . does Hamilton claim exclusive executive power for the president." Such a claim would effectively collapse the separation of powers into a massive, executive-centered, bureaucratic edifice.[13]

Indeed, the report laid out a plan for centralizing all administrative functions under twelve great departments, including the folding in of all independent boards and commissions, and bringing all personnel functions directly under presidential control. Furthermore, it called for more clearly defined control over financial and budgetary decisions, centering them in the Treasury Department and removing the independent status of the comptroller. The details of these proposals were expanded upon at great length in five companion studies commissioned by FDR. Stephanie Newbold and Larry Terry have examined them in depth and find evidence that the authors "were guided by their knowledge and understanding of American constitutional heritage and the specific application of *Federalist 27* and *Federalist 70* to the contemporary issues affecting executive branch dynamics during the early 20th century."[14]

Newbold and Terry quite rightly tie the entire Brownlow project to "the preservation of the nation's democratic institutions." As Rohr describes in his treatment, this was an important objective at the time, given the threat of war and world domination by authoritarian and totalitarian regimes. Many people, including many Americans, questioned whether democratic republics could remain viable against such threats, especially since their economies had failed so badly with the Great Depression. It became imperative to show that American democracy could still work and that its constitutional heritage still mattered. As such, the distinguished authors of these companion reports explicitly tied their analyses and proposals to Hamilton's *Federalist* essays, specifically to his concept of energy in the executive.[15] Interestingly, Newbold and Terry list the four elements Hamilton included in the concept but then immediately focus on UNITY, capitalized as it was by Hamilton, and described by him in *Federalist* essay 70 as "one of the best distinguishing features of our constitution." They then note that "it is precisely this point that served as the philosophical foundation of the five accompanying studies that represent the complete Brownlow Report."[16] Their subsequent analysis of the reports bears that out.

The problem is that the reports focused on *unity* exclusively and spoke of responsibility only in terms of the increased capacity of the president to manage and hold the subordinate administration accountable. The first report, for example, proposed a Central Personnel Agency that was to serve as a "management arm of the president" and then "suggested 20 ways that such an agency would improve the president's administrative capabilities," as well as twenty more ways to improve personnel administration itself. Among the latter, it recommended that Congress and the president develop "a unified system of personnel administration, particularly for nonpolitical positions."[17] This refers of course to the politics/administration dichotomy made popular in Progressive Era principles of scientific management. The core of the Brownlow report's analysis hinged itself to this simplistic distinction, declaring Congress the controlling policy maker, but with the details of administration left to the executive. The report then proceeded to describe virtually every meaningful function of government as pertaining to administrative management. John Rohr succinctly characterizes the approach: "This tidy arrangement . . . was central to the committee's strategy. By describing virtually every governmental activity as some kind of *administrative management*—personnel management, fiscal management, planning management, or administrative reorganization—the committee asserted the president's power over the government as a whole."[18] Newbold and Terry's analysis of the exhaustive companion reports confirms their adherence to this formulation. In fact, the authors of these reports reinforced it with their detailed management analyses and recommendations. Nowhere in their analyses is there a suggestion that civil servants are constitutional officers in their own right, obliged to follow the law first rather than act as mere agents of the executive. Even duration is treated strictly (and ever so briefly) in instrumental terms as a better means for applying neutral expertise systematically to complex problems. The permanent civil service should be expanded "upward, outward, and downward" and exclusively as the arm of the executive.

Rohr concludes that while "Publius would have approved the Brownlow Committee's broad understanding of administration," he would have been puzzled by the distinction between politics and administration because he "assigned to administration a political task of the highest order; it was through sound administration that the loyalties of the people would gradually be transferred from the states to the federal government."[19] The analysis offered in the preceding chapters shows that Hamilton went much further, treating and training subordinates at all levels as republican exemplars and tying their professionalism in normative terms to honor, to fidelity to the rule of law, and to an abiding sense of the public good. They would be employed to govern and serve the public and, in so doing, play a constitutive role in forming new habits and sensibilities suited to life in a commercial republic. Hamilton believed that the Constitution's shared powers, contributing to the elements of executive energy, were intended to provide this kind of tone to the public service as a whole and that it should exhibit a wholesome measure of independent bearing and judgment in the process.

A Unitary Executive?

The presidencies of Andrew Jackson, Theodore Roosevelt, and FDR illustrate what has become a common tendency to expand executive power: claiming exclusive control over the subordinate public administration and treating it as the instrument for achieving personal agendas. The basis for their claims rested on the assertion of democratic mandates from the people, elevating the executive to a supreme status over the other branches because it captures the broadest representation. Presidents speak for the whole people, or at least a majority of them, while members of Congress represent only their state constituents. This way of thinking is now deeply embedded in the American political psyche and excites public fascination with, and demand for, great national leaders. Jackson was the first president to invoke this plebiscitary model and initiate the claim for exclusive control over the public administration. Theodore Roosevelt touted the persuader and stewardship roles shorn of meaningful constitutional tethers, and FDR fused them with a managerial mindset that would eventually turn the White House into an edifice of centralized administrative control. While each of them brought much-needed changes to fruition, they also laid open the path to the kind of leader the founders viewed as the most common existential threat to republics—the demagogue, an unprincipled leader who exploits fear, stirs up the disaffected segments of the population, and offers himself as a savior. In this classic scenario, many people end up demanding an authoritarian leader to resolve what they see as impending chaos and to establish peace and order in its place. Such leaders are notorious for welding the fears of the populace to an ugly and mean-spirited nationalist agenda. Ominously, the present era shows substantial evidence of a return to such strongman rule around the globe, with the current US president imitating the model.

It is hardly surprising that, as presidents carved this path, their thinking would reshape our common understanding of executive power as controlling over all the public administration. In juridical circles, it birthed the late-twentieth-century legal doctrine of the unitary executive, advocated ironically by some who claim to be originalists in regard to constitutional interpretation and who often invoke Hamilton in support of it.[20] Lessig and Sunstein examine in detail the legal and administrative practices of the founding era and find the doctrine wanting on all fronts. "We think that the view that the framers constitutionalized anything like this vision of the executive is just plain myth. . . . It derives from twentieth century categories applied unreflectively to an eighteenth century document." They argue that the founders used the term "executive" in a more limited sense than many constitutionalists do today. They find strong evidence

that the framers wanted to constitutionalize just some of the array of power a constitution-maker must allocate, and as for the rest, the framers intended Congress (and posterity) to control as it saw fit. Modern constitutionalists find it so hard to see this undeveloped design as the framers' design because modern constitutionalists treat the term "executive" or "legislative" or "judicial" as describing fully developed categories that carve up the world of governmental power without remainder, as if governmental power were the genus, and executive, legislative, or judicial were only the species. But the founders' vision was not so complete, their ideas not so developed, their experience not so extensive, and their intent to constitutionalize just a part of the many issues of governmental power that they understood to confront any government.[21]

The framers freely admitted that their work constituted a grand experiment, and in the nature of such experiments, they had to leave many questions about their design unanswered and many of its clauses ambiguous and puzzling—in part because they could agree neither on a single republican vision nor on how to exactly apportion powers by their abstract categories. Uppermost in their minds, however, lay the experience of abusive executive power under the British monarchy, and that fed their penchant for centering control in a legislative body. Advocates of the unitary executive doctrine thus "ignore strong evidence that the framers imagined not a clear executive hierarchy with the President at its summit, but a large degree of congressional power to structure the administration as it thought proper."[22] Hamilton stood out for his attempt at balancing executive power against the legislative vortex and for touting its aggressive exercise in the face of extreme congressional jealousy, but never did he advance the idea that the president should monopolize the implementation of law.

The Pathology of Instrumental Administration

Throughout this book I have noted the constitutive nature of Hamilton's administrative theory and practice. He deemed the public administration an integral manifestation of the constitutional framework, with its many officials contributing to the character and policies of the new republic. They share fully in its governing. Brian Cook contrasts this aspect of public administration with its instrumental aspect and argues that the first Congress missed a vital opportunity with their statutory *Decision of 1789* to secure recognition of its formative roles. Instead, their close vote to give the president sole power of removal of his principal officers set a powerful precedent for treating all sub-

ordinate officials as mere instruments. A strictly instrumentalist conception of public administration increases its susceptibility to partisan
and electoral manipulation, as well as to misconceiving administrative work as something distinct from both politics and law. It denies
a legitimate political role for the public administration, even though
it cannot help but be political. This sets in motion all kinds of patho-
logical dynamics.[23]

First, it diminishes the stature of public administrators in the eyes
of elected officials and the public and makes it all too easy to dismiss
their political competencies. Second, it deprives them of meaningful
normative guidance for articulating values and ordering priorities and
for responsibly exercising the discretionary powers assigned to them.
The lack of such guidance often confines the ethical sense among
publicly employed professionals to the standards of their specialized
professions, without any overarching sense of how they may be normatively grounded by values in the broader political system. And as
Cook indicates, it reduces formal government ethics training to the
minimal task of "preventing bad behavior." This can lead to a kind of
professional and bureaucratic myopia that eschews politics in general
as irrational and antithetical to effective work and reduces the official to one who instrumentally balances trade-offs among aggregated
preferences.[24] Michael Spicer addresses this problem head on in *In
Defense of Politics*, where he criticizes the field of public administration
for embracing a morally arid social-scientific approach that "down-
plays the conflict and uncertainty" that is endemic to governing and
ignores the capacity of politics to reason about and resolve "conflict
among competing ends or conceptions of the good . . . without recourse to any sort of scientific algorithm." This critique is very much
in line with Hamilton's excoriation of empirics and their abstract refinements that travel beyond the bounds of human nature.[25]

Third, and relatedly, Cook argues that intrumentalism enervates
the role of administrators as civic educators, who should bring insights
on governance to bear in public forums and thereby "contribute to
the *formative popular political experience* that sustains and advances the
regime." It weakens their ability and resolve to keep salient public
values in play as private interests seek their own advantage.[26]

Fourth, instrumentalism promotes excessive responsiveness to popular and constituent demands, and this "exacerbates the mutability of
public policy" and its administration, especially when the views and
demands of the public and its elected officials are polarized. Program-

matic fluctuations and reversals amplify with each swing in partisan control.[27]

Fifth, the claimed neutrality of instrumental administration is continually betrayed by the fact that subordinates all the way to the street-level exercise significant degrees and types of discretion. In recent decades, this realization has led elected policy makers to push at-will employment status further down agency hierarchies to make them yet more accountable and responsive, deepening the mutability of administration as it goes.[28]

Finally, the mutability in administration is amplified further through the ritual of reorganization carried out by successive administrations under the banner of improving administrative efficiency. Since the Progressive Era, reformers have argued that the science of management and organization would save money while improving services. But there is usually little science involved and little, if any, savings, because more often than not the overarching agenda is to further centralize, or recentralize, executive control over the public administration. That was the primary aim of FDR's massive reorganization effort, and it produced a never-ending train of reorganization efforts thereafter, with much the same goal in mind. Significantly, however, such efforts have provoked institutional responses by Congress and the courts to challenge the expanding executive reach. Despite repeated attempts to transcend the separation of powers design, the logic of blended powers under the Constitution remains in play, with the branches pushing and pulling for their share of control over the public administration.

The Rough Continuity of Separate Branches Sharing Powers

Since its inception, the Constitution's design of separate branches sharing governing power has engendered constant and jealous efforts to control the public administration. During much of the nineteenth century, the balance tipped in favor of congressional dominance and states' rights doctrine, but the press of wars and depressions animated presidential assertions of power that would eventually put the executive branch in the lead. Hamilton predicted that the executive power might grow out of its bounds for exactly these reasons. By the nature of its design, the executive enjoys the power of initiative and the ability to respond immediately to emergencies, and this gives it an advantage over the deliberative design of Congress and the courts.

However, every presidential gain is eventually met by institutional responses from the other branches. For example, David Rosenbloom describes how Congress gradually adapted to the burgeoning of executive power during the New Deal era by reorganizing its committee structure, adding congressional staff to improve budgetary review, passing the Administrative Procedure Act of 1946 to structure agency rulemaking and adjudicative processes, and delegating time-consuming constituent services to relevant agencies. In the years since, it has steadily increased its oversight and vastly improved its program evaluation and budget management capacities through new institutions such as the Congressional Budget Office that now rival the capabilities and reputations of executive branch counterparts.[29] Likewise, the courts responded by applying more scrutiny to executive agency powers and processes and to the impact of these powers and processes on individuals, groups, public personnel, and a variety of agency and policy fronts. The courts at times also have imposed remedial orders on agencies for egregious and repeated violations of rights and have supervised agency responses over extended periods.[30] In other work, Rosenbloom has illustrated how each branch imposes its values and processes on agency operations and routinely contributes to their ongoing governance.[31]

To at least a modest degree, then, the constitutional superstructure has operated as intended, though under tremendous strain. The power of the presidency is now frightening in its magnitude and continually bolstered by what seems a condition of perpetual military conflict and economic disruption. Such conditions contribute significantly to the erosion of public confidence and trust, the very things Hamilton deemed essential to the viability of the republic. He hoped that presidents would provide confident, centripetal leadership as a counter to the centrifugal forces inherent to a regime of separate powers operating in a milieu of factional politics and disruptive events. Given the subsequent history and dynamics of the presidency, it seems problematic at best to expect consistent exercise of such leadership. Moreover, the size and scope of the federal government today is so great that it requires centripetal leadership at many levels and across many venues, and public administrators are well positioned to exercise it.

The primary work of centripetal leadership is to knit together stable relationships between the branches in such a way that they can be relied upon to mute and channel conflicts, preserve at least a rough balance of power, facilitate mutual understanding and agreements, and preserve the viability and roles of the players. Such work must often proceed in a low-key manner, under the surface as it were, and that is how most administrators operate. Many of them already exercise centripetal leadership, though without any formal recognition of its significance. Substantial evidence exists, however, that the role has steadily declined in the senior administrative ranks of the federal government. A significant factor in this decline has much to do with the establishment of the Senior Executive Service (SES) under the provisions of the Civil Service Reform Act of 1978.

The stated intent by the designers of the SES was to establish a corporate-styled cadre of management generalists who could be deployed across agencies to help improve interbranch and interagency cooperation, as well as internal agency administration. The intentions never panned out because the design required the sacrifice of civil service protections in exchange for promises of enhanced pay and generous bonus incentives. As executive officials, they became subject to the whims of political appointees and White House agendas. In-depth, periodic studies of the SES have consistently discovered low morale, increased turnover, failed promises, and increasing politicization. Most significantly, these senior executives lost the capacity they once had to bridge and sustain mutual understandings and close relationships across the branches. Thus, the institutional knitting frayed at the highest levels of the superstructure.[32] Rebuilding these relationships seems imperative, but that cannot happen without the provision of a meaningful measure of independence and substantial duration in senior administrative positions. That at least would meet Hamilton's criteria for a senior public service capable of exercising effective centripetal roles.

Peri Arnold argues, however, that Hamilton's "ideal of public service for effective administration . . . was short-lived in practice because the Constitution contained no institutional means to maintain it against the contradictory forces within separate institutions sharing powers."[33] He may be right, but it seems plausible that a statutory fix along similar lines to the SES, but with the requisite protections against politicization, might suffice. It may require thinking in terms of a cadre that reports to both Congress and the president, much like Hamilton and the comptroller of the treasury did. Recall that the Treasury was not designated an executive department. It floated between the branches. The current office of the comptroller of the currency, first established in the Lincoln administration, comes to mind as a rough correlate. It is an independent regulatory bureau within the Treasury Department whose mission is to preserve the integrity of the federal banking system. The comptroller is appointed for a five-year term by the president with the consent of the Senate and oversees a significant professional cadre who help maintain interagency relationships and operations. Designing and implementing a similar institution for a select body of senior administrators poses some daunting challenges, but those are probably easier to meet, under the right conditions, than the challenges of amending the Constitution.

Furthermore, the dearth of centripetal leadership is most acute at the top level, but the federal government is huge and flung far across the country and world in myriad agencies and authorities. As stated in the opening chapter, much of that complex inter-organizational field continues to operate effectively with routine and relatively harmonious interbranch relations despite periodic attempts at cutting budgets and disrupting operations and despite the continual press of influential, co-opting interests. Thus, the Hamiltonian legacy has not been entirely compromised, frittered away in the sea of jarring interests, or completely gridlocked. Moreover, the corpus of his administrative theory and practice remains salient in many respects and constitutes perhaps the most prominent administrative tradition in our system.[34] It has had much, though certainly not everything, to do with bringing his vision of a bustling commercial republic to fruition.

While the internal stresses and messiness of our constitutional system pose many problems, few of them seem to present an existential threat. But those that do should receive our rapt attention. Immense presidential power made sympathetic to the clamor for strongman rule poses a dangerous challenge but not an impossible one, especially if the officials and institutions arrayed around and under the executive are prepared to temper and resist it. A fuller understanding of Hamilton's theory of administrative responsibility makes it clear that the public service should play a significant role.

Contemplating "the Evils Concomitant with Temporal Blessing"

The founders, and Hamilton specifically, took seriously Aristotle's maxim that regimes tend to die from an excess of their own virtues. Thus, they feared that taking democracy too far would threaten individual rights and thereby lead a republic into despotism. Correspondingly, they feared that taking rights too far would jeopardize the ability to govern effectively. They wrestled with the problem of giving too much power to govern as well as giving too little. And they worried

over the prospect that a limited government, devoted primarily to enhancing the material conditions of political society, would erode civic
virtue and thereby unleash, in Hamilton's words, "all those vices which
corrupt government, enslave the people and precipitate the ruin of
a nation." The Constitution of 1787 represented their best collective attempt at moderating these extremes. On paper, it presented an
elegant design, and yet they all knew that the document reflected a
bundle of compromises and a host of uncertainties and ambiguities
for those who governed to work out as they and the American people
saw fit. And despite their hopes, few if any of them expected that the
experiment would last much longer than a generation or two.

That our commercial republic has endured to this day would shock
them, and it should amaze us. We are now far more democratic in
spirit and prolific with rights claims. Both conditions pose serious
challenges, but we appear able to cope with them, to keep them in a
workable if tenuous balance. The more insidious and seemingly in-
exorable problem manifests itself in the effects of economic success—
"the evils concomitant with temporal blessing." As Hamilton might
have expected, we have reached a stage of such opulence and devotion to capitalism that the market principle now pervades all sectors
and institutions of society. We tout it as a panacea and yet bemoan its
rampant materialism, its proliferation of vice and luxury, its enerva-
tion of social capital, and its corrosion of traditional institutions. We
turn citizens into consumers and too often neglect or even revile public things. Such conditions unleash the greed and mendacity of capitalists who "throw trade into channels inimical to the public interest"
and, by steady degrees, drive the wedge of extreme inequality into the
heart of the political order. Hamilton doubted that in the long run
we could avoid these extremes, and they are now ours to confront.

Ameliorating these conditions requires thoughtful reforms on many
fronts, many of which must come from the ground up. However, it
is the federal government that must address the disparities in power
and wealth that exacerbate inequality. Without that, it will be impossible to regain the public's confidence that national government is
there to serve the people as a whole in meaningful ways. We now know
from experience how to reduce such extreme disparity through policies affecting employment, education, taxation, public finance, and
the economy.

In the arenas of taxation, public finance, and the economy, we can
still benefit from Hamilton's insight and attitude. He sought to use
wealth for public purposes, to channel it for public benefit. He had

no intention of turning his commercial republic into a commercial oligarchy. Though he never got the chance to achieve it, he anticipated establishing a broad spectrum of taxes in a progressive manner, thus drawing the bulk of revenue from those whose extensive wealth derived in part from economic polices favorable to their success. He helped design the engine of wealth through public finance, and to this day it still bolsters and subsidizes the financial system and the economy as a whole. But he would be alarmed at how that system now concentrates wealth for private agendas without the corresponding public benefit. He designed it with public-regarding principles in mind—to make it transparent and to enforce upon it standards of simplicity and stability that would convince the general public that the system ultimately served them. His policy of balancing and tempering the promotion of economic development with its firm regulation served the same end. Markets in general do not effectively regulate themselves, and they can operate successfully only on an infrastructure built, maintained, and protected by governments.

We cannot understand Hamilton's theory of public administration without understanding these things. He intended the constitutional design not only to protect the liberties of the American people but also to enhance them with a rich array of occupations and pursuits made possible through a diversified political economy. What is often lost in this, however, is that these twin pursuits also require a robust public life to sustain them. Hamilton's theory of administrative responsibility directs our attention to public things: to the need for public institutions and protocols, to public morality, and to the abiding need for public-spiritedness. His theory presumes, therefore, that economic rationality must ultimately be guided and limited by a broader set of public values that should inform political rationality. The pervasiveness of economic rationality today thus threatens the viability of public life.

To conclude, the breadth and depth of Alexander Hamilton's public administration theory offer much to ponder in the current era. At the very least, the analysis presented in this book illustrates Hamilton's relevance as a source of perspective and critique. Study of the founding period in general offers much by way of comparison and contrast and provides a means of putting ourselves in dialogue with our past. The normative quality we attribute to the period sustains the salience of the founders' thought and practice and binds us to them even as we depart from their standards in significant ways. We are obligated to explain to ourselves and others why we depart from, reinterpret, or adapt what they constituted. Thus, in the current era, when so many Americans clamor for a return to the Constitution, one can hardly ignore Hamilton. And yet, it is remarkable that in all the assertions and arguments about what constitutional propriety means, no attention is paid in the public square to the central role that public administration plays in his thought and practice. It is simply absent from public discourse in any positive sense. Rather, it is attacked as an illegitimate appendage to the constitutional system, as if somehow the three branches of the national government could and should carry on the affairs of the country without it. If this book does nothing else, it should disabuse readers of that notion.

Hamilton went further than anyone in establishing public administration as an integral extension of the three-branch superstructure of American government. He wanted an ambitious and powerful national government to establish institutions staffed by highly qualified public servants who would carry out the vital functions he believed necessary to a commercial republic. At a minimum, these include institutions for stimulating and regulating a robust political economy for the sake of multiplying the opportunities, occupations, and avocations of the people; for maintaining effective defense and foreign policy establishments; for building, maintaining, and updating the national transportation and communications infrastructure; and for educating, training, and socializing the corps of public servants and military personnel who would administer these affairs.

Americans can and should argue over the extent of federal responsibilities vis-à-vis the states and the other sectors of political society, but it should surprise no one that as the system developed, new responsibilities and demands emerged at all levels of government, especially as reliance on the agrarian communities of the nation gave way to dependence on industrial cities. Mass migration, depressions, exploitation, and the social pressures of urbanization would demand more governmental response and intervention. Hamilton looked forward in time, not satisfied with the status quo, and was clearly ready to adapt and expand governance to such changing needs of the country. He couched law and administrative process in developmental terms, making the administrative machinery of the procedural republic useful for his and succeeding generations.

Hamilton wanted more harmony in administration than the new constitutional system ultimately provided, and the intense partisanship and acrimony he experienced have become persistent features of American governance, in large part because the American people have always held conflicting visions of the kind of republic they want. Over time we have integrated aspects of these competing visions into our administration at all levels of government, but we have done so in the context of an emerging, complex political economy that reflects more of Hamilton's intentions and vision than any other founder's. We fight our political battles on his ground, just as Jefferson feared. The public administration today therefore plays a central rather than a peripheral role in American governance, and Hamilton is its most brilliant advocate.

Abbreviations

Caldwell, *ATH&J*	Lynton K. Caldwell. *The Administrative Theories of Hamilton and Jefferson: Their Contribution to Thought on Public Administration.* 2nd ed. New York: Holmes & Meier, 1988. First published 1944 by University of Chicago Press (Chicago), with second printing 1964 by Russell & Russell (New York).
Chernow, *AH*	Ron Chernow. *Alexander Hamilton.* New York: Penguin, 2004.
Federalist	Alexander Hamilton, James Madison, and John Jay. *The Federalist Papers.* With an introduction, table of contents, and index of ideas by Clinton Rossiter. New York: New American Library, 1961.
Federici, *PPAH*	Michael Federici. *The Political Philosophy of Alexander Hamilton.* Baltimore, MD: Johns Hopkins University Press, 2012.
LPAH	*The Law Practice of Alexander Hamilton: Documents and Commentary.* 5 vols. Edited by Julius Goebel Jr. New York: Columbia University Press, 1964–81.
Lycan, *AH&AFP*	Gilbert L. Lycan. *Alexander Hamilton and American Foreign Policy: A Design for Greatness.* Norman: University of Oklahoma Press, 1970.
McDonald, *AH*	Forrest McDonald. *Alexander Hamilton: A Biography.* New York: W. W. Norton, 1979.
McNamara, *PE&S*	Peter McNamara. *Political Economy and Statesmanship: Smith, Hamilton, and the Foundation of*

the Commercial Republic. DeKalb: Northern Illinois University Press, 1998.

Miller, *AH*   John C. Miller. *Alexander Hamilton: Portrait in Paradox.* New York: Harper & Row, 1959.

PAH   *The Papers of Alexander Hamilton.* 27 vols. Edited by Harold C. Syrett and Jacob E. Cooke. New York: Columbia University Press, 1969–79.

Notes

A note on emphasis in quotations: emphasis will be acknowledged only when it is not original to the quotation.

Introduction

1. Ron Chernow, *Alexander Hamilton* (New York: Penguin, 2004) (hereafter cited as Chernow, *AH*).

2. Edward Delman quoting Lin-Manuel Miranda in "How Lin-Manuel Miranda Shapes History," *Atlantic*, September 29, 2015, http://www.theatlantic.com/entertainment/archive/2015/09/lin-manuel-miranda-hamilton/408019.

3. Rebecca Mead, "All About the Hamiltons: A New Musical Brings the Founding Fathers Back to Life—with a lot of Hip-Hop," *New Yorker*, February 9, 2015, http://www.newyorker.com/magazine/2015/02/09/hamiltons.

4. For an in-depth analysis of the persistent, negative myths about Hamilton, see Stephen F. Knott, *Alexander Hamilton and the Persistence of Myth* (Lawrence: University Press of Kansas, 2002).

5. See Dwight Waldo, *The Administrative State: A Study of the Political Theory of American Public Administration* (New York: Holmes & Meier, 1948).

6. For a typology of constitutional approaches found among these scholars, see Douglas F. Morgan, Richard T. Green, Craig W. Shinn, and Kent S. Robinson, *Foundations of Public Service*, 2nd ed. (Armonk, NY: M. E. Sharpe, 2013), 18–20. For excellent examples of work that contributes to the Constitutional School of public administration, see John A. Rohr, *Ethics for Bureaucrats: An Essay on Law and Values* (Lawrence: University Press of Kansas, 1989); John A. Rohr, *To Run a Constitution: The Legitimacy of the Administrative State* (Lawrence: University Press of Kansas, 1986); David H. Rosenbloom, *Building a Legislative-Centered Public Administration: Congress and the Administrative State, 1946–1999* (Tuscaloosa: University of Alabama Press, 2000); David H. Rosenbloom, *Federal Service and the Constitution: The Development of the Public Employment Relationship* (Ithaca, NY: Cornell University Press, 1971); Morgan, Green, Shinn, and Robinson, *Foundations of Public*

Service, Stephanie P. Newbold and David H. Rosenbloom, eds., *The Constitutional School of American Public Administration* (New York: Routledge, 2016); Phillip J. Cooper, *Public Law and Public Administration*, 4th ed. (Belmont, CA: Thomson-Wadsworth, 2007); Michael W. Spicer, *The Founders, the Constitution, and Public Administration* (Washington, DC: Georgetown University Press, 1995); Michael W. Spicer, *Public Administration and the State* (Tuscaloosa: University of Alabama Press, 2001); and Michael W. Spicer, *In Defense of Politics in Public Administration: A Value Pluralist Perspective* (Tuscaloosa: University of Alabama Press, 2010). Herbert Storing's work is concisely explained in Douglas F. Morgan, Kent A. Kirwan, John A. Rohr, David H. Rosenbloom, and David Lewis Schaeffer, "Recovering, Restoring, and Renewing the Foundations of American Public Administration: The Contributions of Herbert A. Storing," *Public Administration Review* 70, no. 4 (2010): 621–33.

7. Lynton K. Caldwell, *The Administrative Theories of Hamilton and Jefferson: Their Contribution to Thought on Public Administration*, 2nd ed. (New York: Holmes & Meier, 1988), xix (hereafter cited as Caldwell, *ATH&J*).

8. Harvey Flaumenhaft, *The Effective Republic: Administration and Constitution in the Thought of Alexander Hamilton* (Durham, NC: Duke University Press, 1992); Karl-Friedrich Walling, *Republican Empire: Alexander Hamilton on War and Free Government* (Lawrence: University Press of Kansas, 1999); Knott, *Alexander Hamilton and the Persistence of Myth*; Peter McNamara, *Political Economy and Statesmanship: Smith, Hamilton, and the Foundation of the Commercial Republic* (DeKalb: Northern Illinois University Press, 1998) (hereafter cited as McNamara, *PE&S*); John Lamberton Harper, *American Machiavelli: Alexander Hamilton and the Origins of U.S. Foreign Policy* (New York: Cambridge University Press, 2004); Michael Chan, *Aristotle and Hamilton on Commerce and Statesmanship* (Columbia: University of Missouri Press, 2006); Michael Federici, *The Political Philosophy of Alexander Hamilton* (Baltimore, MD: Johns Hopkins University Press, 2012) (hereafter cited as Federici, *PPAH*); and Thomas K. McCraw, *The Founders and Finance: How Hamilton, Gallatin, and Other Immigrants Forged a New Economy* (Cambridge, MA: Belknap-Harvard University Press, 2012).

9. Gerald Stourzh, *Alexander Hamilton and the Idea of Republican Government* (Stanford, CA: Stanford University Press, 1970). David Epstein, *The Political Theory of "The Federalist"* (Chicago: University of Chicago Press, 1984).

10. Flaumenhaft, *Effective Republic*, 2.

11. Flaumenhaft, *Effective Republic*, 3.

12. Herbert Storing, "Political Parties and the Bureaucracy," in *Political Parties U.S.A.*, ed. Robert A. Goldwin (Chicago: Rand McNally, 1964), 147.

13. Forrest McDonald, *Alexander Hamilton: A Biography* (New York: W. W. Norton, 1979) (hereafter cited as McDonald, *AH*). Also see Forrest McDonald, *Novus Ordo Seclorum: The Intellectual Origins of the Constitution* (Lawrence: University Press of Kansas, 1985), and *We the People: The Economic Origins of the Constitution* (New Brunswick, NJ: Transaction, 1992).

14. Leonard D. White, *The Federalists: A Study in Administrative History* (Westport, CT: Greenwood, 1948), 478. Hamilton's definition occurs in

Alexander Hamilton, James Madison, and John Jay, *The Federalist Papers*, with an introduction, table of contents, and index of ideas by Clinton Rossiter (New York: New American Library, 1961), no. 72, 435–36 (hereafter cited as *Federalist*).

15. Caldwell, *ATH&J*, xiv.

16. See Clinton Rossiter, *Alexander Hamilton and the Constitution* (New York: Harcourt, Brace & World, 1964), 254; Flaumenhaft, *Effective Republic*, passim.

17. Chernow, *AH*, 4.

18. McDonald, *AH*, 3.

19. Hamilton to Robert Morris, April 30, 1781, *The Papers of Alexander Hamilton*, 27 vols., ed. Harold C. Syrett and Jacob E. Cooke (New York: Columbia University Press, 1969–79), 2:617–18 (hereafter cited as *PAH*).

20. See Hamilton's *Continentalist* no. 4, *PAH*, 2:669–74; *Report on Manufactures*, *PAH*, 10:230–340. For a good summary of Hamilton's predictions concerning economic and regulatory policy, see Caldwell, *ATH&J*, 63–79.

21. See chapter 6 for elaboration of this point.

22. Flaumenhaft, *Effective Republic*, chap. 6, 69–81.

23. See Flaumenhaft, *Effective Republic*, 2–3. Clinton Rossiter noted Hamilton's warning that "the American political system would crash in ruins . . . if a science of administration did not come in time to replace the very vague and confined notions of the practical business of government." Rossiter, *Alexander Hamilton and the Constitution*, 174. Caldwell said, "Hamilton anticipated an objective science of administration." Caldwell, *ATH&J*, 3.

24. Richard B. Morris, *The Basic Ideas of Hamilton* (New York: Pocket, 1957), xix; Rossiter (quoting Morris), *Alexander Hamilton and the Constitution* (New York: Harcourt, Brace & World, 1964), 10.

25. Chernow, *AH*, 4.

26. Hamilton was born in Charleston on Nevis Island. Though he claimed to have been born in 1757, there is more evidence (no definitive proof) that he was born in 1755. See Chernow, *AH*, 16–17. For an extensive account of his illegitimacy, see Chernow, *AH*, 7–28.

27. Chernow, *AH*, 29–30.

28. Chernow, *AH*, 30–40.

29. Chernow, *AH*, 42–43.

30. Chernow, *AH*, 43.

31. Chernow, *AH*, 53.

32. Hamilton made his famous *Speech in the Fields* on July 6, 1774, in New York City, where he impressed several leaders of the independence movement. His first pamphlet, *A Full Vindication of the Measures of the Continental Congress*, replying to *Free Thoughts on Congress*, by A. W. Farmer (Samuel Seabury), was published on December 15, 1774. Soon thereafter, he published *The Farmer Refuted* in response to Seabury's *A View of the Controversy* (Feb. 1775), and *Remarks on the Quebec Bill, Parts One and Two* (June 1775). See *PAH*, 1:45–176.

33. *PAH*, 1:158. Chernow, *AH*, 61.

34. See Chernow, *AH*, 83–85.

35. For in-depth treatments of Hamilton's role as Washington's aide-de-camp, see Chernow, *AH*, chap. 5; and Broadus Mitchell, *Alexander Hamilton: Youth to Maturity, 1755–1788* (New York: Macmillan, 1957), chaps. 8–14.

36. See Chernow, *AH*, 158, 206.

37. See "Letters to Phocion," *PAH*, 3:483–97, 530–58. For more detail on Hamilton's defense of Tory property rights, see Chernow, *AH*, 197–99.

38. Chernow, *AH*, 198.

39. See *PAH*, 3:686–90; Chernow, *AH*, 220–24.

40. The charge that Hamilton was a monarchist was used very effectively thereafter by his opponents as a political weapon. It was refuted by Hamilton himself, as well as by later historians, biographers, and analysts. For example, see Mitchell, *Alexander Hamilton: Youth to Maturity*, 393–403; James Madison, *Notes of Debates in the Federal Convention of 1787*, ed. Adrienne Koch (Athens: Ohio University Press, 1966), 129–39, 152–53; and *PAH*, 25:536–39 and 26:147–49, for specific rebuttals by Hamilton concerning his monarchism. See Louise Dunbar, *A Study of Monarchical Tendencies in the United States from 1776 to 1801* (Urbana: University of Illinois, 1922), 82–98, 124–26, for a defense of Hamilton against charges of being a monarchist, and Rossiter, *Alexander Hamilton and the Constitution*, 314n1.

That Hamilton's real intent in his speech was to move the center of debate back to the Virginia Plan is supported by Broadus Mitchell and many other biographers and historians. For example, see Mitchell, *Alexander Hamilton: Youth to Maturity*, 392; and John C. Miller, *Alexander Hamilton: Portrait in Paradox* (New York: Harper & Row, 1959), 162–69 (hereafter cited as Miller, *AH*). His desire to retain "the excellencies of republican government" and to have its "imperfections lessened or avoided" is reiterated in *Federalist*, no. 9.

41. Chernow, *AH*, 242.

42. Chernow, *AH*, 271.

43. Chernow, *AH*, 257.

44. See Robert Hendrickson, *Hamilton*, vol. 1 (New York: Mason/Charter, 1976), chap. 24; and Mitchell, *Alexander Hamilton: The National Adventure*, chap. 2.

45. For details on the congressional debate about the Treasury Act, see McDonald, *AH*, 128–33, and *Debates and Proceedings in the Congress of the United States* (Washington, DC: Gales and Seaton, 1834), 592–607, 611–15. Much of the debate centered on the secretary's powers, that is, whether the Treasury should be run by a board or single head, how and what a single head should *report* or *prepare* for Congress' deliberations, and how his accountability to Congress could be insured and balanced with his accountability to the president.

46. The records of Hamilton's law practice are extensive and form a separate collection. See Alexander Hamilton, *The Law Practice of Alexander Hamilton: Documents and Commentary*, 5 vols., ed. Julius Goebel Jr. (New York: Columbia University Press, 1964–81) (hereafter cited as *LPAH*).

47. For example, see Thomas Jefferson to John Adams, October 28, 1813, in *The Adams-Jefferson Letters*, 2 vols., ed. Lester J. Cappon (Chapel Hill: University of North Carolina Press, 1959), 2:388, 391.

48. See Alexander Hamilton to John Jay, March 14, 1779, *PAH*, 2:17–19.

49. Charles A. Beard, *An Economic Interpretation of the Constitution* (New York: Macmillan, 1935), 100–101, 114. Also see Vernon Louis Parrington, *Main Currents in American Thought* (New York: Harcourt Brace, 1927), 1:292–304; and Thomas P. Govan, "The Rich, the Well-born, and Alexander Hamilton," *Mississippi Valley Historical Review* 36, no. 4 (1950): 675–80.

50. Mitchell, *Alexander Hamilton: Youth to Maturity*, xii.

Chapter 1

1. For Madison, see *Federalist*, no. 39, 240–41. For Hamilton, see *PAH*, 5:149–52, and *PAH*, 25:536–37.

2. He first used this term in 1777 in reference to the state of New York. See Alexander Hamilton to Gouverneur Morris, May 19, 1777, *PAH*, 1:255.

3. See Federici's discussion, *PPAH*, 55–61, quote at 60, of works on Hamilton by Darren Staloff, Henry May, and Michael J. Rosano, which characterize him as a thoroughly modern liberal thinker, though they acknowledge some salutary influence from earlier ages. As will be shown, many of the founders mixed classical and Christian tenets with modern liberal ideas. They lived during the transition from ancient to modern principles of governance, and most (but certainly not all) were more eclectic and pragmatic than ideological in their attraction to liberal principles of their day. That was certainly the case with Hamilton. Federici employs this perspective as well, as does Chan in *Aristotle and Hamilton*, 6–9.

4. *PAH*, 25:537.

5. Federici, *PPAH*, 116–17. The influence of these and other jurisprudes will be treated further in chapter 4. As Paul Sigmund notes, "In ancient and medieval thought the law of nations referred to the common elements in all legal systems, rather than to its modern meaning as international law." *St. Thomas Aquinas on Politics and Ethics*, ed. Paul E. Sigmund (New York: W. W. Norton, 1988), 54n7.

6. *Farmer Refuted*, Feb. 23, 1775, *PAH*, 1:87, 136. As McDonald, *AH*, xii, notes, writers such as Hobbes "turned out upon careful study to have thought patterns so different from Hamilton's mode of thinking as to rule out the likelihood of influence." Also see Chan, *Aristotle and Hamilton*, 62–63, 79. For a good description of the "general jurisprudence" of the period, see Edward S. Corwin, *The "Higher Law" Background of American Constitutional Law* (Ithaca, NY: Cornell University Press, 1928); William Winslow Crosskey, *Politics and the Constitution in the History of the United States* (Chicago: University of Chicago Press, 1953), vol. 1, chaps. 18, 19; James Kent, *Commentaries on American Law*, 4 vols. (New York: D. Halsted, 1826; Da Capo Press, 1971), 1:1–169; and Stourzh, *Alexander Hamilton and the Idea of Republican Government*, 11–24. For a brief review of the origins and development of natural law, see Paul E. Sigmund, *Natural Law in Political Thought* (Cambridge, MA: Winthrop, 1971).

7. Jacques Maritain, *Man and the State* (Chicago: University of Chicago Press, 1951), 50.

8. Maritain, *Man and the State*, chap. 2. This formulation had crystal-

lized in the writings of Jean Bodin in the sixteenth century and provided the basis for French royal absolutism.

9. Maritain, *Man and the State*, chap. 2. Maritain provides an excellent analysis of the original meaning of sovereignty, and argues persuasively that the term "sovereignty" should be abandoned because its meaning is hopelessly confused in applications to modern liberal republics.

10. *PAH*, 8:98. The formal definition of plenary power from that time fits the way I use it here. See the *Oxford English Dictionary*.

11. See "A Letter from Phocion to the Considerate Citizens of New York" and "Second Letter from Phocion," 1784, *PAH*, 3:485, 548–49. The Second Letter is especially valuable for seeing the relation of positive law and government to principles of natural law and justice. The analysis presented here also generally follows that of McDonald, *AH*, chap. 3, 49–69; Federici, *PPAH*, 105–13; Stourzh, *Alexander Hamilton and the Idea of Republican Government*, chap. 2, 38–75. Also see People v. Croswell, 3 Johns, 337 (NY 1804), where Hamilton argues that the common law's foundation is also in natural law.

12. See Federici, *PPAH*, 105–13; Stourzh, *Alexander Hamilton and the Idea of Republican Government*, 58–61, and Ernest Barker, *Traditions of Civility* (Cambridge, 1948), 341. Also note the following statement from Hamilton regarding the sovereignty of the government in relation to the presidency, in marked contrast to that of the king under the British constitution: "But in our Constitution the President is not the Sovereign; the sovereignty is vested in the Government, collectively; and it is of the sovereignty, strictly and technically speaking, that a public officer holds his office." *PAH*, 25:571.

13. *Federalist*, no. 15, 110, 112. See Federici's elaboration of these points at *PPAH*, 105–13.

14. *PAH*, 2:662.

15. *PAH*, 2:663.

16. *Federalist*, no. 23, 156.

17. Federici, *PPAH*, 112.

18. Chernow, *AH*, 289. Hamilton's administrative jurisprudence is addressed at length in chapter 3.

19. Tully no. 3, *PAH*, 17:160.

20. Samuel J. Konefsky, *John Marshall and Alexander Hamilton: Architects of the American Constitution* (New York: MacMillan, 1964), 9.

21. Federici, *PPAH*, 54.

22. Alexander Hamilton to Edward Carrington, May 26, 1792, *PAH*, 11:443.

23. See Mitchell, *Alexander Hamilton: Youth to Maturity*, 83–84.

24. Alexander Hamilton to Timothy Pickering, February 21, 1799, *PAH*, 22:492. Also see Chernow, *AH*, 73.

25. Alexander Hamilton to Lafayette, January 6, 1799, *PAH*, 22:404.

26. *Federalist*, no. 17, 119.

27. Herbert J. Storing, *What the Anti-Federalists Were FOR: The Political Thought of the Opponents of the Constitution* (Chicago: University of Chicago Press, 1981), 71.

28. See Chernow, *AH*, chaps. 15, 18.

29. *PAH*, 26:148; and *New York Ratifying Convention: Notes for Speech of July 12, 1788*, New York Ratifying Convention, *PAH*, 5:149–51.

30. Flaumenhaft, *Effective Republic*, 50–51.

31. Flaumenhaft, *Effective Republic*, 58.

32. Federici, *PPAH*, 133–34.

33. Federici, *PPAH*, 134.

34. See Rohr, *To Run a Constitution*, 185n31.

35. White, *The Federalists*. For a historical treatment of the saga of representation in federal hiring, see Douglas F. Morgan, Richard T. Green, Craig W. Shinn, and Kent S. Robinson, "A Political History of Public Personnel Administration," in *Foundations of Public Service*, 2nd ed. (Armonk, NY: M. E. Sharpe, 2013), 199–232.

36. Treasury Department Circular to the Captains of the Revenue Cutters, *PAH*, 8:432–33.

37. Chernow, *AH*, 292.

38. *PAH*, 8:432–33.

39. Caldwell, *ATH&J*, 35.

40. Madison and Hamilton borrowed these insights from David Hume, *Philosophical Works*, vol. 3, *Essays: Moral, Political, and Literary*, ed. T. H. Gross (Boston: Little Brown, 1889), 39–41.

41. Storing, *What the Anti-Federalists Were FOR*, 7.

42. See *Federalist*, no. 6, 56; and *Federalist*, no. 8, 71. Also see McNamara's treatment of the same at 108–13. This analysis follows mainly his work and that by Storing and McDonald.

43. Patrick Henry, speaking at the Virginia Ratifying Convention. See Herbert J. Storing, *The Complete Anti-Federalist*, vol. 5 (Chicago: University of Chicago Press, 1981), 5:214.

44. Storing, *The Complete Anti-Federalist*, 6:158.

45. Storing, *The Complete Anti-Federalist*, 7:23.

46. McDonald, *Novus Ordo Seclorum*, 106–7.

47. McDonald, *Novus Ordo Seclorum*.

48. McDonald, *Novus Ordo Seclorum*, 109 and 131.

49. Adam Smith, *An Inquiry into the Nature and Causes of the Wealth of Nations*, 2 vols., 4th ed. (Dublin, 1785), 1:26–27, 456. See McDonald's discussion in *Novus Ordo Seclorum*, 124.

50. McDonald, *Novus Ordo Seclorum*, 134–35.

51. McDonald, *Novus Ordo Seclorum*, 135.

52. *Federalist*, no. 6, 54.

53. *Federalist*, no. 6, 56–57.

54. *Federalist*, no. 7, 60–66.

55. Chan, *Aristotle and Hamilton*, 185–212, quotation at 186. Chan is drawing from passages in Aristotle's *Nicomachean Ethics*, Book 4, and his *Politics*, Book 7. Flaumenhaft also mentions Hamilton's advocacy of liberality in both foreign and domestic concerns in Camillus no. 22 (1795), where he "commended America for making it a policy to bottom our system with regard to foreign nations upon 'those grounds of moderation and equity,

by which reason, religion, and philosophy had tempered the harsh maxims of more early times'—'these salutary advances toward improvement in true civilization and humanity.'" Flaumenhaft, *Effective Republic*, 33.

56. Flaumenhaft, *Effective Republic*, 188–89.

57. *PAH*, 19:383–84.

58. *PAH*, 19:383–84.

59. Chan, *Aristotle and Hamilton*, 194.

Chapter 2

1. Brian J. Cook articulates the constitutive qualities of American public administration, distinguishing this from the common view of it as a mere instrument of policy makers. Hamilton treated public administration explicitly in constitutive terms. See Brian J. Cook, *Bureaucracy and Self-Government: Reconsidering the Role of Public Administration in American Politics*, 2nd ed. (Baltimore, MD: Johns Hopkins University Press, 2014).

2. Flaumenhaft, *Effective Republic*, 72. A critical comment by Hamilton about opponents who advocated laissez-faire doctrine is perhaps telling in this regard. The flaws in their thinking were "proved by numerous examples too tedious to be cited; examples which will be neglected only by indolent and temporizing rulers, who love to loll in the lap of epicurean ease, and seem to imagine that to govern well, is to amuse the wondering multitude with sagacious aphorisms and oracular sayings." *PAH*, 25:467.

3. For example, see *Federalist*, no. 23, 155; *Federalist*, no. 30, 190; and *Federalist*, no. 31, 193.

4. Epstein, *Political Theory of "The Federalist."* See chapter 4 and the conclusion for an elaboration of the concept of "honorable determination." It is the acknowledgment and respect by republican government of man's "honorable insistence on their faculty of opining" about, and at times engaging in, matters of governance, 125. Hamilton and Madison disagreed over the extent to which the public should become directly involved in governance at the national level. Hamilton's stated role for the public was generally more passive than Madison's, but he did not adhere to this in his own behavior after leaving office. In fact, he was engaged to the point of being downright meddlesome at times during the Adams administration. He did hold an appointment during Adam's tenure, which gave him access to its operations even after stepping down. For a general discussion of their differences on this matter, see Colleen Sheehan, "Madison v. Hamilton: The Battle over Republicanism and the Role of Public Opinion," *American Political Science Review* 98, no. 3 (August 2004): 405–24.

5. *Federalist*, no. 1, 35. Flaumenhaft, *Effective Republic*, 90.

6. *Federalist*, no. 23, 156. Hamilton used the concept of *safety* in republican government in two senses. In the sense used here, "being safely vested with requisite powers" refers to safety against governmental tyranny. In the other sense, safety means government protecting the rights and liberties of individuals from the tyranny of others. At times, Hamilton seems to have applied the term in both senses.

7. Hamilton, "New York Ratifying Convention," *PAH*, 5:100. Hamil-

ton addresses the necessity of state governments to the American republic in *Federalist*, nos. 17 and 27, and in his speeches to the New York Ratifying Convention, *PAH*, 5:100–104 and 116–17. His only real concern about the states was the potential influence of the larger ones in the national councils. Because of this, he would have preferred that all the states be small and relatively equal in size. See Hamilton's letters to Edward Carrington and Jonathan Dayton in Hamilton, *PAH*, 11:443–44 and 23:604; and Caldwell, *ATH&J*, 33.

8. *PAH*, 5:100. These remarks were made in the New York Ratifying Convention, in part as a refutation of his desire to eliminate the states altogether. For an elaboration of Publius's treatment of the partition of state and local governments and his bias in favor of the national government, see Flaumenhaft, *Effective Republic*, 61–65; Federici, *PPAH*, 93–95, 229–30, 245; and Epstein, *Political Theory of "The Federalist,"* 51–58.

9. *PAH*, 5:100.

10. Storing (quoting James Monroe), *What the Anti-Federalists Were FOR*, 59.

11. On the problem of confusion between the British and American models, Hamilton warned that "many mistakes have arisen from fallacious comparisons between our government and theirs." *PAH*, 5:54. A perusal of just about any part of Madison's notes on the debates at Philadelphia will reveal the great extent to which the British model influenced and confused various framers' thoughts on American government, despite James Wilson's and Charles Pinckney's early admonishments against applying the British model to the American situation. See Madison, *Debates*, 85, for Wilson's comments, 186–87 for Pinckney's.

12. In the constitutional debates, the representational role for senators was contested. They may not effectively represent their states because two senators could cancel each other's vote for their own state's interests in Congress. Hamilton viewed them as representatives of the nation.

For an in-depth discussion of the confusion about and misunderstanding of the proposed constitution in relation to the more commonly understood systems of government, see Storing, *What the Anti-Federalists Were FOR*, chapter on complex government, 53–63. Also, note that Federici argues that Hamilton was a proponent of mixed government, by which he appears to mean mixed *principles* rather than *forms* of government. I find that his discussion of this matter just adds to the confusion, and I argue that his point is inadequately based on one brief reference in one secondhand account of Hamilton's remarks in the New York Ratifying Convention, *PPAH*, 22, 77, and 258–59n28.

13. *Federalist*, no. 47, 302–3.

14. *Federalist*, no. 66, 401–2.

15. *Federalist*, no. 47, 303.

16. For example, see Madison's and Lansing's notes on Hamilton speaking to the Constitutional Convention in which he "prevailed on them [delegates] to tone their Government as high as possible." Lansing recounted it as "[Hamilton] is for tuning the Government high." *PAH*, 4:218–19.

17. *Federalist*, no. 52, 330. Six-year terms for senators are the longest of

any elected official and were intended to bring permanence and stability to the government as a whole.

18. A review of Madison's record of the debates is indicative of this point. For example, see *Debates*, the remarks of Hamilton, 135, 608; Wilson, 197–98, 588, 601; Madison, 68, 83, 92, 110–11, 193–95, 228, 433, 535, 601; Morris, 255–56, 302, 487; Randolph, 110, 113–14, 527; Franklin, 62; Sherman, 60, 316; Ellsworth, 481; Pinckney, 487; Dickenson, 77; and Gerry, 46.

19. Hamilton, *PAH*, 5:68.

20. See Rohr, *To Run a Constitution*, chap. 3, "The Senate as Executive Establishment" (quotations at 28, 36–37). Significantly, however, Rohr argued that the Senate failed to realize the intentions of its design and that the public administration today fulfills that purpose.

21. Alexander Hamilton to George Washington, May 5, 1789, *PAH*, 5:337.

22. See *Federalist*, no. 75, 452–54; and *PAH*, 20:68. Also see Flaumenhaft's discussion of the matter in *Effective Republic*, 88.

23. See Walling, *Republican Empire*, for a full discussion of the matter. Quotes are at 127, 149.

24. *Federalist*, no. 77, 459. See Brian J. Cook, *Bureaucracy and Self-Government: Reconsidering the Role of Public Administration in American Politics*, chap. 2, for an extended discussion of the implications of the *Decision of 1789* for an exclusively instrumental view of public administration. His main points will be discussed in the concluding chapter relative to a strained and unbalanced view of Hamilton's principle of unity in the executive. For an example of an intriguing Supreme Court case stemming from the broadened removal doctrine, see Morrison v. Olson, 487 U.S. 654, (1988).

25. Jeremy Bailey, "The New Unitary Executive and Democratic Theory: The Problem of Alexander Hamilton," *American Political Science Review* 102, no. 4 (November 2008): 453–65, quote at 459. This chapter and chapters 5 and 8 describe Hamilton's extant points on duration and their implications for public administration in general. Also see Jeremy Bailey, "The Traditional View of Hamilton's *Federalist* No. 77 and an Unexpected Challenge: A Response to Seth Barrett Tillman," *Harvard Journal of Law & Public Policy* 33, no. 1 (2010): 169–84. Rohr, who held the *musing* view, nevertheless illustrates how Hamilton and one of his most ardent opponents, Federal Farmer, agreed on the need for a "stable and competent civil service" but differed over how to achieve it. See Rohr, *To Run a Constitution*, 36–37.

26. Notably, President Adams retained Washington's cabinet, but the practice came to an end with Jefferson's presidency. See Stanley Elkins and Eric McKitrick, *The Age of Federalism: The Early American Republic, 1788–1800* (Oxford: Oxford University Press, 1993), 539, 736–41.

27. Epstein, *Political Theory of "The Federalist,"* 191.

28. *Federalist*, no. 78, 467.

29. See Madison, *Debates*, 32. For a general discussion on this proposal by Madison, Wilson, Franklin, Mason, and others, see 46, 61–64, 79–81, 336–43, and 461–62.

30. See letter of President Washington to the Chief Justice and the Asso-

ciate Justices of the Supreme Court of the United States, April 3, 1790, in *John Jay's Correspondence and Public Papers*, 3:396; and *Report on Public Credit*, Jan. 9, 1790, *PAH*, 6:106–7.

31. Alexander Hamilton to James Duane, Sept. 3, 1780, *PAH*, 2:404–5. Though this was directed at the Continental Congress, Hamilton held to this view under the new constitution as well. See *Federalist*, no. 35. The House of Representatives was most closely analogous to the Continental Congress in character.

32. See *Federalist*, no. 35, 214–16, for Hamilton's discussion of the nature and manner of representation desired for the popular assembly. Not every group or class was to be directly represented. Representatives need only to be sensible of general interests such as commerce and agriculture, which bind various classes together.

33. Caldwell, *ATH&J*, 35–36.

34. See White, *The Federalists*, 119.

35. Flaumenhaft, *Effective Republic*, 87. Alexander Hamilton to Otho Williams is at *PAH*, 12:49–50. Also in this regard, see Hamilton's interesting discussion of the treaty power in *Federalist*, no. 75, 450–51.

36. See 1 Stat. 65, Chap. 12, "An Act to Establish the Treasury Department," Sept. 2, 1789, *Public Statutes at Large of the United States of America*, 1:65–67. The acts establishing the Departments of War and Foreign Affairs are in the same volume at 49–50 and 28–29. The act fixing salaries is at 67–69 (1 Stat. 67). Though no direct evidence exists on Hamilton's contribution to the Treasury Act, most historians and biographers believe it was substantial. Leonard D. White believed "he did in fact largely determine the form of the Treasury Act." White, *The Federalists*, 118n3. Also see Lawrence Lessig and Cass Sunstein's treatment of the Treasury Act as an alternative structure to the strictly hierarchical model imposed on the other two departments in "The President and the Administration," *Columbia Law Review* 94, no. 1 (January 1994): 1–123, discussion at 17, 26–28. They also note that Madison believed the comptroller of the treasury should hold office for a fixed tenure (17), presaging the establishment of independent boards and agencies.

37. Hamilton's position on the status of the secretary of the treasury as an executive official is clearly set forth in the memo "To the Select Committee Appointed to Examine the Treasury Department," March 24, 1794, *PAH*, 16:193–94.

38. See White, *The Federalists*, 77–87, regarding more general assertions of congressional power, and 330–31, for discussion of their attempts to control through line-item appropriations.

39. *PAH*, 6:106–7. In congressional deliberations on the measure, the Speaker of the House was pulled out of the bill and the secretary of state added, likely at Jefferson's maneuvering behind the scenes—which was his preferred style of playing politics.

40. See White, *The Federalists*, 52, 116–28, 450–59. For an example of Hamilton's defense and use of administrative adjudication, see Treasury Circular, July 20, 1792, 12:57–62. He also contemplated early on the existence of regulatory boards that would promulgate their own rules pursu-

ant to statute. In 1780, he recommended that the Continental Congress establish a board of trade (preferable to a single director) "as the regulations of trade are slow and gradual and require prudence and experience (more than other qualities), for which boards are very well adapted." *PAH*, 2:408.

41. For a concise account of Washington's style of leadership during his presidency, see Joseph J. Ellis, *His Excellency: George Washington* (New York: Alfred A. Knopf, 2004), chap. 6, 188–240.

42. The concept of centripetal leadership is taken from Federici, *PPAH*, 110–11. For an account that complements Federici's concept, see Caldwell, *ATH&J*, 35–41.

43. Ellis, *His Excellency*, 200.

44. Ellis, *His Excellency*, chap. 6.

45. For example, see *Federalist*, no. 71, 432, where Hamilton speaks of "men who flatter [the people's] prejudices to betray their interests." As will be explained in chapter 4, his ideal leaders were those who guard the people's durable interests by "withstand[ing] the temporary delusion in order to give them time and opportunity for more cool and sedate reflection," and Washington epitomized this type.

46. Ellis, *His Excellency*, 209.

47. Federici, *PPAH*, 84. In the Constitutional Convention, Hamilton spoke of Senators with much the same language, as embodying "a permanent will" and a "weighty interest" in public affairs that would draw them to "the sacrifice of private affairs which an acceptance of public trust would require." Charles C. Tansill, ed., "Debates in the Federal Convention of 1787 as Reported by James Madison," in *Documents Illustrative of the Formation of the Union of the American States* (Washington, DC: Government Printing Office, 1927), 222.

48. *Federalist*, no. 71, 432.

49. *Federalist*, no. 68, 411–15.

50. See Kendall v. U.S. ex Rel. Stokes, 37 U.S. 524 (1838). Jackson was an early proponent of a plebiscitary presidency in which the president serves through direct electoral mandate and centralizes all executive powers and functions under his office.

51. David Epstein, in his analysis of the *Federalist Papers*, identified two broad objects of government under which all other ends could be classed. They are *justice* and the *public good*. As Epstein points out, justice is the more fundamental object and is characterized by its "negative merit." That is, government is concerned with establishing and preserving justice, namely, avoiding, refraining from, or preventing abuse of private rights. Government must keep itself and others from committing injustice. It must protect rights. "But while private rights must be respected by government, it is the public good which is to be pursued by government." Hence, the public good involves *positive merit*. It requires "the more active attention of a 'good government.'" Epstein, *Political Theory of "The Federalist,"* 162–65. In *The Federalist Papers*, both Hamilton and Madison contribute to the discussion of these ends. See *Federalist*, nos. 23, 37, 45, 51, and 62.

52. In the arenas of finance and trade, Hamilton early on (under the

Articles of Confederation) spotted a tension between directors of finance and trade. "I know not, if it would be a good plan to let the Financier be President of the Board of Trade; but he should only have a casting voice in determining questions there. There is a connection between trade and finance, which ought to make the director of one acquainted with the other; but the Financier should not direct the affairs of trade, because for the sake of acquiring reputation by increasing the revenues, he might adopt measures that would depress trade." Alexander Hamilton to James Duane, September 1780, *PAH*, 2:409. He used similar logic in forming the boards of the Bank of the United States and the sinking fund.

53. Federici, *PPAH*, 80.

54. *Federalist*, no. 72, 437, no. 71, 433.

55. *Federalist*, no. 70, 423.

56. *Federalist*, no. 70, 424.

57. *Federalist*, no. 70, 426.

58. *Federalist*, no. 70, 426.

59. *PAH*, 2:408.

60. *Federalist*, no. 71, 431, 436.

61. *Federalist*, no. 71, 435, 437.

62. *Federalist*, no. 71, 447–49.

63. *Federalist*, no. 71, 450–51, 456–57.

64. See Caldwell, *ATH&J*, 96–97; and Catullus, no. 3, Sept. 29, 1792, *PAH*, 12:499. Also see Flaumenhaft's discussion (*Effective Republic*, 76) of department heads who must preside and advise as much as direct the affairs of their departments.

65. These figures are taken from Chernow, *AH*, 339; and White, *The Federalists*, 122–23.

66. White, *The Federalists*, 117.

67. White, *The Federalists*, 117.

68. White, *The Federalists*, 120.

69. White, *The Federalists*, 121.

70. See Chernow's lengthy description of the Adams/Hamilton rift at *AH*, 596–600, 611–26. Chernow aptly describes Hamilton as going far out of bounds with his stridency against Adams, no doubt reflecting his depression, exhaustion, and anxiety over the direction of things at the time.

Chapter 3

1. *Federalist*, no. 78, 467.

2. See *LPAH*, 1:46–50, for details of his legal study.

3. McDonald, *AH*, 50–51. At the time, New York followed the English legal profession in distinguishing between attorneys who performed routine legal work and those who practiced before the courts (called barristers in England).

4. See Goebel, "Practice and Procedure," in *LPAH*, 1:37–54, for what is perhaps the best detailed account we have of the adaptation of common law to the new American republic. Hamilton played a significant and controversial role in establishing a federal common law that coexists with the

common law of the states (Louisiana would become the lone exception with its French-based code law system).

5. McDonald, *AH*, 52.

6. An extensive description of these acts and Hamilton's many cases arising under them are provided in *LPAH*, 1:225–316.

7. McDonald, *AH*, 49.

8. William Blackstone, *Commentaries on the Laws of England* (1765; Oxford: Clarendon, 2001), 1:125–26. Also see McDonald, *AH*, 61.

9. McDonald, *AH*, 50.

10. McDonald, *AH*, 50.

11. McDonald, *AH*, 52. Quotations of Hamilton are from *The Continentalist*, *PAH*, 3:76–77.

12. Emmerich de Vattel, *The Law of Nations, or, Principles of the Law of Nature, Applied to the Conduct and Affairs of Nations and Sovereigns*, "Preliminaries," para. 6n, xlii–xliv, quoted in McDonald, *AH*, 54.

13. "Letter from Phocion to the Considerate Citizens of New York," *PAH*, 3:495. Also see Federici, *PPAH*, 35.

14. McDonald, *AH*, 56.

15. This point is elaborated upon in Walling, *Republican Empire*, chap. 8, and will be addressed at length in chapter 6, this volume.

16. Rossiter, *Alexander Hamilton and the Constitution* (New York: Harcourt, Brace & World, 1964), 186.

17. See McDonald, *AH*, 198–204, for general description of the role of the compromise over location of the capital in the bank/constitutionality debate. Quotes are at 202.

18. *PAH*, 7:103. Also see Walling, *Republican Empire*, 164.

19. Jefferson believed he was violating the Constitution, but he did it anyway for the good of the nation and then anguished about it for the rest of his life. See Stephanie Newbold, *All but Forgotten: Thomas Jefferson and the Development of Public Administration* (Albany: State University of New York Press, 2010). Though the decision clearly benefited the nation, the exercise of a statesman's prerogative to exceed the bounds of the Constitution poses the very danger the founding generation most feared. Hamilton and Madison thought strict construction, complemented by openness to periodic revolution, a dangerous philosophy. Such disruptions almost always resulted in periods of anarchy, which too easily lead to despotism and tyranny. They believed that political upheaval on that scale would put public institutions and the economy at severe risk and incite fears that can induce populist demand for powerful leaders who will establish order at the cost of liberty. Revolutions and other fundamental changes in political society that required extralegal action were to be embarked upon only in the direst circumstances. See Madison's *Federalist*, no. 49.

20. John C. Miller, *Alexander Hamilton and the Growth of the New Nation* (New Brunswick, NJ: Transaction, 2004), 267. Countless biographers, historians, political scientists, and legal scholars agree on this point and regard Hamilton's opinion as a crucial foundation for the American republic. For example, see Chernow, *AH*, 350–55; and Rossiter, *Alexander Hamilton and the Constitution*, 185–90.

21. Rossiter, *Alexander Hamilton and the Constitution*, 188, 190.

22. February 1791, *PAH*, 8:104–5.

23. *PAH*, 8:98–101. As early as 1781, Hamilton, Madison, and James Wilson had advocated the implied powers doctrine in an attempt to bolster the authority of the old Congress. However, as Clinton Rossiter observed, "It was left to Hamilton to convert it into a fortress of logic from which John Marshall was able to beat off the assault of the strict constructionists in McCulloch v. Maryland." Rossiter, *Alexander Hamilton and the Constitution*, 200. Also see *PAH*, 2:245, 400–402; *The Works of James Wilson*, vol. 1, ed. James D. Andrews (Chicago: Callaghan, 1896), 556.

24. *PAH*, 8:106. Hamilton also stated here that the blended powers structure of American government increased the potential for constitutional struggles over meaning as well as power.

25. *PAH*, 8:107–8.

26. *PAH*, 8:103–4.

27. *PAH*, 8:119. Opponents replied that giving such power to the federal government would make it too powerful vis-à-vis the states, but Hamilton countered that the need for such power was all the greater for the federal government, given the ends charged to its care, and that the states possessed more than sufficient powers to stave off federal encroachment.

28. *PAH*, 8:111.

29. *PAH*, 8:103.

30. Federici, *PPAH*, 145.

31. *Federalist*, no. 78, 466–67.

32. *PAH*, *The Examination*, no. 14, 25:550–51.

33. Federici, *PPAH*, 146. Federici distinguishes "liberal construction" from "loose construction" (142–47), with Hamilton's liberal construction tied only to means in pursuit of fixed ends. The problem, of course, is that the enumerated ends are themselves very broad and ambiguous, to the point illustrated more than once in this work that they permitted vastly different visions among the founders of the kind of nation that should either be preserved or brought about under the Constitution's auspices. This poses a conundrum for ardent originalists.

34. McNamara, *PE&S*, 113.

35. Paul Freund suggested as much, arguing, "Although the conception of national economic power had not crystallized by the time of the New Deal, there were decisions . . . which would have sufficed in the hands of a Marshall to validate the major measures taken in the depression." Samuel Konefsky, citing Freund, stated, "The same is basically true of Hamilton." See Paul A. Freund, "Umpiring the Federal System," *Columbia Law Review* 54 (1954): 561, 565. This passage quoted in Konefsky, *John Marshall and Alexander Hamilton*, 10. Freund was a New Deal lawyer as well as a distinguished Harvard Law professor.

36. Federici, *PPAH*, 139.

37. *Federalist*, no. 84, 510–11.

38. *Federalist*, no. 84, 512.

39. *Federalist*, no. 84, 513.

40. Federici, *PPAH*, 140; quotes of Hamilton at *Federalist*, no. 84, 513.

41. *Federalist*, no. 84, 514.

42. *People v. Croswell.* What remains of the records of this case, along with much of its context and dynamics, are provided in *LPAH*, 1:775–848. The quotation is at 775.

43. McDonald, *AH*, 359. Hamilton's 15 propositions are found in *LPAH*, 1:840–41.

44. *Federalist*, no. 84, 515.

45. Rossiter, *Alexander Hamilton and the Constitution*, 193–94. See especially his chap. 6, "Hamilton's Constitutional Law and Theory," 185–225.

46. *Federalist*, no. 33, 201–5; *PAH*, 25:500–506, esp. essay no. 9.

47. See *PAH*, 4:77–79, 222. His position, of course, stands in stark contrast to the insistence of Anti-Federalists and their progeny that the federal government under the new Constitution remained as a mere agent of the states, lacking any sovereignty whatever.

48. *Federalist*, no. 17, 118–22. Also see Alexander Hamilton to Theodore Sedgewick, Feb. 2, 1799, *PAH*, 22:452–54, and Alexander Hamilton to Jonathan Dayton, October 1799, *PAH*, 23:599–604, for Hamilton's proposals for defending national supremacy in the face of the Virginia and Kentucky resolutions.

49. *Federalist*, no. 22, 143–45; nos. 30–35, passim; no. 23, 152–57; Poughkeepsie, June 27, 1788, *PAH*, 5:97–98; *Report on Public Credit*, *PAH*, 6:51–168, passim; *Opinion on the Bank*, *PAH*, 8:97–108; *Report on Manufactures*, *PAH*, 10:302–4, 311–13, 337. Also see Rossiter's in-depth analysis of Hamilton's position on each of these powers in *Alexander Hamilton and the Constitution*, 200–225.

50. Poughkeepsie, June 27, 1788, *PAH*, 5:97–98.

51. Hamilton was pragmatic about specific types of taxation. Different circumstances could warrant a change in taxation schemes wherein even poll or capitation taxes would be used. See his discussion on taxes appropriate to eighteenth- and nineteenth-century American circumstances in *Report on Manufactures*, *PAH*, 9:311–13. For a review of the Hylton case, see *LPAH*, 4:297–353.

52. Rossiter, *Alexander Hamilton and the Constitution*, 203.

53. *PAH*, 10:303.

54. *Federalist*, no. 23, 153–54.

55. See Alexander Hamilton to James McHenry, March 21, 1800, *PAH*, 24:350.

56. *The Examination*, no. 1, *PAH*, 25:454–56, and 21:461–62; Alexander Hamilton to John Marshall, *PAH*, 25:130, also see 130–39; 24:349–50; White, *The Federalists*, chap. 26, passim; *Federalist*, no. 73.

57. Pacificus, no. 1, June 29, 1793, *PAH*, 15:39. See Walling, *Republican Empire*, 146–49, for a lucid discussion of Hamilton's view of foreign affairs and war powers in relation to Locke's *federative* powers. On war and treaty-making powers generally, and in relation to the "War Powers Resolution," see Robert Scigliano, "The War Powers Resolution and the War Powers," in *The Presidency in the Constitutional Order*, ed. Bessette and Tulis, 115–53 (Baton Rouge: Louisiana State University Press, 1981). For an excellent critique of Hamilton's position on the executive power, see John A. Rohr,

"Public Administration, Executive Power, and Constitutional Confusion," *Public Administration Review* 49, no. 2 (March/April 1989): 108–14.

58. Pacificus, no. 1, *PAH*, 15, 42. See Alexander Hamilton to George Washington, March 26, 1796, *PAH*, 20:86–103, for an elaboration of the president's treaty powers relative to negotiations and private papers and of Hamilton's assertion that Congress should follow the president's leadership in treaty-making with requisite appropriations. Also see Alexander Hamilton to George Washington, July 9, 1795, *PAH*, 18:428, in which Hamilton argues the primacy of treaty-making powers over existing laws (local, state, or federal) so long as constitutional provisions are not violated.

59. *Federalist*, no. 36, 223.

60. *Federalist*, no. 36, 223; *Federalist*, no. 25, 167. There is real insight here in regard to state constitutions. They are much longer documents replete with restrictions, they are much more easily and more often amended, and they receive little if any of the reverence accorded to the national constitution, even among state officials.

61. For general references by Hamilton to the necessity of giving the government powers adequate to deal with emergencies, see *Federalist*, no. 22, 148; *Federalist*, no. 25, 167; *Federalist*, no. 28, 178; *Federalist*, no. 36, 223; *Federalist*, no. 70, 423; *Federalist*, no. 72, 439; *Federalist*, no. 73, 446; *PAH*, 1:48–51; *PAH*, 3:173, 540, 549; *PAH*, 4:131–32; and *PAH*, 6:436.

62. See *The Examination*, nos. 12–17, by Lucius Crassus; *PAH*, 25:529–76.

63. See Rossiter, *Alexander Hamilton and the Constitution*, 224.

64. *Federalist*, no. 78, 466.

65. Rossiter, *Alexander Hamilton and the Constitution*, 221; Marbury v. Madison, 5 U.S. 137 (1803). Marshall had first asserted the power of judicial review on June 20, 1788, in the Virginia ratifying convention. In his speech, he used language from *Federalist*, no. 78 through no. 82. If he had forgotten this language by 1803, he was reminded of it by Charles Lee, Marbury's counsel. Jonathan Elliot, ed., *The Debates in the Several State Conventions on the Adoption of the Federal Constitution*, 2nd ed. (Philadelphia, 1876), 3:553. Also see Samuel J. Konefsky, *John Marshall and Alexander Hamilton: Architects of the American Constitution* (New York: MacMillan, 1964), 81–85, for further analysis of Hamilton's and Marshall's agreement on the theory of a limited constitution.

66. Alexander Hamilton to Jonathan Dayton, October 1799, *PAH*, 23: 600–601.

67. Chernow, *AH*, 648. Alfred H. Kelly, Winfred A. Harbison, and Herman Belz, *The American Constitution: Its Origins and Development*, 6th ed. (New York: W. W. Norton, 1983), 184.

68. *Marbury v. Madison*, 5 U.S. 137 (1803) (quotes at 177, 170).

69. Rossiter, *Alexander Hamilton and the Constitution*, 242.

70. Stephen Skowronek, *Building the New American State: The Expansion of National Administrative Capacities, 1877–1920* (New York: Cambridge University Press, 1982), 27–28.

71. U.S. v. Peters, 5 Cranch 115 (1809); Fletcher v. Peck, 6 Cranch 87 (1810); *LPAH*, 4:420–31, quotation at 420–21.

72. Dartmouth College v. Woodward, 4 Wheaton 518 (1819). Quotation

from Peter Zavodnyik, *The Age of Strict Construction: A History of the Growth of Federal Power, 1789–1861* (Washington, DC: Catholic University of America Press, 2007), 111. Other significant cases flowing from *Fletcher* and *Dartmouth* include New Jersey v. Wilson, 7 Cranch 164 (1812); Terrett v. Taylor, 9 Cranch 43 (1815); and Green v. Biddle, 8 Wheaton 1 (1823).

73. Albert J. Beveridge, *The Life of John Marshall* (Boston: Houghton Mifflin, 1916–19), 4:276. Also see Kelly, Harbison, and Belz, *American Constitution*, 193.

74. Hamilton's views were also published in pamphlet form. *LPAH*, 4:420–21. Also see Benjamin F. Wright, *The Contract Clause of the Constitution* (Cambridge, MA: Harvard University Press, 1938), 14, 21–22, 26, 29, 244; Rossiter, *Alexander Hamilton and the Constitution*, 240; and Konefsky, *John Marshall and Alexander Hamilton*, 123.

75. Gibbons v. Ogden, 9 Wheaton 1 (1824) 213–14, 227–28. The term "interstate commerce" was not used by any of the Federalist judges but was instead introduced as an unfortunate gloss later in the nineteenth century. The meaning of commerce "among the states" was broader in meaning during the founding era. Interstate commerce was interpreted more narrowly, limiting the reach of the federal government until New Deal lawyers and judges put the liberal constructionist gloss on it.

76. Martin v. Hunter's Lessee, 1 Wheaton 304 (1816); Cohens v. Virginia, 6 Wheaton 264 (1821).

77. Rossiter, *Alexander Hamilton and the Constitution*, 241. Also see Konefsky, *John Marshall and Alexander Hamilton*, 105–8.

78. McCulloch v. Maryland, 4 Wheaton 316 (1819), 407.

79. *McCulloch v. Maryland*, 410.

80. *McCulloch v. Maryland*, 421.

81. See Wright, *The Contract Clause of the Constitution*. As Wright indicates, the vital functions served during most of the nineteenth century by Hamilton's and Marshall's interpretation of the contract clause were eclipsed by the due process clauses.

82. For an older but exhaustive review of legal commentaries, histories, textbooks, casebooks, and articles that employ Hamiltonian doctrines and/or direct citations of Hamilton, see Rossiter, *Alexander Hamilton and the Constitution*, passim. (esp. 345–47n95). More recent examples are: Lawrence M. Friedman, *A History of American Law* (New York: Simon & Schuster, 1973); and Kermit L. Hall, *The Magic Mirror: Law in American History* (New York: Oxford University Press, 1989).

83. See Rossiter, *Alexander Hamilton and the Constitution*, chap. 7, for an extensive literature review showing the lack of recognition of Hamilton's role in constitutional history. Edward S. Corwin, *The Constitution of the United States of America: Analysis and Interpretation; Annotations of Cases Decided by the Supreme Court of the United States to June 30, 1952* (Washington, DC: US Government Printing Office, 1953), 381; Wright, *The Contract Clause of the Constitution*, 21; Kelly, Harbison, and Belz, *American Constitution*, 1:190–93.

84. Perry Miller, *The Life of the Mind in America: From the Revolution to the Civil War* (New York: Harcourt, Brace & World, 1965), 109–11.

85. See Perry Miller, *The Legal Mind in America: From Independence to the*

Civil War (Ithaca, NY: Cornell University Press, 1962), 83–92; also see Friedman, *History of American Law*, 278–92.

86. Rossiter, *Alexander Hamilton and the Constitution*, 243–44; W. W. Story, ed., *Life and Letters of Joseph Story* (Boston, 1851), 1:144, 195–96; 2:258, 420.

87. Rossiter, *Alexander Hamilton and the Constitution*, 243.

Chapter 4

1. *Federalist*, no. 76, 457.

2. See McDonald, *AH*, 183, viz., "Unlike Hamilton, but like Washington, [Robert] Morris was of a class and a generation that made no distinctions between private and public interest." Also see McDonald, *AH*, 79–84, for an encounter of this sort by Hamilton while a practicing attorney in the 1780s. It involved political intrigue by some leading national figures regarding Philadelphia's Bank of North America, all entered into for the sake of enriching themselves.

3. Alexander Hamilton to John Laurens, May 22, 1779, *PAH*, 2:53.

4. McDonald, *AH*, 86.

5. Publius, Letter 1, October 1778, *PAH*, 1:562–63.

6. Publius, Letter 3, November 1778, *PAH*, 1:580–81.

7. Chernow, *AH*, 118.

8. Paraphrased by McDonald, *AH*, 55.

9. Hamilton explained this distinction several times in his career. A succinct statement is found in *The Examination*, no. 17, March 1802, *PAH*, 25:570–71.

10. Cicero, *On Duties*, ed. M. T. Griffin and E. M. Atkins (Cambridge: Cambridge University Press, 1991), 113, 116, quoted in Federici, *PPAH*, 86.

11. Federici, *PPAH*, 85–86, 89–90. The connection to liberality is made via Chan, *Aristotle and Hamilton*.

12. Federici, *PPAH*, 89. Gordon Wood and Bernard Bailyn perhaps best represent those historians who overstate the role of lower passions and motives in the work of the framers, along with unduly downplaying the role of classical and Christian influences. McDonald provides the most thorough and overwhelming evidence of Hamilton's deep attachment to synthesizers of classical, Christian, and Enlightenment ideas. The more recent works on Hamilton by Chernow, Federici, Chan, McNamara, Sellers, Bederman and Richard echo McDonald's characterization. See Gordon Wood, *Empire of Liberty: A History of the Early Republic, 1789–1815* (Cambridge: Oxford University Press, 2009); Carl J. Richard, *Greeks and Romans Bearing Gifts: How the Ancients Inspired the Founding Fathers* (Lanham, MD: Rowman & Littlefield, 2009); Mortimer Sellers, *American Republicanism: Roman Ideology in the United States Constitution* (New York: NYU Press, 1994); David J. Bederman, *Classical Foundations of the Constitution: Prevailing Wisdom* (Cambridge: Cambridge University Press, 2008).

13. Hamilton demonstrated his intense concern for his public reputation by the manner in which he dealt with a terrible personal blunder. During his tenure as secretary of the treasury, he was enticed into an adulterous affair with a woman (Maria Reynolds) who apparently colluded with her

own husband (James Reynolds) to extort money and compromise Hamilton's character. Long story short, Hamilton made sporadic blackmail payments over about five years until Mr. Reynolds sold the information to one or more members of the Republican opposition. When Hamilton learned this through veiled public attempts to cast suspicion on his decisions as secretary, he immediately crafted a long letter explaining in excruciating detail the whole affair and, against his friends' advice, published it for public consumption. He did this to stop any attempts to impugn his service in office and suffered instead with utter shock and embarrassment to his wife and family. This is one of the most remarkable actions ever taken by a public official for the sake of upholding public trust at the cost of private disaster. For a full account of the matter, see Chernow, *AH*, 364–70, 529–46, 533–36, 576–77.

14. See Douglas Adair, *Fame and the Founding Fathers*, ed. Trevor Colbourn (New York: Norton, 1974); Maynard Smith, "Reason, Passion and Political Freedom in *The Federalist*," *Journal of Politics* 22, no. 3 (August 1960): 525–44; Stourzh, *Alexander Hamilton and the Idea of Republican Government*, 90–97.

15. Federici, *PPAH*, 85–88.

16. See Hamilton's nuanced discussion of the effects of a conflict-of-interest law at Treasury in his "Report on the Improvement and Better Management of the Revenue of the United States," January 31, 1795, *PAH*, 18:223–24.

17. See McDonald, *AH*, 137. McDonald noted that no other man, including Washington, saw fit to do this. Chernow echoes the point, *AH*, 287.

18. Chernow, *AH*, 88–90, 152–53, 293.

19. Thomas Flexner, *George Washington: Anguish and Farewell, 1793–1799* (Boston: Little, Brown), 476. Flexner was citing Hamilton's own words from Washington's correspondence. Washington wanted more friendship from Hamilton and was hurt by his studied avoidance of it.

20. *The Examination*, no. 17, March 1802, *PAH*, 25:570. Harold Syrett notes that these essays received little public attention at the time because Hamilton was out of the government, and the essays joined with many other diatribes against the new Jefferson administration. Moreover, they are seldom referred to by most scholars because they are more strident in tone and lack the cogent and concise reasoning in his other works. Nevertheless, the essays contain many insights still useful for understanding his thinking about public office late in his life. See *PAH*, 25:444–53.

21. First quote from *Federalist*, no. 77, 462; second from *PAH*, 25:445.

22. McNamara, *PE&S*, 142–43.

23. Ian Crowe, *Patriotism and Public Spirit: Edmund Burke and the Role of the Critic in Mid-Eighteenth-Century Britain* (Stanford, CA: Stanford University Press, 2012). The subject of patriotism will be discussed at some length in association with nationalism in chapter 6.

24. See McDonald, *AH*, 382–83n24. Jacques Necker, *Treatise on the Administration of Finances of France*, trans. Thomas Mortimer (London, 1785).

25. McDonald quoting Necker, *AH*, 84. In Necker's text at 1:cxlvi–cxlvii.

26. McDonald quoting Necker, *AH*, 85. *Federalist*, no. 72, 437.

27. *Federalist*, no. 72.

28. Caldwell, *ATH&J*, 90.

29. *The Examination*, no. 12, *PAH*, 25:532–33.

30. *The Examination*, no. 12, *PAH*, 25:470. The implication here is that either Congress or the president may by law remove subordinate officers; Caldwell, *ATH&J*, 88–91; *PAH*, 5:84–86.

31. Caldwell, *ATH&J*, 87. Presidents Jackson and Reagan subsequently popularized this Anti-Federalist view of public office.

32. Caldwell, *ATH&J*, 67–68.

33. These accoutrements are gleaned from several of Hamilton's papers, as well as from secondary sources. See *PAH*, 8:292; 21:78; 18:218–19, 223–24; Caldwell, *ATH&J*, 87–91; Mitchell, *Alexander Hamilton: Youth to Maturity*, 441; Flaumenhaft, *Effective Republic*, chap. 11; Chernow, *AH*, 564–65.

34. Alexander Hamilton to William Hamilton, *PAH*, 21:78.

35. "Report on the Improvement and Better Management of the Revenue of the United States," January 31, 1795, *PAH*, 18:223–24.

36. "Report on the Improvement and Better Management of the Revenue of the United States," January 31, 1795, *PAH*, 18:218–19, 223–24.

37. Mitchell, *Alexander Hamilton: The National Adventure*, 441.

38. Chernow, *AH*, 564.

39. Alexander Hamilton to George Washington, April 17, 1791, *PAH*, 8:292.

40. Alexander Hamilton to James McHenry, March 21, 1800, *PAH*, 24:349–50. This letter is significant as well because in it Hamilton disputed a doctrine advanced by an accounting officer "that no authority short of Congress can make allowances to an Officer beyond the emoluments fixed to his Office by law." Hamilton saw this as a dangerous limitation on executive discretion.

41. Caldwell, *ATH&J*, 87. Also see Chan, *Aristotle and Hamilton*, 77. These points are derived in part from Hamilton's remarks at the New York Ratifying Convention, June 21, 1788, *PAH*, 5:41–43.

42. *PAH*, 5:43. He advanced this argument in the same speech.

43. Caldwell, *ATH&J*, 96.

44. Metellus, October 24, 1792, *PAH*, 12:616.

45. Metellus, October 24, 1792, *PAH*, 12:616–17.

46. "To the Select Committee Appointed to Examine the Treasury Department," March 14, 1794, *PAH*, 16:193–94. Remember that the Treasury Act designated the secretary as an executive official even though the Treasury Department's status was left undesignated.

47. Cf., Alexander Hamilton to Otho H. Williams, Treasury Dept., July 19, 1792, *PAH*, 12:46.

48. Cf., Alexander Hamilton from Benjamin Lincoln, November–December 1789, *PAH*, 5:580–81.

49. McDonald, *AH*, 139.

50. Treasury Circular, December 18, 1789, *PAH*, 6:18–19.

51. Treasury Circular, September 30, 1790, *PAH*, 7:83.

52. A perusal of almost any of his circulars confirms the validity of this

description. See especially his early circulars, for example, *PAH*, 7:66–67, 83–84, 87–88, 207, and 368–72. For a full account of the Duer incident, see Chernow, *AH*, 381–84.

53. Treasury Dept. Circular to the Collectors of the Customs, July 20, 1792, Hamilton, *PAH*, 12:59.

54. Treasury Dept. Circular to the Collectors of the Customs, July 20, 1792, Hamilton, *PAH*, 12:58–60.

55. Treasury Dept. Circular to the Collectors of the Customs, July 20, 1792, Hamilton, *PAH*, 12:60.

56. Treasury Dept. Circular to the Collectors of the Customs, July 20, 1792, *PAH*, 12:60.

57. Alexander Hamilton to James McHenry, September 16, 1799, *PAH*, 23:423–29.

58. For example, see White, *The Federalists*, passim.; Paul Van Riper, *History of the United States Civil Service* (Evanston, IL: Row, Peterson, 1958), chaps. 1–2.

59. Caldwell, *ATH&J*, 7.

60. Federici, *PPAH*, 60. John Lamberton Harper advances a contrary view of Hamilton as a faithful Machiavellian. His fine work on Hamilton's foreign policy pairs Hamilton's thought with Machiavelli's work. However, even he admits that Hamilton rarely ever cited Machiavelli, noting that the author of *The Prince* did not enjoy much popularity among Americans in general. He was in fact looked down upon. Moreover, his concentration on Machiavelli leads him to ignore or greatly downplay Hamilton's exhaustive references to Vattel and other writers at odds with the Machiavellian thesis, namely, that leaders need "to learn how not to be good." Harper focuses more on Hamilton's actions and spots moments of deceit on Hamilton's part as proof of his thesis. I find his evidence rather thin, speaking more to exceptions and moral lapses than to routine practices in the Machiavellian spirit. Little if any evidence exists that Hamilton was willing to trade his soul for the glory of achieving great things for the republic. See Harper, *American Machiavelli*, chap. 2, 8–15. Federici uses the accounts of Hamilton's last days of life to suggest that he abandoned politics to return to his religious moorings, seeking redemption instead through the church. Federici, *PPAH*, 48–49. As noted in chapter 2, McDonald also rejected the characterization of Hamilton as a Machiavellian. Vattel's treatise, *The Law of Nations or, Principles of the Law of Nature, Applied to the Conduct and Affairs of Nations and Sovereigns*, was widely read at the time and is still considered a classic in international law and diplomacy.

61. *PAH*, 19:59–60.

62. *PAH*, 19:59.

63. Alexander Hamilton to Robert Morris, *PAH*, 2:616–18.

64. Publius, Letter 3, November 1778, *PAH*, 1:582 (temerity meaning "excessive boldness, audacity," OED).

65. *PAH*, 19:59.

66. Federici, *PPAH*, 7–9. Hamilton quotes are from Alexander Hamilton to Rufus King, October 1798, *PAH*, 22:192.

67. See Mark H. Moore, *Creating Public Value: Strategic Management in Gov-*

ernment (Cambridge, MA: Harvard University Press, 1995). Interestingly, Hamilton ventured into an entrepreneurial experiment with Tench Coxe, his assistant secretary of the treasury, by helping to establish the Society for Establishing Useful Manufactures or SEUM, which served as a pilot project of sorts to innovate with various arrangements supporting the development of manufacturing, including the development of manufacturing towns. The venture opened at Patterson, New Jersey, in the early 1790s and was, as described by Chernow, *AH*, 372–74, "operated by private interests that would enjoy the general blessings of government," including an initial investment of government bonds and at least tacit support of "industrial espionage" to speed gains in manufacturing machinery.

68. See McDonald, *AH*, 137–39, for an extended discussion of this point.

69. "First Speech of June 21, 1788, New York Ratifying Convention," *PAH*, 5:43.

70. *PAH*, 4:192.

71. Chan, *Aristotle and Hamilton*, 76–77.

72. Chan, *Aristotle and Hamilton*, 76–77.

73. Chan, *Aristotle and Hamilton*, 76–77; Hamilton quote from *PAH*, 5:42.

74. David Hume, "On the Independence of Parliament," in Gross, *Philosophical Works*, 3:39–41. See McDonald's treatment at *AH*, 189–90. He notes that Hamilton borrowed Hume's phrases and maxims extensively in his pamphlets and speeches, often without attribution—a practice common among the founding generation. He quoted Hume directly and extensively in his early essay *The Farmer Refuted*, *PAH*, 1:94–95. On the general influence of Hume on Hamilton, see Rossiter, *Alexander Hamilton and the Constitution*, 115, 120–26, 130, 138–39, 148, 174, 182–83; Stourzh, *Alexander Hamilton and the Idea of Republican Government*, 21, 30, 40, 42–43, 117–19. The most in-depth treatment of Hume's influence is McDonald's *Novus Order Seclorum*, passim.

75. *PAH*, 19:59–60.

76. *PAH*, 19:59–60.

77. Rosemary O'Leary, *The Ethics of Dissent: Managing Guerilla Government* (Washington, DC: CQ, 2014).

78. See John A. Rohr, *Public Service Ethics and Constitutional Practice* (Lawrence: University Press of Kansas, 1998); J. Patrick Dobel, *Public Integrity* (Baltimore, MD: Johns Hopkins University Press, 1999). For a summation of Rohr's arguments on public morality in general, see Richard T. Green, "The Centrality of Public Morality in John Rohr's Work," *Administrative Theory and Praxis* 34, no. 4 (December 2012): 629–34.

79. See, for example, James L. Perry, Annie Hondeghem, and Lois Recascino Wise, "Revisiting the Motivational Bases of Public Service: Twenty Years of Research and an Agenda for the Future," *Public Administration Review* 70, no. 5 (September/October 2010): 681–90; James L. Perry and Annie Hondeghem, *Motivation in Public Management: The Call of Public Service* (Oxford: Oxford University Press, 2008).

80. Arthur Schlesinger Jr., *The Cycles of American History* (Boston: Houghton Mifflin, 1986), 28–29.

81. The attitudes and behaviors of financial regulators during this period are well documented. See, for example, US Senate, *Wall Street and the Financial Crisis: Anatomy of a Financial Collapse*, US Senate Permanent Subcommittee on Investigations, Committee on Homeland Security and Governmental Affairs, Carl Levin, chairman, Tom Coburn, ranking minority member (Washington, DC: Government Printing Office, 2011), accessed at http://www.hsgac.senate.gov; Michael Lewis, ed., *Panic: The Story of Modern Financial Insanity* (New York: W. W. Norton, 2009); James Kwak, "Cultural Capture and the Financial Crisis," in *Preventing Regulatory Capture: Special Interest Influence and How to Limit It*, ed. Daniel Carpenter and David Moss (New York: Cambridge University Press, 2013).

Chapter 5

1. Susan Hoffmann, *Politics and Banking: Ideas, Public Policy, and the Creation of Financial Institutions* (Baltimore, MD: Johns Hopkins University Press, 2001), chaps. 1–2.

2. McDonald, *AH*, 161.

3. McDonald, *AH*, 3, 227, 235.

4. *PAH*, 10:24–26.

5. For more on this, see Flaumenhaft's treatment of Hamilton's *Federalist*, nos. 8–9, and his Camillus essays of 1795, in *Effective Republic*, 18–22.

6. McDonald, *Novus Ordo Seclorum*. The following paragraphs are derived primarily from his chap. 4, 97–142.

7. McDonald, *Novus Ordo Seclorum*, 110.

8. McDonald, *Novus Ordo Seclorum*, 119.

9. McCraw, *Founders and Finance*, 3–7. McCraw also notes that "four of the first six secretaries of the treasury were born oversees" (3) and that "being rootless themselves, they were better able to appreciate the rootlessness of money" (6).

10. McDonald, *AH*, 135.

11. McDonald, *AH*, 136.

12. Michael Lewis, "The Trouble with Wall Street: The Shocking News That Goldman Sachs Is Greedy," Money (section), *New Republic*, February 4, 2013, http://www.newrepublic.com/article/112209/michael-lewis-goldman-sachs. For a succinct analysis of how this financial boom-and-bust came about, see Richard T. Green, "Plutocracy, Bureaucracy, and the End of Public Trust," *Administration & Society* 44, no. 1 (2012): 109–43.

13. McDonald, *AH*, 143.

14. McCraw, *Founders and Finance*, chap. 6; Mitchell, *Alexander Hamilton: The National Adventure*, 16.

15. McCraw, *Founders and Finance*, 47.

16. McCraw, *Founders and Finance*, 64–68, 94–95.

17. McCraw, *Founders and Finance*, 94–95. Regarding the nature and extent of early debt and budget deficits, also see John Steele Gordon, *Hamilton's Blessing: The Extraordinary Life and Times of Our National Debt* (New York: Walker, 1997), 2–17; Richard Sylla, "Financial Foundations: Public Credit,

the National Bank, and Securities Markets," in *Founding Choices: American Economic Policies in the 1790s*, ed. Douglas A. Irwin and Richard Sylla (Chicago: University of Chicago Press, 2011); and James E. Ferguson, *The Power of the Purse: A History of American Public Finance* (Chapel Hill: University of North Carolina Press, 1961), 330–33.

18. Syrett and Cooke, the editors of Hamilton's papers, note Hamilton's immersion in the periodicals and news accounts on financial affairs in Europe as well as the influence of the mentioned authors. Notable among the works of these authors are: Sir James Steuart, *An Inquiry into the Principles of Political Oeconomy* (1767); Malachy Postlethwayt, *Universal Dictionary of Trade and Commerce* (1751); Wyndham Beawes, *The Merchant's Directory* (1751); Richard Price, *Observations on the Nature of Civil Liberty* (1776), and *Additional Observations on the Nature and Value of Civil Liberty* (1777); Jacques Necker, *Essai sur la législation et le commerce des grains* (1775), *Compte rendu au roi* (1781), and *Traité de l'administration des finances de la France* (1784), translated by Thomas Mortimer (1785); Jean Baptiste Colbert, *Mémoires sur les affaires de finance de France* (ca. 1663); *Lettres, instructions et mémoires de Colbert* (ca. 1680); and William Pitt, *Parliamentary Speech on Establishment of a Sinking Fund* (1786). McDonald's account of the influence of these works on Hamilton's thinking remains the best source in an overall sense, though several works, such as those mentioned in footnote 4 above, go deeper into some narrower aspects of his and other founders' thinking on these subjects.

19. Gordon, *Hamilton's Blessing*, 2–4; McDonald, *AH*, 161, 194.

20. Alexander Hamilton to Edward Carrington, May 26, 1792, *PAH*, 11:442.

21. McDonald, *AH*, 128–34, quote at 133.

22. Hamilton's famous reports are found in *PAH* at 6:51–168 (Public Credit); 7:210–342 (Bank of the United States); 462–606 (Mint); and 10:1–340 (Manufactures). In addition to these, Hamilton submitted supplemental reports on public credit and on his fiscal measures generally. His valedictory reports on *Public Credit* (January 16, 1795) and *Defense of the Funding System* (July 1795) are valuable, though often ignored, analyses of all his measures, with prescriptions for America's future. See *PAH*, 18:47–148; *PAH*, 19:1–73.

23. *PAH*, 6:68–69.

24. McDonald, *AH*, 158–59.

25. *PAH*, 6:68–69. His remark that the declining provision for public debts overthrows all public morality is taken from his later "Defense of the Funding System," July 1795, *PAH*, 19:59.

26. *PAH*, 6:69–70.

27. *PAH*, 6:69–70. The quote on debt as a "mechanism of national affairs" is from his *Report on Manufactures*, Dec. 5, 1791, *PAH*, 10:266. Chernow quote at *AH*, 292.

28. The analysis here is derived from McDonald, *AH*, 144–49, 167–69.

29. McDonald, *AH*, 149.

30. These accommodations are explained by McDonald, *AH*, 169–70. They are significant but do not require extensive treatment here.

31. McCraw, *Founders and Finance*, 97–99.

32. McDonald, *AH*, 175. His chapter on funding and assumption (163–88) describes the machinations in Congress in fine detail.

33. McDonald, *AH*, 184–85.

34. Per Swanson and Trout, "Congress rejected all but one of Hamilton's conversion options: that granting the creditor a combination of two perpetual 6 percent annuities, one to begin payment at once and one with payment deferred for ten years. To this package, Congress added a 3 percent annuity. For the creditor the result was an effective interest rate of slightly above 4 percent. What is important is that nearly 70 percent of the new securities—the two 6 percent annuities—would contain a limited redemption feature assuring creditors that they could not suffer wholesale redemption and lose an interest-bearing asset. This was an especially valuable feature if prevailing interest rates dropped, as Hamilton predicted they would, and market value of the securities rose above par." Donald F. Swanson and Andrew P. Trout, "Alexander Hamilton's Hidden Sinking Fund," *William and Mary Quarterly* 49 (1992): 108–16, quote at 111. Quote on loan commission system in White, *The Federalists*, 349.

35. *PAH*, 6:97.

36. Swanson and Trout, "Alexander Hamilton's Hidden Sinking Fund," 111; Donald F. Swanson, *The Origins of Hamilton's Fiscal Policies*, University of Florida Monographs, Social Sciences, no. 17 (Gainesville: University of Florida Press, 1963), 51; *PAH*, 6:106–8.

37. Swanson, *The Origins of Hamilton's Fiscal Policies*.

38. Swanson and Trout, "Hamilton's Hidden Sinking Fund," 114.

39. Swanson, *The Origins of Hamilton's Fiscal Policies*.

40. Jefferson to Washington, Sept. 9, 1792, as quoted in Swanson, *The Origins of Hamilton's Fiscal Policies*, 65. Swanson also points out that Jefferson believed it contrary to the laws of nature to extend debts into subsequent generations for payment. Hence, no debt should exist for more than about twenty years. Implicit in Hamilton's orientation is the view that debt was a way of providing a stable political-economic base for future generations to inherit. It would only be fair that they help pay for what they inherited.

41. Jefferson to Washington, Sept. 9, 1792, as quoted in Swanson, *The Origins of Hamilton's Fiscal Policies*, 71, 84. Also see *Report on a Plan for the Further Support of Public Credit*, January 16, 1795, *PAH*, 18:89–90, where Hamilton makes explicit provision for relaxed sinking fund operations in time of war.

42. Herbert R. Ferleger, *David A. Wells and the American Revenue System, 1865–1870* (Philadelphia: Porcupine, 1977), 7. Also see Henry C. Adams, *Public Debts* (New York: D. Appleton, 1887), 274–79; Edward Ross, "Sinking Funds," *Publication of the American Economic Association* 7 (1892): 54, 98. For a defense of Hamilton as a great financier, see C. F. Dunbar, "Some Precedents Followed by Alexander Hamilton," in *Economic Essays*, ed. D. M. W. Sprague (New York: MacMillan, 1904); and Robert James Parks, *European Origins of the Economic Ideas of Alexander Hamilton* (New York: Arno, 1977).

43. McDonald, *AH*, 189.

44. *Report on a National Bank*, *PAH*, 7:325, 329.

45. McNamara, *PE&S*, 127.

46. *Report on a National Bank, PAH*, 7:305. The longer title styled it as *The Second Report on the Further Provision Necessary for Establishing Public Credit*, indicating that he treated the bank as an integral part of his funding system.

47. McDonald, *AH*, 190.

48. *PAH*, 7:307–9.

49. Chernow, *AH*, 349.

50. *PAH*, 7:310.

51. See Chernow, *AH*, 348–49.

52. McDonald, *AH*, 193.

53. McDonald, *AH*, 194.

54. *PAH*, 7:310–11.

55. *PAH*, 7:316–25, quotes at 316–17.

56. McDonald, *AH*, 195.

57. See Robert A. Love, *Federal Financing: A Study of the Methods Employed by the Treasury in Its Borrowing Operations* (New York: Columbia University Press, 1931), 33–34, for an appraisal of the extensive use of the bank in the founding era.

58. See Bray Hammond, *Banks and Politics in America from the Revolution to the Civil War* (Princeton, NJ: Princeton University Press, 1991), 128–31, 643, quote at 209.

59. For an excellent elaboration of this and subsequent bank controversies, see Hammond, *Banks and Politics*, passim.

60. Hammond, *Banks and Politics*, 250.

61. White, *The Federalists*, 139–43.

62. *Report on the Mint, PAH*, 7:572.

63. McDonald, *AH*, 197; Chernow, *AH*, 355–56.

64. McDonald, *AH*, 198.

65. Chernow, *AH*, 341.

66. White, *The Federalists*, 335–36.

67. McDonald, *AH*, 197.

68. *PAH*, 7:226–31.

69. U.S. v. Hylton, 3 U.S. 171 (1796). For evidence of Hamilton's support of progressive taxation, see his speech of June 28, 1788, New York Ratifying Convention, *PAH*, 5:119, wherein he speaks of laying the "principal [tax] burthens on the wealthy"; and *Report on Manufactures, PAH*, 10:312, where he speaks of the injustice of general fixed rate taxes "to the industrious poor."

70. *PAH*, 10:2–3.

71. Hamilton quoted in McCraw, *Founders and Finance*, 123. McCraw notes at 130 that 150 years later, Joseph Schumpeter characterized Hamilton's report as "applied economics at its best."

72. McNamara, *PE&S*, 128.

73. McCraw, *Founders and Finance*, 125–26.

74. See, for example, Kenneth W. Rowe, *Mathew Carey: A Study in American Economic Development* (Baltimore, MD: Johns Hopkins University Press, 1933), 29–35, 68, 115; Mathew Carey, *Essays on Political Economy* (New York: Augustus M. Kelly, reprint, 1968, [1822]), no. 9. List's work in Europe

would influence the German historical school of economics, offering ideas that cycled back to the United States during the Progressive Era. For sources on this influence, see M. Curtis Hoffman's "Paradigm Lost: Public Administration at Johns Hopkins University 1884–96," *Public Administration Review* 62, no. 1 (2002): 12–23; and Spicer's *Public Administration and the State*.

75. *PAH*, 10:263–74.

76. *PAH*, 10:266–70.

77. *PAH*, 10:266–70.

78. See David Moss, *When All Else Fails: Government as the Ultimate Risk Manager* (Cambridge, MA: Harvard University Press, 2002), chaps. 2–3. Moss illustrates in detail how US and state policies have consistently provided subsidies and limited risk through legal devices such as corporations and through public insurance where private insurance was not viable.

79. *PAH*, 10:268. His discussion of regulation occurs at 309.

80. *PAH*, 10:309–10.

81. *The Continentalist, PAH*, 3:76–77; McDonald, *AH*, 55, 157. If Alan Greenspan had adopted this view in his nineteen-year tenure as federal reserve chief, he would likely have headed off or seriously reduced the extent of the financial crash of 2007–8. He subsequently admitted in testimony before Congress that there was a flaw in the free-market philosophy that guided his inattention to Wall Street speculators.

82. *PAH*, 10:268–69.

83. *PAH*, 10:302–3.

84. *PAH*, 10:269–82, quote at 282.

85. *PAH*, 10:286–87.

86. McCraw, *Founders and Finance*, 131.

Chapter 6

1. Walling, *Republican Empire*.

2. Chernow, *AH*, chaps. 23–26, 431–81.

3. Walling, *Republican Empire*, 3–5. Walling reviews the literature that treats Hamilton as a militarist with imperial pretensions and finds it lacking attention to important distinctions and nuances in both Hamilton's writings and his actions. (See especially his critique of Gerald Stourzh's equation of empire with imperialism or rule by force at page 97.) Though Hamilton never gave a definition of empire in his work, he used the term in ways clearly not given to militarism and imperialism. For example, he referred to various states, including New York, as empires, to areas of land as empires, and to instruments of rule as elements of empire. Thus, Walling draws from the Latin source of the term, *imperare*, which means "to rule," and argues that for Hamilton, "it meant the ability to direct and attach the passions of the people to the national government" (97). It was connected to his attachment to rule by consent as a means of establishing political authority. In conjunction with the biographers, historians, and thematic analyses employed here, I find Walling's assessment of Hamilton's approach more convincing and his critique of the militarist thesis compelling.

4. *The Continentalist*, no. 3, 660; *Federalist*, no. 6, 57. Also see Alexander

Hamilton to James Duane, *PAH*, 2:403, for an illustration of the continual state of war in the leagues of Grecian republics. This early letter projects much of Hamilton's agenda in his subsequent career.

5. *Federalist*, no. 8, 68.

6. *Federalist*, no. 8, 68–69.

7. *Federalist*, no. 8, 69.

8. For an elaborate description of the whole affair, see Chernow, *AH*, chap. 26, 468–81.

9. Chernow, *AH*, chap. 26, 471.

10. Chernow, *AH*, chap. 26, 477. Of course, many political opponents did not share this view of things and used the affair in later political battles as more evidence that both Washington and Hamilton secretly harbored monarchist designs. In the short run, however, a favorable view of the administration's handling of the matter prevailed in the press and left the opposition temporarily deflated.

11. Walling, *Republican Empire*, 5. Walling also establishes Hamilton's view of judicial review and independent courts as part of the bulwark of liberty that makes a powerful military possible without descending to a state of force over the citizenry. See his chaps. 6 and 7, 123–72.

12. "A Letter from Phocion to the Considerate Citizens of New York," *PAH*, 3:485.

13. "Second Letter from Phocion," *PAH*, 3:553–54. Also quoted in Walling, *Republican Empire*, at 74.

14. Alexander Hamilton to James Duane, *PAH*, 2:406. Also see Hamilton's *Report on a Military Peace Establishment* to the Continental Congress, *PAH*, 3:378–83.

15. In his 1791 *Report on Manufactures*, Hamilton recommended that Congress consider this measure as a "usual practice of Nations" at the time. "There appears to be an improvidence, in leaving these essential instruments of national defence to the casual speculations of individual adventure; a resource which can less be relied upon, in this case than in most others; the articles in question not being objects of ordinary and indispensable private consumption or use. As a general rule, manufactories on the immediate account of Government are to be avoided; but this seems to be one of the few exceptions, which that rule admits, depending on very special reasons." *PAH*, 10:317.

16. Alexander Hamilton to James Duane, *PAH*, 2:406.

17. Alexander Hamilton to James Duane, *PAH*, 2:408–11.

18. Walling, *Republican Empire*, 59. Hamilton's words on this distinction are in Alexander Hamilton to John Dickinson, *PAH*, 3:454.

19. Walling, *Republican Empire*, 66–70. Walling drew these insights from Charles Royster's fine book, *A Revolutionary People at War: The Continental Army and the American Character, 1775–1783* (Chapel Hill: University of North Carolina, 1979), especially 194–95.

20. *Federalist*, nos. 24 and 25, 157–67.

21. *Federalist*, no. 24, 162. Gilbert Lycan pointed out that in 1802 Jefferson sounded more like Hamilton when he wrote that New Orleans was the "one single spot, the possessor of which is our natural and habitual enemy,"

implying that taking it by force might well be necessary. A year later, Napoleon's offer of the Louisiana Purchase rendered the whole matter moot. Gilbert L. Lycan, *Alexander Hamilton and American Foreign Policy: A Design for Greatness* (Norman: University of Oklahoma Press, 1970), 415 (hereafter cited as Lycan, *AH&AFP*).

22. *Federalist*, no. 25, 166–67. Also see *Federalist*, nos. 28 and 29, 178–87.

23. See White, *The Federalists*, 145–53. Federici gives much the same account that Hamilton's thinking on the matter stood against the conventional wisdom of the day, which held that standing armies were "instruments of monarchies and oppressive governments that needed to suppress their people" and that popular governments therefore did not need them. Militias could mount defenses sufficient to defend the states from foreign as well as domestic aggressors and deflate imperial pretensions to boot.

24. White, *The Federalists*, 156–57.

25. White, *The Federalists*, 160–63.

26. Alexander Hamilton to James McHenry, *PAH*, 24:76.

27. For a brief outline of some of his proposals, see Alexander Hamilton to Oliver Wolcott, June 5, 1798, *PAH*, 21:485–88, and letters from Alexander Hamilton to James McHenry, *PAH*, 22:341–66; *PAH*, 421; *PAH*, 24:69–75, 306–11. Also see "An Act giving eventual authority to the President of the United States to augment the Army" (1 Stat. 725–27), March 2, 1799; and "An Act authorizing the President to raise a Provisional Army" (1 Stat. 558–61), May 28, 1798.

28. Mitchell, *Alexander Hamilton: The National Adventure*, 438–39, 449–51.

29. Chernow, *AH*, 564; White, *The Federalists*, 147–55.

30. See, for example, Alexander Hamilton to Louis Le Begue Du Portail, *PAH*, 22:29.

31. Chernow, *AH*, 564.

32. See Alexander Hamilton to James McHenry, *PAH*, 24:69–75; *PAH*, 22:204, 356–57.

33. *PAH*, 22:41–42, 163, 202, 377.

34. *PAH*, 22:377.

35. *PAH*, 22:555, 350–51.

36. *PAH*, 22:352–54.

37. *PAH*, 22:357–58, 342–43. For details of the Washington administration's personnel policy, see White, *The Federalists*, 253–66; and Van Riper, *History of the United States Civil Service*, chap. 1.

38. *PAH*, 22:349–50.

39. *PAH*, 22:268, 350–51.

40. *PAH*, 22:269, 421, 431.

41. *PAH*, 22:421, 431.

42. Walling, *Republican Empire*, 160–61. Walling addresses the charges by a few authors that Hamilton was an ardent militarist with imperial pretensions and, upon close analysis of Hamilton's work and theirs, finds them wanting for evidence.

43. Lycan, *AH&AFP*, 132.

44. Americanus, no. 1, *PAH*, 15:670.

45. Americanus, no. 1, *PAH*, 15:671.

46. Chernow, *AH*, 392.

47. Alexander Hamilton to George Washington, April 14, 1794, *PAH*, 16:267.

48. Lycan, *AH&AFP*, 214.

49. For an elaborate description of the many grievances and political dynamics against both Great Britain and France regarding US commercial shipping during the European war, see Lycan, *AH&AFP*, chaps. 10 and 11, 175–225; and Harper, *American Machiavelli*, chaps. 7–9, 88–126. Their chapters also address the Spanish-held lands on the southern and western borderlands as a complicating factor in those political dynamics.

50. *PAH*, 16:167.

51. Quoted in Lycan, *AH&AFP*, 213, from Washington's fifth annual message to Congress, December 3, 1793.

52. Hamilton's insights on foreign affairs are found in essays penned as Pacificus, Americanus, Camillus, Metellus, and Lucius Crassus, in essays titled *No Jacobin*, *The Warning*, and *Federalist*, nos. 23–39, and in his many letters to President Washington on executive powers relating to foreign affairs and military preparedness. His letter to Washington on April 14, 1794, is considered one of his most influential works because it convinced the president to follow the policy of strict neutrality. Washington had been ambivalent up to that point. The antics of Genêt no doubt also made it easier to see the wisdom in Hamilton's counsel.

53. Mitchell, *Alexander Hamilton: Youth to Maturity*, 102.

54. Pacificus, no. 2, *PAH*, 15:57–60.

55. Pacificus, no. 4, *PAH*, 15:85–86. Also see Federici, *PPAH*, 172.

56. Pacificus, no. 2, 56–63.

57. Pacificus, no. 2, 57–60.

58. Pacificus, no. 2, 58.

59. Pacificus, no. 2, 58–59.

60. Lycan, *AH&AFP*, 198.

61. Pacificus, no. 4, *PAH*, 15:85.

62. Pacificus, no. 4, *PAH*, 15:85.

63. Pacificus, no. 4, July 1793, *PAH*, 15:84.

64. Pacificus, no. 4, July 1793, *PAH*, 15:83–85.

65. Alexander Hamilton to George Washington, Sept. 15, 1790, *PAH*, 7:43–44.

66. *The Warning*, no. 3, *PAH*, 20:519–20.

67. Pacificus, no. 2, July 1793, *PAH*, 15:60.

68. Pacificus, no. 2, July 1793, *PAH*, 15:62. Also see Lycan, *AH&AFP*, 156–57.

69. "Draft of Washington's Farewell Address," July 30, 1796, *PAH*, 20:284–85.

70. Chernow, *AH*, 438.

71. Chernow, *AH*, 440–41.

72. Harper, *American Machiavelli*, 117. Genêt quoted in Elkins and McKitrick, *The Age of Federalism*, 348–49.

73. Chernow, *AH*, 447.

74. Chernow, *AH*, 488–90.

75. *Washington's Farewell Address,* July 30, 1796, *PAH,* 20:284.
76. Harper, *American Machiavelli,* 96.
77. Federici, *PPAH,* 183–84. Quote from Lukacs is found at 184. See John Lukacs, *Democracy and Populism: Fear and Hatred* (New Haven, CT: Yale University Press, 2005), 31, 36.
78. Federici, *PPAH,* 184.
79. John Schaar, "The Case for Patriotism," *American Review,* no. 17 (May 1973): 59–101.
80. An example of the kind of introspection needed today, and one that matches Hamilton's realist perspective very closely, is found in the works of Andrew Bacevich. See, for example, his *New American Militarism: How Americans Are Seduced by War* (New York: Oxford University Press, 2013); *American Empire: The Realities and Consequences of U.S. Diplomacy* (Cambridge, MA: Harvard University Press, 2002); *The Imperial Tense: Prospects and Problems of American Empire* (Chicago: Ivan R. Dee, 2003); and *The Limits of Power: The End of American Exceptionalism* (New York: Metropolitan Books, Henry Holt, 2008). Bacevich relies heavily on the Christian realism of Reinhold Niebuhr in all his work.

Conclusion

1. Lawrence Lessig and Cass Sunstein have argued along this same line, though casting it more in terms of the founders in general. Their exegesis of the words and actions of the founders reinforces the sense that they were pragmatic, permissive, and often tentative in their application of constitutional clauses and structures. Furthermore, they argue persuasively that the founders in general held a more limited view of executive power than is attributed to them today, finding that significant administrative functions, such as prosecution, some treasury operations, postal duties, some judicial administrative duties, and even state-level execution of federal laws fell beyond the reach of presidential control. I must thank Brian Cook for calling my attention to their fine law review article late in my work on this book. See Lessig and Sunstein, "The President and the Administration," *Columbia Law Review* 94, no. 1 (January 1994): 1–123, especially page 69.
2. Lessig and Sunstein, "The President and the Administration," 78–83, quotes at 80, 81. Lessig and Sunstein point out that the Supreme Court later narrowed the decision in *Kendall* to purely ministerial (nondiscretionary) matters as determined by law. In that case, the postmaster general had been ordered by law to pay grieving contractors the money owed to them by contract—a ministerial instruction. In effect, this preserved presidential claims to exclusive control over all discretionary matters of administration.
3. Cook, *Bureaucracy and Self-Government,* 96, 107.
4. Peri Arnold, "*Federalist* No. 70: Can the Public Service Survive in the Contest between Hamilton's Aspirations and Madison's Reality?" *Public Administration Review,* special issue (December 2011): 105–11, quotations at 105.
5. See Theodore Roosevelt, *The Autobiography of Theodore Roosevelt* (New York: Scribner's, 1913). In foreign affairs, Roosevelt meddled in other

countries' affairs to build his own political reputation as a leader, with little regard to a realist sense of national interests per se. A fine analysis of Roosevelt's stewardship theory as held together by his conception of statesmanship can be found in Randall L. Robinson, "The Stewardship Theory of the Presidency: Theodore Roosevelt's Political Theory of Republican Progressive Statesmanship and the Foundation of the Modern Presidency," PhD dissertation, Claremont Graduate School, 1997.

6. For example, see Sidney Milkis, "The Rhetorical and Administrative Presidencies," *Critical Review: A Journal of Politics and Society* 19, no. 2–3 (2007): 379–401; Sidney Milkis and Michael Nelson, *The American Presidency: Origins and Development, 1776–2002* (Washington, DC: CQ, 2003), 204; Jeffrey K. Tulis, *The Rhetorical Presidency* (Princeton, NJ: Princeton University Press, 1987), chap. 4. Cook, *Bureaucracy and Self-Government,* 143–46.

7. Cook, *Bureaucracy and Self-Government,* 144.

8. Cook, *Bureaucracy and Self-Government,* 152–53. Also see Rohr, *To Run a Constitution,* chap. 5, where he shows that Wilson, in his early works, clearly advocated amending the Constitution to make the president's cabinet part of the legislative branch, much as in parliamentary government.

9. Cook, *Bureaucracy and Self-Government,* 168.

10. See Milkis, *The President and the Parties: The Transformation of the American Party System since the New Deal* (Oxford: Oxford University Press, 1993), 41, quoted in Cook, *Bureaucracy and Self-Government,* 168.

11. Cook, paraphrasing Milkis, *Bureaucracy and Self-Government,* 169.

12. Cook, *Bureaucracy and Self-Government,* 171.

13. See Rohr, *To Run a Constitution,* chap. 9, quotes at 112, 139, 141. Brownlow Report: Louis Brownlow, Charles Merriam, and Luther Gulick, *Administrative Management in the Government of the United States* (Washington, DC: President's Committee on Administrative Management, 1937).

14. Stephanie P. Newbold and Larry D. Terry, "The President's Committee on Administrative Management: The Untold Story and the Federalist Connection," *Administration & Society* 38, no. 5 (November 2006): 522–55, quote at 525.

15. Among the authors of these companion reports were such notable scholars and public figures as Floyd Reeves and Paul David, Arthur E. Buck and Harvey C. Mansfield, Robert Cushman, James Fesler, Herbert Emmerich, James Hart, and Edwin Witte.

16. Newbold and Terry, "President's Committee on Administrative Management," 526.

17. Newbold and Terry, "President's Committee on Administrative Management," 529–30.

18. Rohr, *To Run a Constitution,* 138.

19. Rohr, *To Run a Constitution,* 138.

20. For notable examples, see Steven G. Calabresi and Kevin H. Rhodes, "The Structural Constitution: Unitary Executive, Plural Judiciary," *Harvard Law Review* 105, no. 1153 (1992); Theodore B. Olson, "Separation of Powers Principle Is No 'Triviality' (*Bowher v. Synar*)," *Legal Times,* July 21, 1986.

21. Lessig and Sunstein, "President and the Constitution," quotes at 2, 41–42.

22. Lessig and Sunstein, "President and the Constitution," quotes at 2.

23. Cook, *Bureaucracy and Self-Government*, passim.

24. Cook, *Bureaucracy and Self-Government*, 251.

25. Spicer, *In Defense of Politics in Public Administration*, i.

26. Cook, *Bureaucracy and Self-Government*, 254.

27. Cook, *Bureaucracy and Self-Government*, 255.

28. See, for example, James S. Bowman and Jonathon P. West, *American Public Service: Radical Reform and the Merit System* (Boca Raton, FL: CRC, Taylor and Francis Group, 2007).

29. Rosenbloom, *Building a Legislative-Centered Public Administration*.

30. See, for example, Phillip J. Cooper, *Civil Rights in Public Service* (New York: Routledge, 2017); Cooper, *Public Law and Public Administration*; Phillip J. Cooper, *Cases on Public Law and Public Administration* (Belmont, CA: Thomson-Wadsworth, 2005); Phillip J. Cooper, *Hard Judicial Choices: Federal District Court Judges and State and Local Officials* (New York: Oxford University Press, 1988); Rosenbloom, *Federal Service and the Constitution*.

31. David H. Rosenbloom, "Public Administration Theory and the Separation of Powers," *Public Administration Review* 43, no. 3, 219–27; David H. Rosenbloom, Robert S. Kravchuk, and Richard M. Clerkin, *Public Administration: Understanding Management, Politics, and Law in the Public Sector*, 8th ed. (New York: McGraw-Hill, 2015); David H. Rosenbloom, Rosemary O'Leary, and Joshua Chanin, *Public Administration and Law*, 3rd ed. (New York: Routledge, 2010).

32. See, for example, Patricia W. Ingraham and David H. Rosenbloom, eds., *The Promise and Paradox of Civic Service Reform* (Pittsburgh: University of Pittsburgh Press, 1992); James P. Pfiffner and Douglas A. Brook, eds., *The Future of Merit: Twenty Years after the Civil Service Reform Act* (Baltimore, MD: Johns Hopkins University Press, 2000). It is important to note that Louis Fisher saw the fraying of interbranch relations beginning in the early 1970s, before the SES came into being, so other causes such as the abuses during the Nixon administration also pertain. See Louis Fisher, *Presidential Spending Power* (Princeton, NJ: Princeton University Press, 1975).

33. Arnold, "*Federalist* No. 70," 105–11, quotations at 105.

34. My work with Morgan, Shinn, and Robinson in our book *Foundations of Public Service* identifies four distinct administrative traditions engendered at the founding by the unresolved problem of how to provide safety from tyranny while providing effective but limited government marked by responsiveness, protection of rights and access, and ample opportunities for civic engagement.

Bibliography

Adair, Douglass. *Fame and the Founding Fathers.* Edited by Trevor Colbourn. New York: W. W. Norton, 1974.

Adams, Abigail, John Adams, and Thomas Jefferson. *The Adams-Jefferson Letters.* 2 vols. Edited by Lester J. Cappon. Chapel Hill: University of North Carolina Press, 1959.

Adams, Henry C. *Public Debts.* New York: D. Appleton, 1887.

An Act to Establish the Treasury Department. *Public Statutes at Large of the United States of America.* 1 Stat. 65, Chap. XII (Sept. 2, 1789): 1:65–69.

Arnold, Peri. "*Federalist* No. 70: Can the Public Service Survive in the Contest between Hamilton's Aspirations and Madison's Reality?" *Public Administration Review,* special issue (December 2011): 105–11.

Bacevich, Andrew J. *American Empire: The Realities and Consequences of U.S. Diplomacy.* Cambridge, MA: Harvard University Press, 2002.

———. *The Imperial Tense: Prospects and Problems of American Empire.* Chicago: Ivan R. Dee, 2003.

———. *The Limits of Power: The End of American Exceptionalism.* New York: Metropolitan Books, Henry Holt, 2008.

———. *New American Militarism: How Americans Are Seduced by War.* New York: Oxford University Press, 2013.

Bailey, Jeremy D. "The New Unitary Executive and Democratic Theory: The Problem of Alexander Hamilton." *American Political Science Review* 102 (2008): 453.

———. "The Traditional View of Hamilton's *Federalist* No. 77 and an Unexpected Challenge: A Response to Seth Barrett Tillman." *Harvard Journal of Law & Public Policy* 33, no. 1 (2010): 169–84.

Barker, Ernest. *Traditions of Civility.* Cambridge: Cambridge University Press, 1948.

Baxter, Lawrence. "Capture in Financial Regulation: Can We Redirect It Toward the Common Good?" *Cornell Journal of Law and Public Policy* 21 (2011): 175–200.

Beard, Charles A. *An Economic Interpretation of the Constitution.* New York: Macmillan, 1935.

Beawes, Wyndham. *The Merchant's Directory,* 1751.

Bederman, David J. *Classical Foundations of the Constitution: Prevailing Wisdom*. Cambridge: Cambridge University Press, 2008.

Beveridge, Albert J. *The Life of John Marshall*. 4 vols. Boston: Houghton Mifflin, 1916–19.

Blackstone, William. *Commentaries on the Laws of England*. Vol. 1. 1765. Oxford: Clarendon Press, 2001.

Bowman, James S., and Jonathon P. West. *American Public Service: Radical Reform and the Merit System*. Boca Raton, FL: CRC, Taylor and Francis Group, 2007.

Brownlow, Louis, Charles Merriam, and Luther Gulick. *Administrative Management in the Government of the United States*. Washington, DC: President's Committee on Administrative Management, 1937.

Calabresi, Steven G., and Kevin H. Rhodes. "The Structural Constitution: Unitary Executive, Plural Judiciary." *Harvard Law Review* 105, no. 1153 (1992).

Caldwell, Lynton K. *The Administrative Theories of Hamilton and Jefferson: Their Contribution to Thought on Public Administration*. 2nd ed. New York: Holmes & Meier, 1988. First published 1944 by University of Chicago Press (Chicago), with second printing 1964 by Russell & Russell (New York).

Carey, Mathew. *Essays on Political Economy*. 1822. Reprint, New York: Augustus M. Kelly, 1968.

Chan, Michael. *Aristotle and Hamilton on Commerce and Statesmanship*. Columbia: University of Missouri Press, 2006.

Chernow, Ron. *Alexander Hamilton*. New York: Penguin, 2004.

Cicero. *On Duties*. Edited by M. T. Griffin and E. M. Atkins. Cambridge: Cambridge University Press, 1991.

Cohens v. Virginia, 6 Wheaton 264 (1821).

Colbert, Jean Baptiste. *Lettres, instructions et mémoires de Colbert*. Ca. 1680.

———. *Mémoires sur les affaires de finance de France*. Ca. 1663.

Cook, Brian J. *Bureaucracy and Self-Government: Reconsidering the Role of Public Administration in American Politics*. 2nd ed. Baltimore, MD: Johns Hopkins University Press, 2014.

Cooper, Phillip J. *Cases on Public Law and Public Administration*. Belmont, CA: Thomson-Wadsworth, 2005.

———. *Civil Rights in Public Service*. New York: Routledge, 2017.

———. *Hard Judicial Choices: Federal District Court Judges and State and Local Officials*. New York: Oxford University Press, 1988.

———. *Public Law and Public Administration*. 4th ed. Belmont, CA: Thomson-Wadsworth, 2007.

Corwin, Edward S. *The Constitution of the United States of America: Analysis and Interpretation; Annotations of Cases Decided by the Supreme Court of the United States to June 30, 1952*. Washington, DC: US Government Printing Office, 1953.

———. *The "Higher Law" Background of American Constitutional Law*. Ithaca, NY: Cornell University Press, 1928.

Crenson, Matthew A. *The Federal Machine: Beginnings of Bureaucracy in Jacksonian America*. Baltimore, MD: Johns Hopkins University Press, 1975.

Crosskey, William Winslow. *Politics and the Constitution in the History of the United States.* Vols. 1 and 2. Chicago: University of Chicago Press, 1953.

Crowe, Ian. *Patriotism and Public Spirit: Edmund Burke and the Role of the Critic in Mid-Eighteenth-Century Britain.* Stanford, CA: Stanford University Press, 2012.

Dartmouth College v. Woodward, 4 Wheaton 518 (1819).

Davies, Phil. "The Bank That Hamilton Built." *Region* (Federal Reserve Bank of Minneapolis), September 1, 2007. https://minneapolisfed.org /publications/the-region/the-bank-that-hamilton-built.

Debates and Proceedings in Congress of the United States. Washington, DC: Gales and Seaton, 1834.

Delman, Edward. "How Lin-Manuel Miranda Shapes History." *Atlantic,* September 29, 2015. http://www.theatlantic.com/entertainment/archive /2015/09/lin-manuel-miranda-hamilton/408019.

Dillon, John F., ed. *John Marshall: Life, Character and Judicial Services as Portrayed Addresses and Proceedings on Marshall Day.* 3 vols. Chicago: Callaghan, 1903.

Dobel, Patrick. *Public Integrity.* Baltimore, MD: Johns Hopkins University Press, 1999.

Dunbar, C. F. "Some Precedents Followed by Alexander Hamilton." In *Economic Essays,* edited by D. M. W. Sprague. New York: MacMillan, 1904.

Dunbar, Louise. *A Study of the Monarchical Tendencies in the United States from 1776 to 1801.* Urbana: University of Illinois, 1922.

Elkins, Stanley, and Eric L. McKitrick. *The Age of Federalism: The Early American Republic, 1788–1800.* Oxford: Oxford University Press, 1993.

Ellis, Joseph J. *His Excellency: George Washington.* New York: Alfred A. Knopf, 2004.

Elliot, Jonathan, ed. *The Debates in the Several State Conventions on the Adoption of the Federal Constitution.* 2nd ed. Philadelphia, 1876.

Epstein, David. *The Political Theory of "The Federalist."* Chicago: University of Chicago Press, 1984.

Federici, Michael. *The Political Philosophy of Alexander Hamilton.* Baltimore, MD: Johns Hopkins University Press, 2012.

Ferguson, E. James. *The Power of the Purse: A History of American Public Finance.* Chapel Hill: University of North Carolina Press, 1961.

Ferleger, Herbert R. *David A. Wells and the American Revenue System, 1865–1870.* Philadelphia: Porcupine, 1977.

Financial Crisis Inquiry Commission. *The Financial Crisis Inquiry Report: Final Report of the National Commission on the Causes of the Financial and Economic Crisis in the United States.* Washington, DC: US Government Printing Office, 2011. Available from bookstore.gpo.gov.

Fisher, Louis. *Presidential Spending Power.* Princeton, NJ: Princeton University Press, 1975.

Flaumenhaft, Harvey. *The Effective Republic: Administration and Constitution in the Thought of Alexander Hamilton.* Durham, NC: Duke University Press, 1992.

Fletcher v. Peck, 6 Cranch 87 (1810).

Flexner, James T., ed. *George Washington: Anguish and Farewell, 1793–1799.* Boston: Little, Brown, 1969.

Freund, Paul A. "Umpiring the Federal System." *Columbia Law Review* 54 (1954): 561–78.

Friedman, Lawrence. *A History of American Law.* New York: Simon & Schuster, 1973.

Gibbons v. Ogden, 9 Wheaton 1 (1824).

Gordon, John Steele. *Hamilton's Blessing: The Extraordinary Life and Times of Our National Debt.* New York: Walker, 1997.

Govan, Thomas P. "The Rich, the Well-born, and Alexander Hamilton." *Mississippi Valley Historical Review* 36, no. 4 (1950): 675–80.

Green, Richard. "The Centrality of Public Morality in John Rohr's Work." *Administrative Theory and Praxis* 34, no. 4 (December 2012): 629–34.

———. "Common Law, Equity, and American Public Administration." *American Review of Public Administration* 32, no. 3 (September 2002): 263–94.

———. "Institutional History and New Public Governance: Lessons from Banking History and the Financial Disaster of 2007–8." In *New Public Governance: A Regime-Centered Perspective,* edited by Douglas F. Morgan and Brian J. Cook. Armonk: M. E. Sharpe. 2014.

———. "Plutocracy, Bureaucracy, and the End of Public Trust." *Administration & Society* 44, no. 1 (2012): 109–43.

Green v. Biddle, 8 Wheaton 1 (1823).

Hall, Kermit L. *The Magic Mirror: Law in American History.* New York: Oxford University Press, 1989.

Hamilton, Alexander. *The Law Practice of Alexander Hamilton: Documents and Commentary.* 5 vols. Edited by Julius Goebel Jr. New York: Columbia University Press, 1964–81.

———. *The Papers of Alexander Hamilton.* 27 vols. Edited by Harold C. Syrett and Jacob E. Cooke. New York: Columbia University Press, 1969–79.

Hamilton, Alexander, James Madison, and John Jay. *The Federalist Papers.* With an introduction, table of contents, and index of ideas by Clinton Rossiter. New York: New American Library, 1961.

Hammond, Bray. *Banks and Politics in America from the Revolution to the Civil War.* Princeton, NJ: Princeton University Press, 1991.

Harper, John Lamberton. *American Machiavelli: Alexander Hamilton and the Origins of U.S. Foreign Policy.* New York: Cambridge University Press, 2004.

Hendrickson, Robert. *Hamilton.* Vols. 1 and 2. New York: Mason/Charter, 1976.

Hoffman, M. Curtis. "Paradigm Lost: Public Administration at Johns Hopkins University 1884–96." *Public Administration Review* 62, no. 1 (2002): 12–23.

Hoffmann, Susan. *Politics and Banking: Ideas, Public Policy, and the Creation of Financial Institutions.* Baltimore, MD: Johns Hopkins University Press, 2001.

Hume, David. *Philosophical Works.* Vol. 3, *Essays: Moral, Political, and Literary,* edited by T. H. Gross. Boston: Little, Brown, 1876.

Ingraham, Patricia W., and David H. Rosenbloom, eds. *The Promise and*

Paradox of Civic Service Reform. Pittsburgh: University of Pittsburgh Press, 1992.

Jackson, Andrew. First Annual Message, December 8, 1829. Online by Gerhard Peters and John T. Woolley, *The American Presidency Project.* http://www.presidency.ucsb.edu/ws/?pid=29471.

Jay, John. *The Correspondence and Public Papers of John Jay.* Vol. 3, *1782–1793,* edited by Henry P. Johnston, A.M. New York: G. P. Putnam's Sons, 1891.

Johnson, Simon, and James Kwak. *13 Bankers: The Wall Street Takeover and the Next Financial Meltdown.* New York: Pantheon, 2010.

Kelly, Alfred H., Winfred A. Harbison, and Herman Belz. *The American Constitution: Its Origins and Development.* 6th ed. New York: W. W. Norton, 1983.

———. *The American Constitution, Its Origins and Development.* 7th ed. Vol. 1. New York: W. W. Norton, 1991.

Kendall v. U.S. ex Rel. Stokes, 37 U.S. 524 (1838).

Kent, James. *Commentaries on American Law.* 4 vols. New York: D. Halsted, 1826. Reprint, New York: Da Capo, 1971.

Khademian, Ann. "The Financial Crisis: A Retrospective." *Public Administration Review* 71 (2011): 841–49.

Konefsky, Samuel J. *John Marshall and Alexander Hamilton: Architects of the American Constitution.* New York: MacMillan, 1964.

Knott, Stephen F. *Alexander Hamilton and the Persistence of Myth.* Lawrence: University Press of Kansas, 2002.

Kwak, James. "Cultural Capture and the Financial Crisis." In *Preventing Regulatory Capture: Special Interest Influence and How to Limit It,* edited by Daniel Carpenter and David Moss. New York: Cambridge University Press, 2013.

Lessig, Lawrence, and Cass Sunstein. "The President and the Administration." *Columbia Law Review* 94, no. 1 (January 1994): 1–123.

Lewis, Michael, ed. *Panic: The Story of Modern Financial Insanity.* New York: W. W. Norton, 2009.

———. "The Trouble with Wall Street: The Shocking News that Goldman Sachs Is Greedy." Money (section), *New Republic,* February 4, 2013. http://www.newrepublic.com/article/112209/michael-lewis-goldman-sachs.

Levy, Beryl H. *Our Constitution: Tool or Testament?* Port Washington, NY: Kennikat, 1965.

Light, Paul. *Thickening Government: Federal Hierarchy and the Diffusion of Accountability.* Washington, DC: Brookings Institution, 1995.

Love, Robert A. *Federal Financing: A Study of the Methods Employed by the Treasury in Its Borrowing Operations.* New York: Columbia University Press, 1931.

Lukacs, John. *Democracy and Populism: Fear and Hatred.* New Haven, CT: Yale University Press, 2005.

Lycan, Gilbert L. *Alexander Hamilton and American Foreign Policy: A Design for Greatness.* Norman: University of Oklahoma Press, 1970.

Madison, James. *Notes of Debates in the Federal Convention of 1787.* Edited by Adrienne Koch. Athens: Ohio University Press, 1966.

Marbury v. Madison, 5 U.S. 137 (1803).

Maritain, Jacques. *Man and the State*. Chicago: University of Chicago Press, 1963.

Marshall, John. *The Life of George Washington*. 5 vols. Fredericksburg, VA: Citizen's Guild, 1926.

Martin v. Hunter's Lessee, 1 Wheaton 304 (1816).

Mason, Alpheus Thomas. *The Supreme Court from Taft to Warren*. Baton Rouge: Louisiana State University Press, 1968.

McCraw, Thomas K. *The Founders and Finance: How Hamilton, Gallatin, and Other Immigrants Forged a New Economy*. Cambridge, MA: Belknap-Harvard University Press, 2012.

McCulloch v. Maryland, 17 U.S. 316 (1819).

McDonald, Forrest. *Alexander Hamilton: A Biography*. New York: W. W. Norton, 1979.

———. *Novus Ordo Seclorum: The Intellectual Origins of the Constitution*. Lawrence: University Press of Kansas, 1985.

———. *We the People: The Economic Origins of the Constitution*. New Brunswick, NJ: Transaction, 1992.

McNamara, Peter. *Political Economy and Statesmanship: Smith, Hamilton, and the Foundation of the Commercial Republic*. DeKalb: Northern Illinois University Press, 1998.

Mead, Rebecca. "All About the Hamiltons: A New Musical Brings the Founding Fathers Back to Life—with a lot of Hip-Hop," *New Yorker*, February 9, 2015. http://www.newyorker.com/magazine/2015/02/09/hamiltons.

Milkis, Sidney. *The President and the Parties: The Transformation of the American Party System since the New Deal*. Oxford: Oxford University Press, 1993.

———. "The Rhetorical and Administrative Presidencies." *Critical Review: A Journal of Politics and Society* 19, nos. 2–3 (2007): 379–401.

Milkis, Sidney, and Michael Nelson. *The American Presidency: Origins and Development, 1776–2002*. Washington, DC: CQ, 2003.

Miller, John C. *Alexander Hamilton: Portrait in Paradox*. New York: Harper & Row, 1959.

———. *Alexander Hamilton and the Growth of the New Nation*. New Brunswick, NJ: Transaction, 2004.

Miller, Perry. *The Legal Mind in America: From Independence to the Civil War*. Ithaca, NY: Cornell University Press, 1962.

———. *The Life of the Mind in America: From the Revolution to the Civil War*. New York: Harcourt, Brace & World, 1965.

Mitchell, Broadus. *Alexander Hamilton: Youth to Maturity, 1755–1788*. New York: Macmillan, 1957.

———. *Alexander Hamilton: The National Adventure, 1789–1804*. New York: Macmillan, 1958.

Moore, Mark H. *Creating Public Value: Strategic Management in Government*. Cambridge, MA: Harvard University Press, 1995.

Morgan, Douglas F., Richard T. Green, Craig W. Shinn, and Kent S. Robinson. *Foundations of Public Service*, 2nd ed. Armonk, NY: M. E. Sharpe, 2013.

———. "A Political History of Public Personnel Administration." In *Foundations of Public Service*, 2nd ed., 199–232. Armonk, NY: M. E. Sharpe, 2013.

Morgan, Douglas F., Kent A. Kirwan, John A. Rohr, David H. Rosenbloom, and David Lewis Schaeffer. "Recovering, Restoring, and Renewing the Foundations of American Public Administration: The Contributions of Herbert A. Storing." *Public Administration Review* 70, no. 4 (2010): 621–33.

Morgenthau, Hans J. "The Mainsprings of American Foreign Policy: The National Interest Versus Moral Abstractions." *American Political Science Review* 44, no. 4 (December 1950): 833–54.

Morrison v. Olson, 487 U.S. 654 (1988).

Morris, Richard B. *Alexander Hamilton and the Founding of the Nation.* New York: Dial, 1957.

———. *Basic Ideas of Hamilton.* New York: Pocket, 1957.

Moss, David. *When All Else Fails: Government as the Ultimate Risk Manager.* Cambridge, MA: Harvard University Press, 2002.

Necker, Jacques. *Compte rendu au roi.* 1781.

———. *Essai sur la législation et le commerce des grains.* 1775.

———. *Treatise on the Administration of Finances of France.* Translated by Thomas Mortimer. London, 1785. Originally published in 1784 as *Traité de l'administration des finances de la France.*

Newbold, Stephanie P., and David H. Rosenbloom, eds. *The Constitutional School of American Public Administration.* New York: Routledge, 2016.

Newbold, Stephanie P. *All but Forgotten: Thomas Jefferson and the Development of Public Administration.* Albany: State University of New York Press, 2010.

Newbold, Stephanie P., and Larry D. Terry. "The President's Committee on Administrative Management: The Untold Story and the Federalist Connection." *Administration & Society* 38, no. 5 (November 2006): 522–55.

New Jersey v. Wilson, 7 Cranch 164 (1812).

O'Leary, Rosemary. *The Ethics of Dissent: Managing Guerilla Government.* 2nd ed. Washington, DC: CQ, 2014.

Olson, Theodore B. "Separation of Powers Principle Is No 'Triviality' (*Bowher v. Synar*)." *Legal Times,* July 21, 1986.

Oster, John E. *The Political and Economic Doctrines of John Marshall.* New York: Burt Franklin, 1914.

Otenasek, Mildred. *Alexander Hamilton's Financial Policies.* New York: Arno, 1977.

Parks, Robert J. *European Origins of the Economic Ideas of Alexander Hamilton.* New York: Arno, 1977.

Parrington, Vernon Louis. *Main Currents in American Thought.* New York: Harcourt Brace, 1927.

People v. Croswell, 3 Johns, Cas. 337 N.Y. 1804.

Perry, James L., Annie Hondeghem, and Lois Recascino Wise. "Revisiting the Motivational Bases of Public Service: Twenty Years of Research and an Agenda for the Future." *Public Administration Review* 70, no. 5 (September/October 2010): 681–90.

Perry, James L., and Annie Hondeghem. *Motivation in Public Management: The Call of Public Service.* Oxford: Oxford University Press, 2008.

Pfiffner, James P., and Douglas A. Brook, eds. *The Future of Merit: Twenty Years after the Civil Service Reform Act.* Baltimore, MD: Johns Hopkins University Press, 2000.

Pickering, Timothy. *Papers.* Massachusetts Historical Society, February 13, 1811.

Pitt, William. *Parliamentary Speech on Establishment of a Sinking Fund.* 1786.

Postlethwayt, Malachy. *Universal Dictionary of Trade and Commerce.* London, 1766.

Price, Richard. *Additional Observations on the Nature and Value of Civil Liberty.* 1777.

———. *Observations on the Nature of Civil Liberty.* 1776.

Reinhart, Carmen M., and Kenneth S. Rogoff. *This Time Is Different: Eight Centuries of Financial Folly.* Princeton, NJ: Princeton University Press, 2009.

Richard, Carl J. *Greeks and Romans Bearing Gifts: How the Ancients Inspired the Founding Fathers.* Lanham, MD: Rowman & Littlefield, 2009.

Robinson, Randall L. "The Stewardship Theory of the Presidency: Theodore Roosevelt's Political Theory of Republican Progressive Statesmanship and the Foundation of the Modern Presidency." PhD dissertation, Claremont Graduate School, 1997.

Rohr, John A. *Ethics for Bureaucrats: An Essay on Law and Values.* Lawrence: University Press of Kansas, 1989.

———. "Public Administration, Executive Power, and Constitutional Confusion." *Public Administration Review* 49, no. 2 (March/April 1989): 108–14.

———. *Public Service Ethics and Constitutional Practice.* Lawrence: University Press of Kansas, 1998.

———. *To Run a Constitution: The Legitimacy of the Administrative State.* Lawrence: University Press of Kansas, 1986.

Roosevelt, Theodore. *The Autobiography of Theodore Roosevelt.* New York: Scribner's, 1913.

Rosenbloom, David H. *Building a Legislative-Centered Public Administration: Congress and the Administrative State, 1946–1999.* Tuscaloosa: University of Alabama Press, 2000.

———. *Federal Service and the Constitution: The Development of the Public Employment Relationship.* Ithaca, NY: Cornell University Press, 1971.

———. "Public Administration Theory and the Separation of Powers." *Public Administration Review* 43, no. 3: 219–27.

Rosenbloom, David H., Robert S. Kravchuk, and Richard M. Clerkin. *Public Administration: Understanding Management, Politics, and Law in the Public Sector.* 8th ed. New York: McGraw-Hill, 2015.

Rosenbloom, David H., Rosemary O'Leary, and Joshua Chanin. *Public Administration and Law.* 3rd ed. New York: Routledge, 2010.

Ross, Edward. "Sinking Funds." *Publication of the American Economic Association* 7 (1892): 54.

Rossiter, Clinton. *Alexander Hamilton and the Constitution.* New York: Harcourt, Brace & World, 1964.

Rowe, Kenneth W. *Mathew Carey: A Study in American Economic Development.* Baltimore, MD: Johns Hopkins University Press, 1933.

Royster, Charles. *A Revolutionary People at War: The Continental Army and the American Character, 1775–1783.* Chapel Hill: University of North Carolina, 1979.

Schaar, John. "The Case for Patriotism." *American Review*, no. 17 (May 1973): 59–101.

Schlesinger, Jr., Arthur. *The Cycles of American History*. Boston: Houghton Mifflin, 1986.

Scigliano, Robert. "The War Powers Resolution and the War Powers." In *The Presidency in the Constitutional Order*, edited by Joseph Bessette and Jeffrey Tulis, 115–53. Baton Rouge: Louisiana State University Press, 1981.

Sellers, Mortimer. *American Republicanism: Roman Ideology in the United States Constitution*. New York: New York University Press, 1994.

Sigmund, Paul E. *Natural Law in Political Thought*. Cambridge, MA: Winthrop, 1971.

———, ed. *St. Thomas Aquinas on Politics and Ethics*. New York: W. W. Norton, 1988.

Sheehan, Colleen. "Madison v. Hamilton: The Battle over Republicanism and the Role of Public Opinion." *American Political Science Review* 98, no. 3 (August 2004): 405–24.

Skowronek, Stephen. *Building the New American Administrative State: The Expansion of National Administrative Capacities, 1877–1920*. New York: Cambridge University Press, 1982.

Smith, Adam. *An Inquiry into the Nature and Causes of the Wealth of Nations*. 2 vols. 4th ed. Dublin, 1785.

Smith, Maynard. "Reason, Passion and Political Freedom in *The Federalist*." *Journal of Politics* 22, no. 3 (August 1960): 525–44.

Spicer, Michael W. *The Founders, the Constitution, and Public Administration*. Washington, DC: Georgetown University Press, 1995.

———. *In Defense of Politics in Public Administration: A Value Pluralist Perspective*. Tuscaloosa: University of Alabama Press, 2010.

———. *Public Administration and the State*. Tuscaloosa: University of Alabama Press, 2001.

Steuart, Sir James. *An Inquiry into the Principles of Political Oeconomy*. London, 1767.

Stever, James A. *The End of Public Administration: Problems of the Professions in the Post-Progressive Era*. New York: Transnational, 1988.

Stinchecombe, William, Charles Cullen, and Leslie Tobias, eds. *The Papers of John Marshall*. Chapel Hill: University of North Carolina Press, 1979.

Storing, Herbert J. *The Complete Anti-Federalist*. Vol. 5. Chicago: University of Chicago Press, 1981.

———. *Essays on the Scientific Study of Politics*. New York: Holt, Rinehart & Winston, 1962.

———. "Political Parties and the Bureaucracy." In *Political Parties U.S.A.*, edited by Robert A. Goldwin. Chicago: Rand McNally, 1964.

———. *What the Anti-Federalists Were FOR: The Political Thought of the Opponents of the Constitution*. Chicago: University of Chicago Press, 1981.

Story, Joseph. *Commentaries on the Constitution of the United States*. 2 vols. Boston: Charles C. Little and James Brown, 1851.

Stourzh, Gerald. *Alexander Hamilton and the Idea of Republican Government*. Stanford, CA: Stanford University Press, 1970.

Swanson, Donald F. *The Origins of Hamilton's Fiscal Policies*. University of

Florida Monographs, Social Sciences, no. 17. Gainesville: University of Florida Press, 1963)

Swanson, Donald F., and Andrew P. Trout. "Alexander Hamilton's Hidden Sinking Fund." *William and Mary Quarterly* 49 (1992): 108–16.

Sylla, Richard. "Financial Foundations: Public Credit, the National Bank, and Securities Markets." In *Founding Choices: American Economic Policies in the 1790s*, edited by Douglas A. Irwin and Richard Sylla. Chicago: University of Chicago Press, 2011.

Tansill, Charles C., ed. "Debates in the Federal Convention of 1787 as Reported by James Madison." In *Documents Illustrative of the Formation of the Union of the American States*. Washington, DC: Government Printing Office, 1927.

Terrett v. Taylor, 9 Cranch 43 (1815).

Tulis, Jeffrey K. *The Rhetorical Presidency*. Princeton, NJ: Princeton University Press, 1987.

U.S. v. Hylton, 3 U.S. 171 (1796).

U.S. v. Peters, 5 Cranch 115 (1809).

US Senate. *Wall Street and the Financial Crisis: Anatomy of a Financial Collapse*. US Senate Permanent Subcommittee on Investigations, Committee on Homeland Security and Governmental Affairs, Carl Levin, Chairman, Tom Coburn, Ranking Minority Member. Washington, DC: Government Printing Office, 2011. Accessed at http://www.hsgac.senate.gov.

Van Riper, Paul P. *History of the United States Civil Service*. Evanston, IL: Row, Peterson, 1958.

Vattel, Emmerich de. *The Law of Nations or, Principles of the Law of Nature, Applied to the Conduct and Affairs of Nations and Sovereigns*. 1758.

Waldo, Dwight. *The Administrative State: A Study of the Political Theory of American Public Administration*. New York: Holmes & Meier, 1948.

Walling, Karl-Friedrich. *Republican Empire: Alexander Hamilton on War and Free Government*. Lawrence: University Press of Kansas, 1999.

White, Leonard D. *The Federalists: A Study in Administrative History*. Westport, CT: Greenwood, 1948.

———. *The Republican Era, 1869–1901*. New York: Macmillan, 1958.

Wilson, James. *The Works of James Wilson*. Vol. 1. Edited by James D. Andrews. Chicago: Callaghan, 1896.

Wright, Benjamin F. *The Contract Clause of the Constitution*. Cambridge, MA: Harvard University Press, 1938.

Wiecek, William M. *Liberty under Law: The Supreme Court in American Life*. Baltimore, MD: Johns Hopkins University Press, 1988.

Wood, Gordon. *Empire of Liberty: A History of the Early Republic, 1789–1815*. Cambridge: Oxford University Press, 2009.

Wright, Benjamin F. *The Contract Clause of the Constitution*. Cambridge, MA: Harvard University Press, 1938.

Zavodnyik, Peter. *The Age of Strict Construction: A History of the Growth of Federal Power, 1789–1861*. Washington, DC: Catholic University of America Press, 2007.

Index